Winning Chess

Endings

Yasser Seirawan
International Grand Master

EVERYMAN CHESS

Published by Gloucester Publishers plc, formerly Everyman Publishers plc, Gloucester Mansions, 140a Shaftesbury Avenue, London, WC2H 8HD

British Library Cataloguing-in-Publication Data
A catalogue record for this book is available from the British Library.

ISBN 1 85744 348 9

Distributed in North America by The Globe Pequot Press, P.O Box 480, 246 Goose Lane, Guilford, CT 06437-0480

All other sales enquiries should be directed to Everyman Chess, Gloucester Mansions, 140a Shaftesbury Avenue, London, WC2H 8HD

Tel: 020 7539 7600   Fax: 020 7379 4060
Email: info@everymanchess.com
Website: www.everymanchess.com

Everyman is the registered trade mark of Random House Inc. and is used in this work under license from Random House Inc.

EVERYMAN CHESS SERIES (formerly Cadogan Chess)
Chief Advisor: Garry Kasparov
Commissioning editor: Byron Jacobs
Cover design by Horatio Monteverde

Printed and bound in Great Britain by Biddles Ltd, *www.biddles.co.uk*

Contents

Acknowledgments

This, the sixth book in the Winning Chess series from Microsoft Press, has become the most collaborative of all the efforts. I would like to express my sincere appreciation and respect to the many authors of those books and magazines that are listed on the Resources page. Truly, I stand on the shoulders of giants who have blazed the path for understanding chess endings. Their work made mine so much easier.

A more hands-on thanks must be given to those who supported me throughout the work. My wife, Yvette, was her ever-supportive self. Many family outings were either delayed or canceled while I plugged away on my PC, surrounded by stacks of books, files full of endgame clips, and magazines. Sometimes the house was a bit of a mess—how I thank her for not cleaning up!

Special thanks belong to my friend IM Nikolay Minev. His clear understanding of endgames and his assistance in ferreting out those perfect examples were greatly appreciated. A hearty handclasp to chess historian Edward Winter; chess has a marvelous history and its endings are no exception. Our many e-mail exchanges were a tremendous help.

Many thanks to those behind the scenes: my acquisitions editor, Christey Bahn, for her faith; my editor, Leslie Eliel, for being such a pleasure to work with. For this, her first chess book, she did remarkably well, only periodically growling about some of the grammatical eccentricities that are common in chess analysis. To her back-up, Joyce Cox, a veteran of the first book, *Play Winning Chess*, for her eagle eye. What a comma-cop! You were all wonderful. Thank you very much! A special word of thanks to my publisher, Microsoft Press; it's been a remarkable ten-year journey, and I've enjoyed every step of the way.

Last, but certainly not least, I would like to dedicate this book to chess coaches everywhere. Thank you all.

Introduction

Studying the ending is like cheating. This is what Michael J. Franett, three-time Washington State Champion and editor of *Inside Chess* Magazine, once told me. It rather stuck in my mind, and I'd like it to stick in your mind as you read this book.

No one likes to study endings. Often the work is solitary and overwhelming. Where do you begin? Which books should you study? Even the most determined and enthusiastic players can be driven nearly to tears with the tedium of trying to study endings. Why? Because most books on endings are insipid, dull, horribly dry tomes. They seem designed to wring out all the joy one could have for chess.

The worst offenders are those works that are written without much explanatory prose, but that force-feed the poor readers reams of variations, leaving them—intelligent players—befuddled as to why a series of moves had to be played in the first place.

Then there are those works *with* explanatory prose. Grueling explanatory prose. If it isn't the reams of analysis putting us to sleep, it is surely the pedantic way the variations are described that do the job! The philosophy of athletes, "No pain, no gain," has been adopted by these pedants of chess and taken to the limit, each page offering us a new and painful agony.

The bad books have a lot to answer for.

Then there are the endings books that are good. Genuinely good! It was Grandmaster Yuri Averbach's classic Russian series on endings that I liked best. This series contained just the right balance of variations and explanatory prose that made a satisfying and edifying mix. Although still a bit dry, it was meaty and readable. By the time I found the Averbach series I was already an accomplished Expert player, and that series undoubtedly helped me over the hump from Expert to Master player. So how did I become a "master" in the endings? Read on.

Despite the tens of thousands of books on chess, and hundreds, if not thousands, that are devoted to the endgame, books on endings *for beginners* are few and far between. The reason for this is partly economic. Books on endings, in general, simply don't sell as well to a wide audience as those devoted to openings, because beginning players just want to get in there and go for the gusto. They are like kids who think they know what's good for them. They want sugar! Lots of sugar, in all kinds of shapes and sizes. Beginning players want to jump right into the heat of battle, hack away, combine with a tactic or two, and then gracefully resign so that they can do it all over again. Exciting titles that promise the moon, like *Scintillating Short Victories*, or *Attacking Like a Grandmaster*, or *Tactics, Combinations, and Brilliancies for Geniuses Only*, feed a beginner's ego, stimulate that sugar craving. On the other hand, mundane titles like *King and Pawn Endings* or *Learning the Endgame* (all these are fictional titles) tell the novice one thing utterly and completely: Run! This book is boring!

In short, books on chess endings suffer a bad reputation. Naturally, such a reputation makes publishers rather nervous. But thanks to readers like you, and the success of my last book, *Winning Chess Openings* (Microsoft Press, 1998), my publisher's fears were assuaged, and I was given an enthusiastic go-ahead to make a book on endings that we hope will be used by generations of players to come.

However, fulfilling such a task wasn't easy. Because endings have traditionally been presented in such an unpalatable manner, the beauty that is inherent in this part of the game is too often lost.

But the beauty won't be lost to you in this book because, in a certain sense, I've won your trust from the other books in the series. To keep your trust, I've tried to make the material entertaining and easily digestible. That's where I've had to be a bit crafty by taking an unusual approach that resonates well with me, as I think it will with you. Much like in *Winning Chess Openings*, I'm going to walk you through the exact same approach that was taught to me when I started learning endings. After getting through a number of basic points, you'll be challenged to think through the strategies for yourself. You'll "take sides" in some classical endings—just as I did. The challenges will be hard, but I guarantee, if you apply yourself, your game will improve dramatically.

Worried about the task ahead? Good! So was I. If any of you are being "forced" to read this book by your chess teacher, coach, or parent, I feel for you. That's a bad break. The only thing that I can say is, let's trick them. Instead of slogging our way through a boring book on endings, let's determine to enjoy ourselves!

Studying the endgame will teach you how to land those "won" positions and to avoid the bad ones. Although some middlegames or openings end in a decisive checkmate or perpetual check, most games come down to an ending in which the game is well balanced and ends in a draw, or one in which the stronger side tries to force the advantage and gain victory. You will have a decided advantage if you have a good grasp on ending strategies.

Furthermore, your skills in all facets of the game will improve. By learning in advance all those positions that are won or drawn, you'll be better able to steer your way through the middlegame. The more experience you have in the ending, the better your own middlegame play becomes. Then, as you get better in the middlegame, you learn to choose openings that suit your middlegame tastes. In short, improving your endgame improves your whole game.

Learning the endings will also allow you to become much more familiar with the power of the pieces. In endings, boards are usually wide open. The Rooks and Bishops can swoop down the board, and Kings often emerge from their protective lair to become powerful pieces. The concepts of centralization, active pieces, and passed pawns are no longer principles; they become real, tangible strategies. Questions such as why a Rook is worth 5 points and a Bishop is worth 3 points get answered. (In openings, Bishops are often more powerful than Rooks, which are clumsy. In the middlegame, the relative value between the Rooks and Bishops has evened up, with the Rooks, for the most part, being a bit more powerful. In endings, there is no contest, as Rooks dominate Bishops and Knights.)

After you've become a bit more familiar with the power of the pieces, suddenly you'll find your game is getting a bit better. Why? Because then you'll know with complete certainty that the ending you're heading for is a win. Or, you'll know it's dead lost. If that's the case, guess what? You will struggle mightily to avoid those lost endings and peddle like heck toward those winning ones.

Much of my success in learning endings can be traced to these key habits:

- I had many chess coaches.

- I studied best-game collections, which all feature well-played endings.

- I played often against strong opponents who pointed out my mistakes.

This book is by no means intended to be your one and only endgame book. No, not at all. I shudder when I think that there are books on endings devoted solely to *certain* endings! For example, when I was in Riga, Latvia, in the old Soviet Union in 1979, a kindly white-haired gentleman came forward and presented me with a special gift. It was a 200-page volume exclusively addressing the position of the Rook and Bishop vs. the Rook. Sadly, this treasure in Russian has been lost in the intervening years, yet I still recall the gist of the author's parting thoughts—in essence, "Much remains to be written about this ending..."

A huge amount of published information has been devoted to the endgame, and you are encouraged to take your studies as far as you'd like. This book will teach you the ending basics of what every serious player absolutely needs to know.

There will be guidelines and principles espoused for nearly all endings, but there is one thing that you should know and steel yourself for right away: *Endings involve calculation*. Intuition takes a back seat and you'll be forced to think hard to discover the secrets of many positions. It is here in the ending that your ability to accurately calculate moves will be most severely tested. One thing I can promise: This book will point you in the direction of calculating the right moves and speeding up those calculations.

If you are one of the few progressive females making your way into this traditionally male-dominated sport, I hope you won't mind chess players being referred to as "he" throughout this and, as far as I know, all chess books. I encourage you to master the endgame and take your new skills into competition. In fact, I'll make a pledge: When the World Championship title (as opposed to the Women's World Championship—why use different standards when the medium is brain, not brawn?) is won by a woman (or a precocious girl!), I will officially break tradition and make whatever book I am writing at the time perhaps the first chess book in history with inclusive language. The challenge is yours, women and girls, to change history on two fronts!

Throughout the book, I've given the advantage to the White side for simplicity. In some cases when I've used positions from tournament games, I've reversed the colors. That is to say, if the winning player had the Black pieces in the game, I've turned the board around and set up the winning position as White. Don't be troubled by this—in real games, Black wins his share of endings, too!

I've also used some chess terms (placed in italics the first time they are introduced) that you are probably familiar with already, but if not, there are good glossaries in *Winning Chess Openings* and also in *Winning Chess Strategies* (Microsoft Press, 1994). Strategic principles and rules of thumb, also in italics for easy reference, pepper the book, and you will find solutions to the quizzes at the end of each chapter. You have all the tools. Just add a little mettle and you are on your way.

Studying the ending is like cheating. It's like knowing the answers to a test that you know you're going to have to take. The silver lining? The opposition is usually so ill-prepared.

Yasser Seirawan
Seattle, Washington

Basic Mates

You might be tempted to skip this first chapter on basic endings. My advice is, don't. In fact, I would encourage you to also pick up my book *Play Winning Chess* (Microsoft Press, 1990), where you can review a good discussion of basic mate strategy. Getting these endings down pat is absolutely vital. Every strong player knows them well. While memorizing them is not necessary, you should know how to win them quickly and efficiently. It helps to remember that you will be gaining the knowledge that every World Champion has!

The hardest basic mate is King, Bishop, and Knight. It took me an entire week to fully master this operation. While I must confess that I've never had to use this particular ending in my tournament practice—my opponents have always politely resigned—this knowledge has nonetheless reaped untold rewards.

The Easy

Rook Ending: Boxing the King

The principle for this operation is the same as with all basic mates: *The stronger side must drive the opposing King to the side of the board*—not necessarily a corner of the board, although that is usually the case. One method that works well is the "box" method, in which the opposing King is placed by the Rook in a box that just gets smaller and smaller until the King is checkmated. The box method is shown in Diagram 1.

As you can see, White is up a Rook, and he has to press Black's King to the side of the board. Note how many

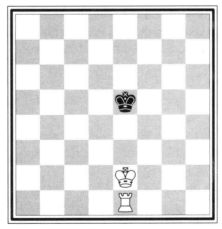

DIAGRAM 1.

squares Black's King can move to. White's plan will be to reduce the number of those squares. White should also be activating his King, and so he begins with:

1.Kd3+

This discovered check means that Black must move off the e-file and decide which file to move to, the d-file or the f-file. As there are more squares on the d-file, the best response is:

1...Kd5

What would have happened after 1...Kf4? White would begin boxing in Black's King because 2.Re3 is likely to follow. Notice that Black's King would then be confined by the Rook to the box of squares: f4-f8-h8-h4-f4. Play might proceed with 2...Kf5 3.Re4, making the box of squares just a little smaller. Black's King would then be confined to the squares f5-f8-h8-h5-f5.

2.Re4

White sets up his first box. Black's King is now confined to the d5-d8-a8-a5-d5 box.

2...Kd6

Black isn't happy about 2...Kc5 3.Rd4 Kb5 4.Rc4, because he realizes the box would shrink.

3.Kc4!

The King has to come up the board and play a role in forcing the opposing King backward. Do you see how Black's King has fewer squares to go to after this move?

3...Kc6

The two Kings are now in *opposition* to one another; that is, they're in a "face off." (Opposition will be discussed in more detail in Chapter Two.) When the Kings are in opposition to one another, the Rook can check the King and force it backward. If Black plays a different third move—for example, 3...Kd7? 4.Kc5!—White's job is only made easier, as Black is quickly herded to the side of the board.

4.Re6+

Another excellent move. Black's King is driven back, dejected.

4...Kc7

This is clearly the best resistance. The box would close even more quickly after 4...Kd7 5.Kd5 Kc7 6.Rd6 Kb7 7.Rc6. We can see that the squares in the box are now b7-a7-a8-b8.

5.Kc5

The Kings are now in opposition, and if it were White's move, he would quickly pounce with Re6-e7+ after the King had been driven to the edge of the board.

5...Kd7

The box becomes a coffin, and Black recoils from 5...Kb7 6.Rc6 Ka7 7.Rb6.

6.Kd5

White protects the Rook and leaves Black with a bleak decision.

6...Kc7

Stepping backward by choosing 6...Kd8 7.Kc6 Kc8 8.Re8 checkmate would only have lightened White's task.

7.Rd6

The box shrinks.

7...Kb7

If Black's King steps back with 7...Kc8, then 8.Kc6, White's King steps forward.

8.Rc6

Just as Black did to White in his fourth move, White has forced Black's King into a small box. The next step is to force the Black King to the side.

8...Ka7

The alternate move, 8...Kb8, would have been no different, whereas the weaker 8...Ka8? would have led to 9.Rc7! Kb8 10.Kc6 and Black's downfall.

9.Kc5

Also strong would have been 9.Kd6 Kb7 10.Kd7 Kb8 11.Rb6+ Ka7 12.Kc7, leading to a mate next move, but the move selected best demonstrates closing of the box.

9...Kb7   10.Kb5 Ka7   11.Rb6

Although Black has resisted, the box is now shut. Black can shuttle his King only between two squares, a8 and a7.

11...Ka8

The position is now as shown in Diagram 2. When we compare Diagrams 1 and 2, it's apparent that White has made tremendous progress, and with Black's King confined to only two squares, there is a danger of stalemate. White must avoid 12.Ka6, which would change a won position into a draw at once. Now wouldn't that be tragic?

12.Kc6 Ka7   13.Kc7 Ka8

14.Ra6 Checkmate

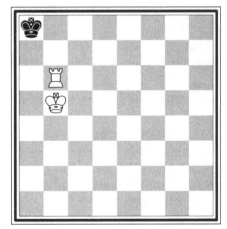

DIAGRAM 2.

The box method is an easy one to master. Play this ending out, putting the pieces in different positions just to be certain that it is absolutely clear.

Queen Ending: A Lot of Power, a Bit of Caution

Because the Queen is so much more powerful than a Rook, she can force a checkmate more easily. It is this very power, however, that increases the danger of stalemate. Thus, an extra touch of caution is required.

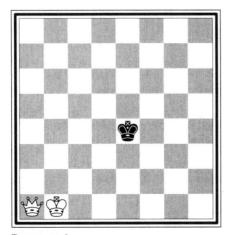

Using the box method is still the plan, but unlike the Rook, the Queen can herd the weaker side's King to the edge of the board by herself, after which her King will waltz up in opposition to help deliver checkmate. From his position in Diagram 3, White decides that his King shouldn't have to go too far:

1.Qf6

White confidently takes the first step in setting up a box.

1...Kd5

Black will try his best to remain as active as possible.

2.Qe7

DIAGRAM 3.

White has his choice of which way to make the box and determines that it would be easiest to push Black to the a-file.

2...Kd4   3.Kc2 Kd5   4.Kc3 Kc6   5.Kc4 Kb6

Note how White's Queen has been so strong that Black's last two moves were forced.

6.Qd7 Ka6   7.Qb5+

This keeps Black's King secured to the a-file. White could have checkmated more quickly with 7.Kc5 Ka5 8.Qa7 checkmate, but I wanted to demonstrate the box method using the Queen. A dreadful move is 7.Qc7, which would be a stalemate.

7...Ka7   8.Kc5 Ka8   9.Kc6

This assures a checkmate on the next move, whereas 9.Qb6 would produce another stalemate, undoing all of White's fine work.

The principle of forcing the King to the side of the board using the box method is straightforward. Remember that either the Rook or the Queen *can* force the King to the edge of the board, and that, despite her immense powers, the Queen can checkmate only a King that has been forced to the edge of the board.

Those two mates were an easy warm-up. Next you'll discover that the King has to be forced into a *corner* to be checkmated.

The Hard

Two Bishops, Two Principles

There is no box strategy for mating with the two Bishops. Instead, there are two principles at work:

- *The Bishops are best when centralized and working side by side.*

- *The player with the two Bishops must utilize his King more aggressively.*

In Diagram 4, the starting position is as poor as it could be for the superior side. White will have to drive Black's King to the side and eventually to one of the four corners. The first order of the day is for White to activate his King.

1.Ke2 Ke4

Black's King moves into opposition and tries to stay as centralized as possible. A weaker choice would be 1...Kc3 2.Ke3, for then Black's King would be quickly herded to the side of the board.

2.Be3

Here we see a standard theme in this ending: Black's King is forced backward.

2...Ke5   3.Kd3 Kd5   4.Bd4

As before, Black's King is forced back.

4...Ke6   5.Ke4 Kd6

Black tries a different tack from trying to oppose Kings.

6.Bc4

DIAGRAM 4.

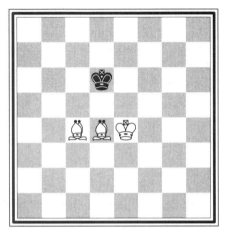

DIAGRAM 5.

As Diagram 5 shows, in a half-dozen moves, White has achieved his objective. Both Bishops are centralized, working side by side with an active King. White needs to make more progress and push Black's King to the side of the board.

6...Kc6

Black tries to make White's task as difficult as possible by refusing to step backward.

7.Ke5 Kd7

Black is doing his best to avoid the a8-corner.

8.Bd5

Denying Black's King the c6-square.

8...Kc7   9.Bc5 Kd7   10.Bd6!

A key move, as Black's King is at last forced to the end of the board.

10...Ke8

Once more, Black tries his best to avoid the corner. If he plays 10...Kc8, then 11.Bc6 will transpose into the *main line*. ("Main line" refers to the line of play actually made by the players, or the variations that the author considers to be the best moves. In this book, the main line appears in bold text.)

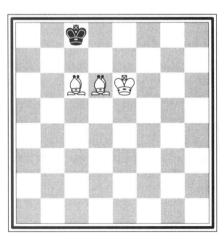

DIAGRAM 6.

11.Ke6

With this, Black's King remains nailed to the back rank.

11...Kd8   12.Bc6

Now Black's King is forced toward the a8-corner.

12...Kc8

Diagram 6 shows the current position, which the two Bishops can typically enforce. Notice how Black's King is forced to shuttle between the d8- and c8-squares. White must reposition his King in order to cover the a7- and b7-squares. The b6-square—a natural choice—beckons White's King.

13.Kd5

As usual, White must be vigilant to avoid 13.Ke7?, which would be a stalemate and produce a draw.

13...Kd8   14.Kc5 Kc8

15.Kb6 Kd8

White is just a few moves away from mate. He must now allow Black's King the opportunity to move to the corner.

16.Bc5 Kc8   17.Be7!

Another key move. Black is forced away from the center and toward the corner.

17...Kb8   18.Bd7!

White uses the same principle as in his previous move.

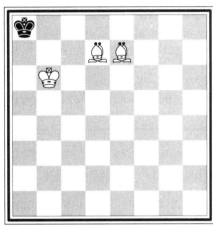

DIAGRAM 7.

18...Ka8

At last, Black is forced into the corner, as shown in Diagram 7. Now the checkmate is simple. White has to make a "pass" move, waiting for the King to move back to the b8-square.

19.Bd8

White has many passing moves. The moves 19.Bc5, 19.Bf8, 19.Be6, and 19.Ka6 would all be as effective as the move he chooses.

19...Kb8   20.Bc7+ Ka8

21.Bc6 Checkmate

Diagram 8 shows the pleasing finale.

This basic mate was rather easy. The two Bishops are tremendously powerful on an open board, covering a lot of territory. Working side by side, two Bishops can keep a King imprisoned, but they need the assistance of the King to force mate. Practice this ending with a friend and try to checkmate in as few moves as possible. This training will help you better understand the power of the two Bishops and remind you that the mighty King is essential to the ending.

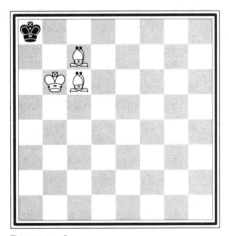

DIAGRAM 8.

Bishop and Knight: A Wall of Force

We are now about to enter the treacherous territory that has made the study of endings so notoriously difficult. A quick glance at Diagram 9 reveals one of the culprits.

Thus far, life has been easy, with the Queen, Rook, and two Bishops making short work of the lone King. The ending of Bishop and Knight is far more difficult—in fact, it's astonishing when you stop and think about it. You know that a Bishop and a Knight are each worth 3 points on the material count, whereas a Rook is worth 5 points. A Bishop and a Knight together total 6 points. Why is it that a superior force count of 6 is more difficult to mate with than a force count of 5? I don't know, but it is.

DIAGRAM 9.

The combination of Bishop and Knight forces a different mating approach. The underlying principles to this ending are complex enough to warrant their own discussion.

There are four important principles to keep in mind in a Bishop and Knight ending:

- *The superior side must use all of his pieces, especially the King, to create a "wall" as opposed to a box.*

- *The weaker King can be mated only in the corner of the same color as the Bishop.*

- *Normally, the King has to be driven to the "wrong" corner first, and then, using the wall technique, driven to the "right" corner.*

- *The defender should try to stay in the center for as long as possible and, when forced, run to the wrong corner.* (Remember that in tournament competition, you have only 50 moves to force the win!)

Unfortunately, this ending is quite difficult and not at all easy to master. But again, much can be gained by applying yourself to this ending. You will learn how to coordinate your pieces and improve your ability to calculate. Let's begin.

1.Bg2

A good start, as would be 1.Bd3. White's first order of business is to drive Black's King back and centralize his own King. Black will try to hang around in the center as long as possible.

1...Kd4   2.Kd2 Ke5

Another reasonable choice would be 2...Kc5 3.Kc3, as Black would still be able to run to the h8-corner. A third, less desirable scenario, 2...Kc4 3.Nd3 Kd4 4.Ke2 Kc4 5.Ke3, would have had Black doing White's work for him, as Black would be driven to the a1-corner—the wrong corner—more quickly than necessary.

3.Ke3 Kf5

Again, Black doesn't want to be too cooperative by retreating before he has to. He will have to be driven to the h8-corner.

4.Nd3

This move simply brings the Knight into play and seals off the e5-square.

4...Kg5   5.Be4

White's fifth move, demonstrating the first effects of the wall, is shown in Diagram 10. Observe how White's pieces combine to cover a whole buffer of squares: f3, f4, f5, e5, d5, and more. White's objective will be to press the wall forward, forcing Black into a corner.

5...Kf6

Black is hovering too close for comfort to the h8-corner, but he had to avoid 5...Kg4? 6.Kd4 Kg5 7.Ke5 Kh6 8.Kf6!, knowing his King would be calmly shepherded over to the h1-corner to be mated.

6.Kd4

DIAGRAM 10.

The line 6.Kf4 Ke6 7.Kg5 Kf7 8.Kf5 is also reasonable, as White also makes progress. I prefer 6.Kd4, however, because of the powerful step into the center.

6...Ke6   7.Kc5 Ke7   8.Kd5

Black's King must now consider which corner to go to. He chooses the best defense and heads toward the h8-corner.

8...Kf6

This is a wise choice, for if he chooses 8...Kd7 9.Ke5 Kd7 10.Bd5 instead, he won't make it to the h8-square.

9.Kd6 Kf7

Black avoids 9...Kg5? 10.Ke5 Kh6 11.Kf6 and is now forced to start his march to the h1-corner.

10.Ke5 Kg7!

After 10...Ke7 11.Bd5!, Black again misses the h8-corner.

11.Ke6 Kg8   12.Ne5!

White is not just centralizing his Knight; he is anticipating that the Knight will be needed to force Black's King out of the h8-corner.

12...Kf8   13.Kf6 Kg8   14.Nf7!

White denies Black's King the corner. This is the only way to win. Note that if, in Diagram 11, Black's King were already on h8, this move would come with check, and that after 14...Kg8 15.Bd3! Kf8 16.Bh7!, Black's King would be forced out of the corner, just as in our main line.

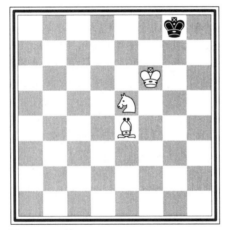

DIAGRAM 11.

14...Kf8   15.Bh7!

At the cost of misplacing his pieces, Black's King is driven back toward the center and away from the wrong corner. Now White faces a difficult juggling act. On the one hand he has to keep Black's King away from the h8-corner, and on the other hand he can't allow Black to slip out to the Queenside and make his way to the a1-square. This is where the wall comes back into play.

15...Ke8   16.Ne5!

With this move, White denies Black's King the use of the d7-square and begins preparing the wall. Black has a choice, as we can see in Diagram 12. The main line is 16...Kd8. If Black goes back to the f8-square, he loses faster.

16...Kd8

This is the best resistance because 16...Kf8 would accelerate defeat. With 17.Nd7+ Ke8 18.Ke6!, White keeps Black's King on the back rank and forces it toward the right corner. Then 18...Kd8 19.Kd6 Ke8 20.Bg6+! stops Black's escape once and for all while releasing the Knight. With 20...Kd8 21.Nc5!, White covers the d7-, b7-, and a6-squares, which severely restricts Black's King. With 21...Kc8 22.Be8!, the Bishop prepares to shift to the better option, the a4-e8 diagonal, where Black's King is prevented from escaping to the Kingside and is further forced toward the right corner. Now 22...Kd8 23.Bc6 Kc8

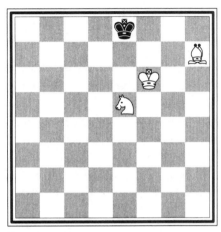

DIAGRAM 12.

24.Bd7+! is the winning point. Black's King is forced into the corner so that with 24...Kb8 (24...Kd8? 25.Ne6 would be checkmate.) 25.Kc6 Ka7 26.Kc7 Ka8 27.Kb6, much like the example of checkmating with the two Bishops, White's King has achieved the ideal square. White checkmates in the next two moves.

17.Ke6 Kc7!

Seeing this move, you might have the feeling that White has blown the win and that his quarry is about to escape. Not so! In Diagram 13, we see White's pieces coordinating to form a wall.

18.Nd7!

Well done! White covers both the b6- and c5-squares, preventing Black's escape.

18...Kb7

Black tries to play ...Kb7-a6 and snake up the a-file. A weaker choice is 18...Kd8 19.Kd6, which transposes to a line given previously.

19.Bd3!

With this move, White covers all the squares on the f1-a6 diagonal. Black's King isn't going to escape its a8-fate.

DIAGRAM 13.

19...Kc6 20.Bc4

White keeps Black's King under guard. It is forced to step back.

20...Kc7

Black resists as best he can. A weaker path is 20...Kb7 21.Kd6! Kc8 22.Nc5 Kd8 23.Bb5, transposing to the winning line given after Diagram 12.

21.Bb5!

The wall continues to press further. Now White is covering the a6-, c6-, and in certain cases, the e8-squares.

21...Kd8

This is the best move, as 21...Kc8 and 21...Kb7 both allow 22.Kd6 and a faster win. White must not allow Black to wiggle back to the Kingside.

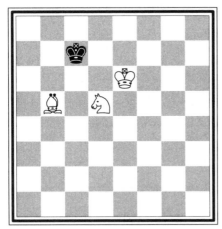

DIAGRAM 14.

22.Nf6 Kc7 23.Nd5+!

Diagram 14 shows how Black's King is beautifully netted. There is no escape either to the Kingside or up the Queenside. Black is walled into the right corner, and it is now up to White to move closer with his King, all the while paying attention to stalemate possibilities.

23...Kd8 24.Kd6 Kc8 25.Ke7!

In this definitive moment, Black is forced to the b-file.

25...Kb8 26.Kd8 Kb7 27.Kd7

Now that White's King has snuggled in closely, it is time to execute the final mating net.

27...Kb8

This is a necessary choice; otherwise 27...Ka7 28.Kc7 Ka8 29.Nb6+ Ka7 30.Nc8+ leads to mate next move.

28.Ba6 Ka7 29.Bc8!

This limits Black's choices to just three squares.

29...Kb8 30.Nb4

Diagram 15 shows that the Knight is able to move now that White's King is ready to cover the b6-square.

30...Ka7 31.Kc7 Ka8 32.Bb7+ Ka7 33.Nc6 Checkmate

That was quite a process, wasn't it? It took 33 moves to win from an inferior position. And a number of the moves were difficult to predict. This process is of such importance that you must be certain you understand it. When my first chess teacher showed me the method, he asked me, "Did you understand it?" "Sure did!" I shot back. "Good. In that case, you can checkmate me." Naturally, I failed altogether and spent the next week trying to nail it down. Because this "basic mate" was difficult for me, I imagine that it will be for you, also. Therefore, we're going to go through it

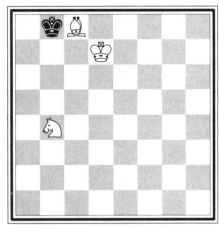

DIAGRAM 15.

again, this time changing the Bishop's color so that you won't try to copy the exact sequence as before.

Set up Diagram 16 and play both sides of the board. Try to checkmate Black's King at least twice. Afterward, read the rest of the chapter and see how many moves you predicted for yourself. You should be able to predict at least half of the moves correctly. For each correct prediction, give yourself a point. Count your points at the end of the sequence to see if you've guessed more than half of the moves.

As you can see from Diagram 16, I've made a conscious effort to totally misplace White's pieces. In the first moves, the guiding principle will be: *Bring the King and the other pieces into the center.*

1.Kb5

Give yourself credit for 1.Nb3, but not for 1.Nc2 Kd3 2.Nb4+ Kc4, which is slow.

1...Kd4

Another point if you were ready to answer 1...Kd5 with 2.Nb3, which would force Black's King away.

2.Nb3+ Kc3   3.Nc5

DIAGRAM 16.

White continues to bring his pieces into the center. Deduct a point if you wanted to play 3.Ka4?, a move that would cut against the grain of centralization.

3...Kd4

Black prepares to run to the h1-corner. After 3...Kc2? 4.Kc4 Kb1? 5.Kb3, White would checkmate in just a few more moves.

4.Bb2+

Black is forced by this move to commit himself. Will he try to run to the a8- or h1-corner?

4...Ke3

Black heads to the safety of the h1-corner. If Black played 4...Kd5, what would you do? Give yourself credit only if you were ready to play 5.Bc3 Kd6 6.Kc4 Kc6 7.Be5 Kb6 8.Kd5, in which White does a superb job of centralizing his pieces.

5.Kc4 Kf4   6.Kd3

Also give yourself credit for 6.Kd5, but only if you were prepared to meet 6...Kf5 with 7.Be5, forcing Black's King back.

6...Kf5

Take a point for keeping Black's King in a net by meeting 6...Kf3 with 7.Be5.

7.Ke3 Kg4   8.Ke4

Good thinking. Now White's plan is becoming plain. Black's King is being forced to the side and, eventually, the corner.

8...Kg3

If Black plays 8...Kg5, how would you handle it? If you were prepared to play 9.Be5 and meet 9...Kg4 with 10.Bf4, or 9...Kg6 with 10.Kf4, give yourself a point.

9.Nd3

Now the Knight is close to the action, controlling the f2-square so that he can rule out possible escape routes.

9...Kg4   10.Bc1!

White cuts Black's King by controlling a lot of important squares on the c1-h6 diagonal. Admittedly, this is cheating a bit. I've told you to centralize your pieces, but that doesn't mean that you can't think for yourself! Give yourself 2 points for this move. Give yourself 1 point if you thought of centralizing your pieces by playing 10.Bf6 Kg3 11.Be5+.

10...Kg3   11.Bf4+ Kg2

Give yourself another point if you were ready for 11...Kg4? 12.Nf2+! Kh4 13.Kf5, a savvy move that keeps Black away from the h1-corner.

12.Ke3 Kf1

If Black had moved with 12...Kh3, how would you respond? If you weren't worried because you understood that Black would be driven to the h8-corner after 13.Kf3 Kh4 14.Nc5 Kh5 15.Kg3 Kg6 16.Kg4 Kf6 17.Bd6, give yourself a pat on the back and 2 points. Note how White's pieces create a wall that will force Black's King into the h8-corner.

13.Kf3 Kg1

Black has defended well by staying close to the h1-corner. Now Black has to be driven out.

14.Nf2!

Subtract a point if you were ready to play a different move.

14...Kf1   15.Bh2!

Ditto: Subtract a point if you didn't plan to make this move, either.

15...Ke1   16.Ne4!

Now that Black has been forced away from the light square's corner, it's time to control his movements, just as before.

16...Kd1

Pause here for a moment. If the move had been 16...Kf1, what would you do? If you were ready with 17.Nd2+ Ke1 18.Ke3, give yourself an additional point.

17.Ke3

Subtract a point for any other move.

17...Kc2

Against 17...Ke1, did you plan 18.Nd2, as in the earlier situation? Good. You don't get any credit, just a tip of the hat.

The moment of truth has arrived. What will you play? Note that the position in Diagram 17 is a mirror image of that in Diagram 13. Don't look! It will give you the answer! Turkey!

18.Nd2!

The star move. If you found it, give yourself a bonus credit of 2 points. White covers the b3- and b1-squares. He has only to prevent Black's King from wandering up the a-file.

18...Kb2   19.Bd6!

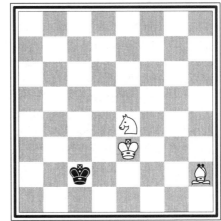

DIAGRAM 17.

It's the only way. Subtract a point for anything else.

19...Kc3   20.Bc5 Kc2   21.Bb4 Kd1

Any other move would lose more quickly. Black is hoping, maybe, to crawl back to the h1-corner.

22.Nf3 Kc2   23.Nd4+!

The wall is firmly in place now. Deduct a point for other moves. Now the trick is to leave the pieces alone and snuggle up with the White King.

23...Kd1   24.Kd3 Kc1   25.Ke2! Kb2   26.Kd2 Kb1

DIAGRAM 18.

Looking at Diagram 18, it's easy to see that if White's King could encroach a bit further—ideally to the c2-square—then checkmate would be easy. For this stage of the operation, the Bishop is needed to ensure that Black's King can't escape up the board.

27.Ba3!

You get only 1 point for this move, although perhaps it deserves 2.

27...Ka2   28.Bc1 Kb1   29.Kd1!

White wins control over the c2-square.

29...Ka1   30.Kc2

Deduct 4 whole points if you played anything else! What were you thinking?

30...Ka2   31.Ne2

Chalk up another point if you couldn't resolve your artistic self between 31.Ne2 and 31.Nb5, which also gets a point. If you played either 31.Nb3 or 31.Bb2, stalemating Black's King in both cases, consider the game of checkers. It, too, is quite challenging.

31...Ka1   32.Bb2+ Ka2   33.Nc1 Checkmate

Now tally your points. Be honest! Subtract those lost points, too. Did you manage to score 17 points? If not, don't worry—it took me a long while. But you're not ready to go on to Chapter Two, so reread this portion of the chapter and then go on.

The Impossible

King and Two Knights vs. King

If you felt that the basic mate of Bishop and Knight vs. lone King was unfairly difficult—I certainly did—you'll be shocked to realize that a King and two Knights can't force checkmate against a lone King! When I was first told this, my reaction was immediate: "Impossible!" I shouted. "Precisely!" responded my teacher.

How confusing! A Knight is worth 3 points, and with both on the board, how could I have a 6-point advantage in the material count and not be able to win? I needed proof. I quickly set up a mating net with both my Knights as illustrated in Diagrams 19 and 20 and, self-satisfied, remarked, "There's checkmate!"

"Very good," replied my teacher, "but you can't force it." He was right. After a struggle that eventually forced my opponent's King into the corner, I always came up with a stalemate.

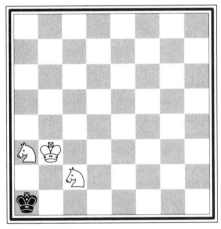 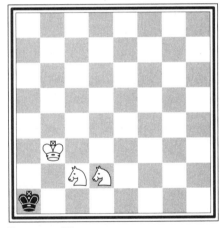

DIAGRAM 19.   **DIAGRAM 20.**

Take a look at Diagram 20 and imagine that White's c2-Knight is on the e2-square, covering the c1-square. White's last move, Nd2+, forced Black's King into the corner. Now the coup de grace is to play Ne2-d4-c2 checkmate. But, unfortunately, Black's King is left stalemated! If Black could only move, checkmate would be a cinch. No matter how I tried, the only way I could checkmate Black's King was with his *cooperation*. I couldn't do it by force. Spend a while on this confounded ending and see for yourself.

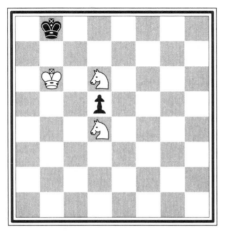

DIAGRAM 21.

The idea that *if only Black could move* has sparked endgame specialists to consider establishing an entire esoteric field of endgame theory. *What if Black had a pawn?* Indeed, this would do the trick. In Diagram 21, I have put a pawn on the board so that Black is now neatly checkmated by 1.Nc6+ Ka8 2.Ne8 d4 3.Nc7 checkmate. Endgame players have delighted in finding the "zone" of how far a pawn has to be blocked before the position is no longer a win. Fortunately, I will spare you a discussion about some of these endings, as their winning procedures are sometimes in the hundreds of moves!

The Crazy

King and Lone Knight vs. King and Pawn

For the moment, let me confound you with two cute examples of a King and lone Knight doing the job with the help of the opponent's pawns.

The first example, shown in Diagram 22, is not a quiz and you will not find the solution in this book. Incredibly, it's White turn to move and win. How can a lone Knight mate, whereas two Knights can't? That is yet another of the beguiling mysteries of chess.

If you weren't very impressed by Diagram 22, take a gander at Diagram 23.

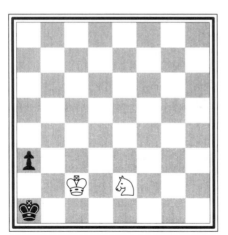

DIAGRAM 22.

QUIZ 1: Can you figure out how the King and Knight will win this position? (Solutions to quizzes can be found at the end of each chapter.)

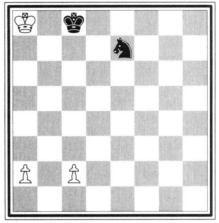

DIAGRAM 23.

Before you try your hand at this quiz, let's first give thanks to Seattle's own Bruce Moreland, programmer of the chess engine Ferret, for sending along this problem. Bruce explains that much work can be done on such endings, and points out that Black can checkmate White in exactly 17 moves. It is truly a tango for the Black Knight and King.

Solutions

(The curly brackets indicate alternative moves that would not have changed the verdict of a win.)

QUIZ 1 (DIAGRAM 23): **1...Nc6! 2.a3** { c3 } **Kc7! 3.a4** { c3 } **Kb6** { Kc8 } **4.a5+** { c3 } **Kc7! 5.a6** { c3 } **Ne5** { Nb8, Kb6, Kc8 } **6.c3** { Ka7 } **Nc4** { Nc6, Nd7 } **7.Ka7 Nb6 8.c4 Nd7 9.Ka8 Kb6 10.c5+ Kc6! 11.Ka7 Kc7! 12.Ka8 Ne5 13.Ka7 Nc6+ 14.Ka8 Kc8 15.a7 Ne5** { Na5, Ne7, Nd4, Nb4, Nd8 } **16.c6 Nc4! 17.c7 Nb6!** Checkmate.

King and Pawn Endings

At all stages of a chess game, timing is vitally important. But timing undergoes curious changes in King and pawn endings. In the opening and middlegame, every move is treasured as a way to enhance our development, protect our King, protect a weakness, or initiate an attack. In chess, each move is a *tempo*, and the plural is *tempi*, which is a synonym for timing. In King and pawn endings, the difference of a single tempo is often the deciding factor. Having an extra move in a pawn race can mean victory or defeat. Interestingly enough, there are some King and pawn endings in which you want your opponent to be on the move, so you *want* to lose a tempo!

To drive home the importance of timing, there's a joke I tell about a bank robber who wouldn't tell prison authorities where he buried the loot, no matter how they tried to pry it out of him. In one of his aging mother's weekly calls, she said she was thinking about planting potatoes in her back garden. Her son, stressing his concern, said, "Mother, you definitely don't want to do that! The ground is extremely hard, and you have to dig deep to plant the potatoes. You would certainly strain your back and might hurt yourself badly. You must promise me you won't plant potatoes. Now is definitely not the time!" "But...," she started to protest, but her son insisted. "Really, Mother, now is not the time." The next week when she called, her son asked, "Mother, how are you?" "Terrible," said his mother. "There are FBI agents and police everywhere, digging up the backyard! It's a mess and I'm in a panic! I don't know what to do!" Calmly, her son replied, "Now is the time to plant your potatoes."

Just as in life, in chess it is sometimes better to wait.

The Tempo Tester

With the importance of tempi and tempo firmly in our minds, we can enjoy a practical example and an exercise I've seen taught around the world. In Diagram 24 on the next page, we see the starting position of the pawns, minus all the pieces. In this example, both players are trying to promote their pawns. The first to

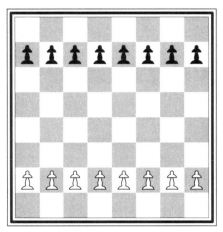

DIAGRAM 24.

promote one of his pawns wins. White starts first. The *tempo tester* game seems easy at first, but bear in mind that I constantly lost to my first teacher! Now I invariably beat my students in the tempo tester game, whether I play Black or White.

In this example of a poorly played tempo tester game, with 1.e4 e5 2.c4? c5 3.a4? a5, White is running out of ways to create an imbalance. White makes one more mistake: 4.g4?, and it turns out to be the decisive one. Then 4...g5 5.h3 h6 6.f3 f6 7.d3 d6 8.b3 b6 brings us to Diagram 25.

It's White's move, and he's dead lost because of it. He would love to pass, but that's not an option. Now imagine that on his first move, White had played 1.e3, and answered 1...e5 with 2.e4, hoping to ape his opponent, just as before. In that case, it would be Black's move in Diagram 25, and *he* would be lost. Play the tempo tester game a few times with a friend. It will improve your calculation skills and teach you the vital importance of controlling the tempo.

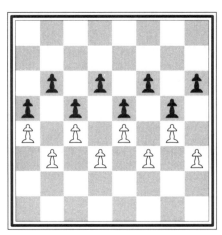

DIAGRAM 25.

In King and pawn endings, the fight for a tempo might mean the difference between a draw and a win. In this section, you will learn to spot any position with King and pawn vs. a lone King that indicates whether the game will be a win or a draw.

Kings in Direct Opposition

It's time to nail down some basics of King and pawn vs. King endings. The first basic principle is this: *If the defender's King is directly in front of the pawn, the ending is drawn.* This is true of all pawns from a to h.

In Diagram 26, Black's King has the perfect defensive position, and the game is drawn. However, there are a number of tricks you must know. Play begins as follows:

1.Kc3 Kb6!

The defending King steps backward on the same file as the pawn.

2.Kc4 Kc6!

This immediately puts the Kings in direct *opposition*. Opposition is a crucial aspect to the King and pawn endgame. The Kings face off, and because neither can advance, one has to give way, and that player "loses" the opposition. In Black's last move, White has to yield, and Black wins the opposition. Every other move loses!

3.Kd4

White tries to trick his opponent into a mistake.

3...Kb5!

Black is quick to step up directly in front of the pawn. The players now repeat the moves just played.

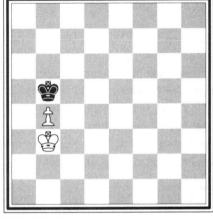

DIAGRAM 26.

4.Kc3 Kb6   5.Kc4 Kc6   6.b5+

Unable to make progress any other way, White advances his pawn.

6...Kb6

The King always steps in the path of the pawn.

7.Kb4 Kb7   8.Ka5 Ka7!

Black's King gains the opposition and saves the game. White again advances his pawn.

9.b6+ Kb7   10.Kb5

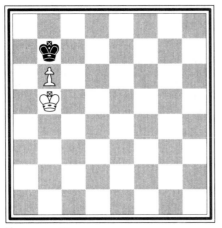

DIAGRAM 27.

Diagram 27 reveals a critical moment, which is repeated time and time again. Black has but one move to save the game.

10...Kb8!

Why would 10...Ka8 or 10...Kc8 have failed?

11.Kc6 Kc8 12.b7+ Kb8 13.Kb6

Stalemate. The ending is drawn.

Note that 10...Kc8 would have lost to 11.Kc6 Kb8 12.b7 Ka7 13.Kc7 when the b-pawn becomes a Queen. This sample tells us that for the pawn to promote, the superior side will need the support of its King, which must cover the queening square to force the pawn's promotion.

Imagine that you are White in Diagram 28. A long, hard-fought game has come down to this position. Will you win or will you draw? Only one move wins.

1.Kf6!

The key move: White *moves his King in front of the pawn to be able to protect the promoting square.* The pawn's mundane advance, 1.f6? Ke8 2.f7+ Kf8 3.Kf6, would be a stalemate and a draw. After Kf6!, Black is forced to move his King out of the way, and he loses.

1...Ke8!

Rats. Neither would 1...Kg8 2.Ke7! have saved Black.

2.Kg7!

White wins. He has covered the f8-square, and with Black's King out of the way, the f-pawn can saunter up the board for a new Queen.

Both the a-pawn and h-pawn present a different problem. In Diagram 29, regardless of who is on move, the game is drawn. White is unable to cover the h8-promotion square.

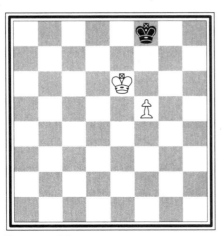

DIAGRAM 28.

1...Kg8 2.Kg6 Kh8

3.h6 Kg8 4.h7+ Kh8

The game is drawn.

In Diagram 30, we can see that the two Kings are in opposition. To win the game, White will have to *step in front of his pawn, gain the opposition, and then secure the promotion square.* This method of escorting the pawn up the board is key to winning many King and pawn endings, even though getting in front of the passer seems to be contrary to the plan of promotion. Imagine the King acting as a football blocker, clearing a path for the pawn.

DIAGRAM 29.

1.Ke4!

The winning move. To rush the pawn up the board with 1.e4? Ke6! would be a mistake. When Black waits for the pawn to advance further with 2.e5 Ke7! 3.Kf5 Kf7, the game ends in a draw.

1...Ke6! 2.e3!

This is White's point. Black's King must give way, losing the opposition and allowing White's King to escort the pawn to its coronation. If White didn't have this little tempo waster with the pawn, he wouldn't win the opposition.

2...Kf6 3.Kd5 Ke7 4.Ke5!

White again gains the opposition and forces Black's King to move aside.

4...Kd7 5.Kf6 Kd8

6.e4 Ke8 7.Ke6 Kf8 8.Kd7!

White wins control of the e8-square, and the pawn successfully marches up the board.

And with that, we have the basics of King and pawn endings. However, if that was all there was to it, learning these endgames would be a snap. Now let's try our hand at something more difficult.

DIAGRAM 30.

25

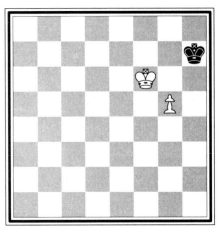

DIAGRAM 31.

The scenario shown in Diagram 31 seems like it would be a piece of cake to play out.

1.Kf7!

White controls the queening square. The weaker choice, 1.g6+? Kh8! 2.g7+ Kg8, would have tossed away the win.

1...Kh8

Sudden panic grips White's heart. He realizes that the pawn can't be pushed right away because of the threat of stalemate. What to do? How can he improve his position? After all, he already controls the queening square.

2.Kg6! Kg8   3.Kh6! Kh8

4.g6 Kg8   5.g7

Black's King must now give way, and White wins:

5...Kf7   6.Kh7

So this exercise gave you a scare? You should now be alerted to the fact that b-pawns and g-pawns give the defender an extra chance to escape, because the defender, being close to the corner, is aided by stalemate possibilities.

To play Diagram 32, imagine that you are White in a tournament game.

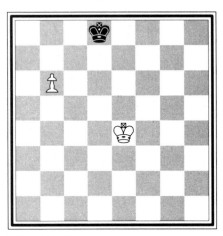

DIAGRAM 32.

Your opponent is the highly esteemed Grandmaster Yasser Seirawan. Happy to have the sunny side of draw, you desperately want to win so that you can boast of your prowess to all your friends.

The first thing you notice is that your pawn is a little too far advanced and is away from your King. This means that you can't step in front of the pawn to try to win the opposition. Worried that it will be captured, you hasten to protect it.

1.Kd5 Kd7   2.Kc5 Kd8

QUIZ 1: That last move was a cunning one, laying a trap. How do you proceed?

Kings in Distant Opposition

We have learned what it means when Kings face one another in direct opposition, but at some earlier point, the Kings are at a distance from one another. To go head-to-head in opposition, they must first get closer. As they approach each other, however, it is important to know which King is likely to gain the opposition. When Kings are not in direct opposition, they are often in a state of *distant opposition*. What do I mean?

In Diagram 33, White wants to escort his pawn up the board, but the Black King is well placed to block its progress. White's only hope is to bring his King up off the first rank and win the opposition by getting in front of the pawn.

1.Kd2

Black is in real trouble. It seems that no matter where he plays his King, he will lose the opposition and the game. For instance, playing 1...Kd5? 2.Kd3 Kc5 3.Kc3 Kd5 4.Kb4 Kc6 5.Kc4 means White wins, as we've seen. No better is 1...Kc5? 2.Kc3!, which transposes into the same line. Attempting this: 1...Kb5 2.Kd3 Kc5 3.Kc3 does likewise, and Black transposes again. Black has one move:

1...Kd6!

With this move, Black steps into a distant opposition. Instead of facing off directly with one square between the Kings, Black keeps three squares between

DIAGRAM 33.

them, achieving a distant opposition, and the game is drawn. When White's King steps up the board, Black's King will also, but he will have gained the opposition.

2.Kc3 Kc5!

Black wins the opposition, and the game is drawn. Had White tried 2.Kd3, then 2...Kd5! would have won the opposition and would also have saved the draw.

Now let's go back to Diagram 33. Suppose White tries:

1.Kb2

In this case, White is hoping to trick Black into allowing the opposition. For instance, 1...Kd5? 2.Kb3! would allow White to win the opposition. After 1.Kb2, Black has a similar way of keeping the distant opposition:

1...Kb6!

Now if White steps up with his King, Black does the same and thus wins the opposition.

2.Kb3 Kb5

Black draws the game, as before.

Learning to think about King and pawn endings using opposition and distant opposition will help you calculate which positions are won or drawn. If in Diagram 33, White can plunk down the move 1.Kc4, we know that White has an automatic win regardless of who is on the move. This is because the tempo c2-c3 will always give White the opposition. If White's pawn were already on the c3-square, we'd need a crucial piece of information: Which player is on the move? When you have practiced opposition and distant opposition, you should be able to tell at a glance the result of the game!

King in the Square

Quite often the King and the pawn are separated from one another, and the pawn races up the board, trying to promote before the defending King can stop it.

In Diagram 34, it is White's move. Black's King is far away from the passed b3-pawn, and White is spending his time calculating whether or not the immediate

1.b4 wins. Calculating the race is quite unnecessary. There is a quick device we can use called *the square*. The b3-pawn is five squares away from queening. We can then draw the square b3-b8-g8-g3-b3. This is called the *queening square*, or simply the square. If the defending King can "step into" the queening square, the game is drawn, as the pawn can't win the race. If the defending King is unable to step into the square, the pawn can race away, unaided, to score a touchdown. As we can see, Black's King is already in the square. White starts first.

DIAGRAM 34.

1.b4?

Now the square has shrunk to b4-b8-f8-f4-b4. After a heavy thinking spell, White figures the pawn makes it home because it is only four squares away from queening. Black must step into the square. Interestingly enough, it doesn't matter which square he chooses: the f6-, the f7-, or the f8-square will put his King into the square.

1...Kf6   2.b5 Ke5

Notice that the square has become smaller and now encompasses only b5-e5-e8-b8-b5, but Black's King is still safely within it.

3.b6 Kd6   4.b7 Kc7   5.b8=Q+ Kxb8

Gotcha!

Learning to use the square to calculate King and pawn endings can save you a lot of time on the clock and can help prevent you from cluttering your mind with useless variations.

QUIZ 2: Go back to Diagram 34 and see if you can find a method for White to win.

QUIZ 3: Grandmasters can tell at a glance what is happening in the position in Diagram 35. Without calculating, and without knowing who is on move, see if you can tell what is going on in this King and pawn endgame.

DIAGRAM 35.

Triangulation: The Art of Losing a Tempo

What makes King and pawn endings so complex is that when you add a few pawns to the position for both sides, a whole new range of problems suddenly seem to pop up. In many cases, the superior side often *wants* to lose the tempo by passing. This is done by a method called *triangulation*.

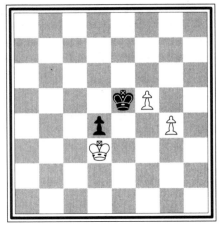

DIAGRAM 36.

Diagram 36 is a fine illustration of triangulation. White's two connected passed pawns are magnificent. Even if Black's King were on the g5-square, White's pawns wouldn't be vulnerable to capture. If the g4-pawn were taken, the f-pawn would rush to its queening square. White knows that with the aid of his King, promoting one of his pawns would be a snap. The problem is that Black's d4-pawn is a bit of a bother. It would be much simpler if its removal could be arranged.

Delving into the deep mysteries of this position, White comes to a startling conclusion: Black's King is overworked. It defends the d4-pawn and covers the f6-square. If only it were Black's move, White could win by capturing the d4-pawn or by running with his f-pawn. White's goal is to reach the same position as in Diagram 36, but with Black to move. That is, White wants to lose the tempo. White arranges the win of the pawn by triangulating with his King.

1.Kd2 Kf6

Black must keep an eye on the f6-pawn. With 1...Kd5? 2.f6 Ke6 3.g5, Black's King will no longer be able to support the e5-pawn without letting the f-pawn queen.

2.Ke2! Ke5

Black would love to play the same little dance as White's King, but the e6-square is guarded.

3.Kd3!

White achieves his goal. By utilizing the d2-, e2-, and d3-squares, White reaches his goal in losing the tempo.

3...Kd5   4.f6 Ke6   5.g5

White will now pick up the d4-pawn and escort a pawn to sweet victory.

Diagram 37 illustrates a slightly more complicated triangulation, but it is still the same idea. Much to his regret, it is White's turn. If only it were Black's move,

Black would have to retreat his King with 1...Kc8, and White could win brilliantly by playing 2.Kb6 and snapping up the a6-pawn. Then he would be able to insure the promotion of one of his pawns. White has to figure out a way to reach the position shown in Diagram 37, with Black to play. He triangulates with his King.

1.Kd5 Kc8!

As we can see, this is the only move for Black. After 1...Kd8? 2.Kd6 Kc8 3.c7, White will have no difficulties promoting his pawn.

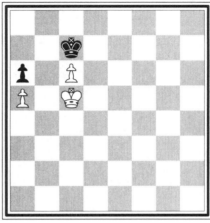

DIAGRAM 37.

2.Kd4!

What's this? White is stepping backward! Why? White's King is doing a little dance between the triangle of squares c4, d4, and d5 to win the opposition! Black can't do a dance with his King on the c7-, c8-, d8-triangle of squares, because the moment Black plays ...Kc7, the answer is revealed: Kc5. White gains the same position as in Diagram 37, but this time it's Black's move.

Grabbing the bull by the horns and storming ahead with 2.Kd6 Kd8 3.c7? Kc8 4.Kc6 would have blown the win completely. Many ending positions require a bit more finesse.

2...Kd8

Black is careful to avoid 2...Kc7 3.Kc5 Kc8 4.Kb6, which is the simple win that White wants.

3.Kc4 Kc8   4.Kd5!

Looks like the cat and mouse game is over. Black's only choice is which way to lose.

4...Kc7

The alternative, 4...Kd8 5.Kd6 Kc8 6.c7 Kb7 7.Kd7, would allow White to promote his pawn.

5.Kc5!

White's triangulation has a handsome reward. The a6-pawn must fall, and the victory is clear:

5...Kc8   6.Kb6 Kb8   7.Kxa6 Kc7   8.Kb5 Kc8   9.a6 Kb8

10.Kc5 Kc7   11.a7

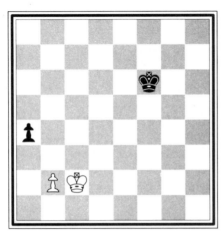

DIAGRAM 38.
C. Dedrle, 1921

As more pawns get added to King endings, the complexity of the endgame increases, sometimes exponentially. Let's start exploring some of these complex, yet typical, endings.

Diagram 38, a study by Cyril Dedrle (1876–1944), features some nice twists in fighting for the opposition. It's White's move. How would you play for victory? Be careful. I'm not in the business of making your life easy.

1.Kb1!!

This is White's only way to approach the a-pawn for a victory. After 1.Kc3 a3 2.b4 Ke5 3.Kb3 Kd5 4.Kxa3 Kc6 5.Ka4 Kb6! is played, the game is a draw. (With 2.bxa3, we'll find Black's King in the square, and then 2...Ke6 makes the game an easy draw.)

1...a3!

Black tries his best shot. After 1...Ke5 2.Ka2 Kd5 3.Ka3 Kc5 4.Kxa4 Kb6 5.Kb4, White would win the opposition and the game, as we saw earlier.

2.b3

Can you determine why 2.b4? or 2.bxa3? would have drawn?

2...Ke5   3.Ka2 Kd5   4.Kxa3 Kc6!

With this, Black slyly lays a trap for White. He must advance his King, but to which square?

5.Ka4!

White avoids the embarrassing 5.Kb4? Kb6, which leads to a draw. But by placing 5.Ka4!, White gains the *opposition on the diagonal* with the single b5-square separating the two Kings.

5...Kb6   6.Kb4

It's a win.

Pawn Races

As we just saw, you often reach a King and pawn ending in which both sides have the same numbers of pawns. In this case, positional factors are paramount. Consider the following:

- Which side has the better placed King?
- Which side has a further advanced pawn?
- Which side has a doubled pawn or another type of structural weakness?

In the examples that follow, White, as usual, will be the superior side.

Diagram 39 shows what appears to be a complete draw. Neither King will be able to stop the opponent's pawns from queening, when the game should be a draw. In such cases, which side queens first, or queens with check, can make a crucial difference. In this case, White promotes his pawn first and is able to put this advantage to good use.

1.f7 h2   2.f7=Q h1=Q

3.Qf3+ Kg1

DIAGRAM 39.

The first note of concern is 3...Kh2 4.Qg3 Checkmate!, which would be a surprising end. Now, however, Black is ready for a Queen swap and a draw.

4.Qe3+! Kf1   5.Qc1+ Kg2   6.Qd2+ Kf1   7.Qd1+ Kg2   8.Qe2+ Kg1

The last series of moves by Black was all forced. But what has White gained? Well, he has managed to bring his Queen close to Black's King. The Queen has also moved away from the f3-square, avoiding a Queen swap, and all of this has been done with tempo.

9.Kg3!

A surprising finish. Despite the even material, Black can't prevent 10.Qe1 Checkmate without losing his Queen. This pattern is seen quite often and is a good one to keep in mind.

Being able to checkmate after both sides have promoted is a clever device, but one that isn't necessarily common in victories that feature pawn races. Usually, one side tries to finesse the other player's King onto a square in such a way that the opponent might queen his pawn with check and thereby win the race.

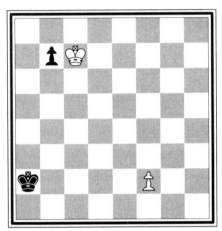

DIAGRAM 40.
A. Mandler, 1938

Diagram 40 is a charming study by Arthur Mandler (1891–1971). When you realize that 1.Kxb7 Kb3 means that Black is in the square, the position seems as good as drawn. The immediate comeback, 1.f4 b5, allows White to Queen first, but nothing will be gained. Is there any way that White can win? Here's a hint: Can White get Black's King to step on the a3-f8 diagonal? If he can, his f-pawn has the potential to queen with check!

1.Kd6!

A startling conception. White intends to use his King to *stop* Black's pawn, *not to capture it*. When I learned it, this move was a total violation of all my greedy impulses to capture the little devil, and I was unable to solve this problem when given the challenge.

1...Ka3

Black has no choice. After 1...b5 2.Kc5 Kb3 3.Kxb5!, White isn't so merciful, and hacks the pawn off the board. With 3...Kc3 4.Kc5 Kd3 5.Kd5, White will be just in time to save his own f-pawn and win the position.

2.Kc5!

He stops Black's b-pawn from advancing. Now it will need the assistance of the Black King.

2...Ka4   3.f4 b5   4.f5 b4   5.Kc4!

Again, White has the option of promoting first. With 5.f6 b3 6.f7 b2 7.f8=Q b1=Q 8.Qa8+ Kb3 9.Qb7+ Kc2, he's left empty-handed. No glorious checkmate this time.

5...b3   6.Kc3! Ka3

White's beautiful play steps into the clear. Black's King has been lured to the a3-square, and that fact will make the difference between a win and a draw.

7.f6 b2   8.f7 b1=Q   9.f8=Q+

Even though Black has queened his pawn first, White has promoted with check! Black must yield to the *skewering* of his King and Queen.

9...Ka4

Even sadder was 9...Ka2 10.Qa8 Checkmate!

10.Qa8+ Kb5   11.Qb7+

And with this, Black's Queen is laid over the coals.

Well, that last one was certainly a rush. But who among us wouldn't have captured the b-pawn? Certainly not I! This pattern of having both sides queen and having the victor in the race skewer the opposing Queen happens often.

Let's try the same concept in a more likely setting. Diagram 41's arrangement is a bit more commonplace. A few things leap out at you. First, notice that Black's King is boxed in and is unable to get back to stop White's g-pawn. That's the bad news. The good news is that the King is optimally placed to escort his own pawn to coronation. But there's one more piece of bad news. The g-pawn is ready to queen with check!

QUIZ 4: How can White use this news to win the game?

DIAGRAM 41.

The Crooked Path

A constant stratagem that is prevalent in many King and pawn endings is what I refer to as the *crooked path*. In geometry class, I learned that the shortest distance between two points is a straight line. Clearly, my geometry teacher wasn't familiar with King and pawn endings. Oftentimes the King does not take a straight path between two squares. Consider a White King on the f3-square, intending to make a lunge for the f8-square. Is 1.Kf4, 2.Kf5, 3.Kf6, 4.Kf7, and 5.Kf8 the quickest way to get there? Not at all. The King may zigzag its way up the board with Kg4-f5-e6-f7-f8, or go out of its way with Ke4-d5 before proceeding to f8. All of these paths take the same number of tempi! Taking a walk on the crooked path is something to keep in mind when trying to win or save your skin. Two beautiful examples that illustrate this concept are shown in Diagrams 42 and 43 on the next page.

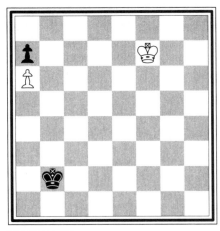

DIAGRAM 42.
Schlage–Ahues
Berlin, 1921

The position in Diagram 42 occurred in a game played in Berlin in 1921. Obviously, White has to move across the board, gobble up the a7-pawn, and promote his a6-pawn if he wants to win. Easier said than done. The game continues with **1.Ke6 Kc3 2.Kd6? Kd4 3.Kc6 Ke5 4.Kb7 Kd6 5.Kxa7 Kc7**, until White finds his King trapped in the corner, and the game is drawn. Instead of this line of play, White's King can walk a crooked path to shoulder Black's King out of the way. This method is highly instructive.

1.Ke6! Kc3 2.Kd5!

Here we have the crucial point, in which Black's King is prevented from getting back up the board.

2...Kb4 3.Kc6 Ka5 4.Kb7 Kb5 5.Kxa7 Kc6 6.Kb8

That's it. White wins.

One of my favorite studies is this next classic, much appreciated by all who have ever witnessed it. The composer was Richard Reti (1889–1921). In Diagram 43, we see that White is impossibly placed if he wants to stop the h5-pawn from queening. Furthermore, his c-pawn is firmly controlled by Black's King. Can White possibly save the position?

1.Kg7

White appears to be going through the motions of inexorable defeat. Black is happy to push his pawn home.

1...h4 2.Kf6 Kb6

Black takes a break from the race. He realizes that 2...h3 3.Ke6 h2 4.c7 would allow White to save the game.

3.Ke5!

DIAGRAM 43.
R. Reti, 1921

A stunning surprise! Now White has a double threat: supporting his pawn's advance, and stepping into the square of the h-pawn with Ke5-f4.

3...h3

Not 3...Kxc6 4.Kf4 h3 5.Kg3 h2 6.Kxh2, which would show the remarkable route of White's King.

4.Kd6 h2   5.c7 h1=Q   6.c8=Q

And White draws.

The Pawn Breakthrough

By now we have quite an arsenal of tricks to help us understand King and pawn endgames. A highlight of these endings—my favorite—is the *pawn breakthrough*. In this device, a player sacrifices a pawn, often two, to pursue a promotion. Recall the tempo tester exercise at the start of this chapter. If you played a few games, you might have found yourself in a position similar to the one shown in Diagram 44.

White has the advantages of a superiorly placed King and pawns that are further advanced. Jeffrey Parsons, my first teacher, playing Black, delighted in saving this ending. Flaunting my natural talent, I'd breezily produce a line like 1.Kf5 Kf7 2.Ke5 Ke7 3.Kd5 Kd7 4.c6+ Kc8 5.Ke6 a6! 6.cxb7+, and yet never come close to winning. After several attempts, I took a deep breath. "Okay," I said, "I'm absolutely certain about my first move, 1.Kf5! Now, why can't I win?"

In the spirit of mercy, Jeffrey charmed me with this breakthrough:

DIAGRAM 44.

1.b6! cxb6   2.a6! bxa6   3.c6!

Because Black's King isn't in the square, the c-pawn queens. Recall the move that I was so cocky about? That move, 1.Kf5? Kf7, brings Black's King into the square and throws away the win! To this day, I can't imagine how Jeffrey was able to keep a straight face.

QUIZ 5: What would you have played after 1.b6 axb6?

DIAGRAM 45.

In Diagram 45 we see an innocent setting. Pleased with the advanced b-pawn, White jumps into a pawn race.

1.a4! h5   2.a5 h4   3.b6 axb6

Now White has to stop to consider his move. He has a choice of which pawn to promote. He makes the right decision.

4.a6! h3   5.a7 h2   6.a8=Q

With this, White queens first and covers the h1-square. This *breakthrough sacrifice* is a common strategy.

Give yourself a pat on the back if you noticed, looking at Diagram 45, that to play 1.Kc4 would have brought White's King into the square of the h7-pawn, like this: 1...h5 2.Kd5 h4 3.Ke4 h3 4.Kf3 h2 5.Kg2. But did you also notice that 5...Kf7 would also have brought Black's King into the square of White's Queenside pawns? In that case, White would only have drawn.

In Diagram 46, we see a mixture of advantages. Black has the much more active King and appears to be pressing matters on the Queenside. Unfortunately for him, this isn't the essential factor in the position. It's the advanced White pawns that are the telling difference.

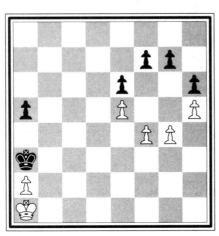

DIAGRAM 46.

1.f5 Kb4

As 1...exf5 2.gxf5 Kb4 3.e6 allows White to Queen, Black is counting on picking up the e5-pawn for an easy win.

2.g5!

The breakthrough sacrifice appears.

2...exf5

White's breakthrough, 2...Kc5 3.f6 gxf6 4.gxh6 or 2...hxg5 3.f6 gxf6 4.h6, is unstoppable.

3.g6! fxg6   4.e6

White promotes his e-pawn and he wins the game.

38

Your Turn on Russian Soil

We are now armed with all the key strategies of King and pawn endings: opposition, distant opposition, the square, triangulation, the crooked path, and pawn breakthroughs. Let's look at some of these in action from my own practice.

In the following example, you will have to play "my" side of the board. That is, you'll be tested to guess each move or series of moves. When making a move, try to articulate to yourself what your justification is for each move. For the purpose of this exercise, it is best if you set the positions up on a chess board, take a deep breath, and cloak yourself in a serious frame of mind. Or, in the parlance of a gunfighter, put on your snake eyes. Use a piece of blank paper to cover the next moves in the book and guess them for yourself.

The position in Diagram 47 is from the 1994 Olympiad I played with International Master Fernando Cruz in Moscow. It was in the tenth round, between the United States and Peru. The U.S. team had had its habitual bad start (I think that jet lag was the culprit) and was just beginning to move up in the tournament standings. Every half point was crucial. For much of the game I had been nursing a positional advantage but was unable to turn it into a material one.

(Some of the following material was borrowed from an article I wrote for my magazine, *Inside Chess* [January 23, 1999]. You can find out more about this fine magazine by visiting my Web site at *http://www.insidechess.com*.)

This Rook ending is quite nice for me. With 48...Rh5 49.Kb4 Rxh2, I can snip a pawn. On the other hand, White's advanced passer, the c4-pawn, will offer good counterplay. I can also consider the pawn ending, 48...Ra5+, trading Rooks. Can this be good for me? I don't think so: White has the outside passed pawn. Once I blockade it (on the c5-square), I can advance my own pawns, with an

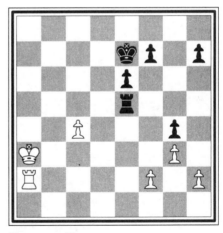

DIAGRAM 47.
Cruz–Seirawan
Moscow Olympiad, 1994

interesting possibility of a breakthrough. After engineering a breakthrough, I'll have sacrificed two pawns. We'll both queen, when I'll be worse off because I'm behind material. Why transpose from a favorable Rook ending to a worse Queen ending? Thus, with a lot of difficulty, I worked out a small 21-move combination.

48...Ra5+!! 49.Kb3 Rxa2 50.Kxa2

My opponent gave me a flabbergasted look and my teammates disappeared from the playing hall. When they returned, their worried expressions said it all. They believed I could only draw. Consequently, the win was especially dramatic. The first thing I had to do was blockade White's passer.

50...Kd6 51.Kb3 Kc5 52.Kc3

In general, such endings favor the side with the outside passer. This is because the passed pawn forces the opposing King to either step into a blockade or move over to win it. Once the King is either on the defensive or out of the way, the other player's King has the opportunity to raid the other side of the board. Each position has its own unique properties; in this case, the favorable position of the g4-pawn keeps White's Kingside structure frozen. White can move his King only back and forth. However, Black can't move his King at all! Instead, he must move his pawns forward, relying on a breakthrough pattern. How would you advance Black's pawns?

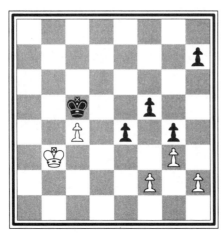

DIAGRAM 48.
Cruz–Seirawan
Moscow Olympiad, 1994

52...e5 53.Kd3 f5!
54.Kc3 e4! 55.Kb3

It is clear, as Diagram 48 illustrates, that Black cannot move his King and must rely on advancing his pawns. Take a moment and decide for yourself how this must be done.

55...h6!

Black wants to advance his pawns to engineer a breakthrough. But he has to be careful with how the pawns are advanced. It is useful to keep White's King away from the Kingside on the less active b3-square. Triangulation isn't the only way to lose a tempo!

56.Kc3 h5 57.Kb3

White can't afford to abandon the protection of the c4-pawn. Follow this line, 57.Kd2 Kxc4 58.Ke3 Kc3! 59.Kf4 Kd2 60.Kxf5 Ke2 61.Kxe4 Kxf2 62.Kf4 Kg2 63.Kg5 Kxh2 64.Kxh5 Kxg3, and you'll see that Black's lone g4-pawn will be a hero.

After White's last move (57.Kb3), Black's position has reached its zenith, and he must make his breakthrough sacrifice.

57...f4!

Black would lose after 57...Kd4 58.Kb4 Kd3 59.c5—did you realize that? And 57...Kc6 58.Kb4 Kb6 59.c5+ Kc6 60.Kc4 is another losing line. If you anticipated that, good job! Such losses are typical for the side on the defense against an outside passed pawn.

58.gxf4

QUIZ 6: Why must White accept the pawn? If White had played 58.Kc3, what would you have done?

58...e3   59.fxe3 h4

With the text, Black will queen. The problem is that after the two-pawn sacrifice, White might queen too.

60.f5!

White isn't going to go gently into that good night. The runaway passer wants to queen with check! What to do?

60...Kd6!

This is the only move as the King steps back to deal with the pawn. Black would have suffered after 60...g3? 61.hxg3 hxg3 62.f6 Kd6 63.c5+! Ke6 64.c6!, in which White would queen with the better game. No dying light this time.

61.Kb4

Did you notice that Black's King could have handled 61.f6 Ke6 62.c5 Kxf6 63.c6 Ke6 64.c7 Kd7, effectively stopping both of White's pawns? If so, bravo! You have made it to the position in Diagram 49.

DIAGRAM 49.
Cruz–Seirawan
Moscow Olympiad, 1994

By first stepping back with the King to the d6-square, White has been forced to waste a tempo with Kb3-b4, as opposed to pushing his c-pawn. Diagram 49 reveals the moment of truth. What do you play?

61...Ke5!!

A lovely move. Before promoting a pawn to a Queen, which can't be prevented, Black first deals with White's passers by eliminating the f5-pawn. It was this move that bogged me down in my calculations. When I realized that the move 61...g3? 62.hxg3 hxg3 63.c5+ Kd7 64.f6 wasn't enough to win, I prepared to abandon the King and pawn ending. Then I saw my King was in the square of both of White's pawns and would be able to deal with them.

Unfortunately, my opponent, reading the blaze in my eyes, now resigned, as he, too, could see the beautiful finish. A pity. I would love to have finished what was on the agenda:

62.c5

White is advancing his other passed pawn? What to do now?

62...Kxf5

In my calculations, I had seen the move 62.c5 but had mentally resisted making this capture, as my King would be moving away from the c5-pawn. Had my King been on, say, the g5-square, playing 62...Kxf5 would have been automatic, as I would have entered the outer edge of the square. Because I love to snack on pawns, I soon overcame my resistance and started licking my chops.

63.c6 Ke6   64.Kb5

White is supporting his passer. Now Black has to make a decision: To which square will he promote his pawn? Can you figure it out?

64...g3   65.hxg3 h3!

The final point. Black will be able to queen with check.

66.Kb6 h2   67.c7 Kd7!   68.Kb7 h1=Q+

Winning, just as I calculated when I entered the King and pawn ending. I was assisted by several factors: One, White could only move his King; two, I was familiar with breakthrough themes; and three, I realized that my King would be in the square, and who doesn't love to queen with check?

In case you think this gold-medal-winning form is the norm for me (I had three draws and seven straight wins for the best individual score), let the following story relieve you of this notion right away.

In Diagram 50, my opponent was the talented Soviet player, Garry Kasparov. I was determined to teach this fine young fellow a lesson. Unfortunately, I had been outplayed throughout the game and was now in an inferior pawn ending. The key factor that gave Garry the superior position was the outside passed pawn. Let me explain. In a situation like this, Black's Queenside pawns are mobile and capable of forcing a passed b-pawn, a factor that forces White's King to remain on guard, preventing the b-pawn from queening. Black has the option to jettison his b-pawn so that when White's King moves over to pick up the passed b-pawn, Black's King can gorge itself on White's Kingside.

Study Diagram 50 carefully. At this point, I was in trouble, running out of time and facing a critical decision. My choice was between 40.Kd4, keeping Black's King at bay, and 40.e4, setting up a wall against Black's King, while advancing a potential passer. What should White play? Cover all the moves but the one you are on with a piece of blank paper and play Black's moves.

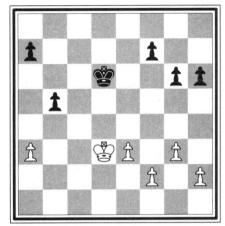

DIAGRAM 50.
Seirawan–Kasparov
Niksic, 1983

40.e4??

This was a losing move from which I never recovered. Though arguable, a guiding principle in such a case is: *An active King move should be chosen over a pawn push.* However, there are hundreds of positions where this principle is false. Consider it to be a general principle, and remember that each position must be assessed according to its own unique factors.

What might have transpired had I played 40.Kd4, the correct choice? From that position, it seems that the game is drawn. White wants to advance his Kingside pawns, but first he decides to keep Black's King at bay. Black, in turn, wants to create a Queenside passer and then raid White's Kingside. Black, therefore, wants to create Kingside weaknesses so that his King will have a clear avenue along which to conduct a raid. In the postmortem, Garry and I decided that Black has two possible choices after 40.Kd4: The first is 40...g5, after which Black would try to isolate White's Kingside pawns and play ...g5-g4, freezing the Kingside (further analysis below). Or Black could have tried 40...f5. Then play continues with:

41.f4!

The only move. After 41.g4? a5, White will find that his e-pawn is a laggard.

41...f6

Black is thinking that he has to be careful to avoid 41...f5? 42.fxg5 hxg5 43.h4!, when White gains an outside passer.

42.e4 a5   43.h4! gxh4

Black tries to break up White's Kingside. If he tries to keep pawns on the board with 43...g4? 44.h5! Kc6 45.e5! fxe5+ 46.Kxe5, White also benefits by creating a protected passed f4-pawn.

44.gxh4 h5

Black has now gained the opposition, as you can see in Diagram 51. White is forced to make the following simplification:

45.e5+ fxe5+ 46.fxe5+ Ke6 47.Kc5 b4 48.axb4 axb4

49.Kxb4 Kxe5 50.Kc3 Kf4 51.Kd2 Kg3 52.Ke1 Kxh4 53.Kf2

The White King is just in time to stop Black's h-pawn from queening, securing the draw.

Let's now go back to move 40 and play out the line following Black's first alternative:

40.Kd4 f5

As before, Black tries to limit White's advance and "cull the herd," that is, create a weak White pawn on the Kingside. If Black is able to create a weakness in White's Kingside structure, he will then use his Queenside majority as a decoy and win White's Kingside pawns.

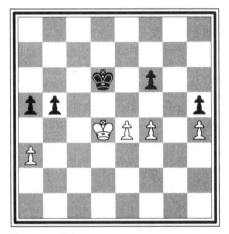

DIAGRAM 51.
Seirawan–Kasparov
Niksic, 1983

41.f4 a5

Black is ready to trade off the Queenside pawns and then attack the Kingside by the route …Kd6-d5-e4, which wins.

42.e4!

White is just in time to trade off the laggard e3-pawn. White's King is still in the square of Black's a-pawn.

42...fxe4

Black prevents 43.e5+ with a protected passed pawn.

43.Kxe4 Kc5 44.g4

At this point the game is drawn, and the concluding moves might well be **44...b4 45.axb4+ axb4 46.f5 gxf5+ 47.gxf5 Kd6 48.Kd4 h5 49.Kc4 Ke5 50.Kxb4 Kxf5 51.Kc3 Kg4 52.Kd2 Kh3 53.Ke2 Kxh2 54.Kf2**.

Now turn your attention to Diagram 52. This reflects the position after I made my blooper on move 40. Your task will be to imitate the yet-to-be-crowned Fédération Internationale des Échecs (FIDE) Champion Garry Kasparov. I assure you the variations are quite difficult, so take your time and study the position. How should Black play?

40...g5!

This move is difficult to anticipate. Black is trying to separate and isolate White's Kingside structure, making it as fragile as possible. His threat is to play …g5-g4, which would freeze White's Kingside majority. White has to respond. If you chose 40…Kc5, pat yourself on the back. That is also an excellent move; however, 40…g5! is the most precise.

41.f4

Now what will you play?

41…gxf4!

Naturally, Black creates two groups of pawn islands. If you wanted to play 42…g4?, allowing 43.e5+, you made a knuckleheaded decision. In that case, White always has the potential of using his e5- and f4-pawns to create a passed pawn, drawing the game.

42.gxf4

Your turn.

42…Kc5!

An excellent move. Black's King is brought to an active position. White can now only wait. If he tries to push his central pawns by 43.f5? f6!, they are weakened and soon lost.

43.Kc3 a5   44.Kd3

The ending has shifted to the position in Diagram 53. How should Black continue?

44…h5!

Here is yet another powerful move that forces further concessions. White can't advance his center pawns because they lack support and will soon fall. Remaining passive with the King, which would mean 45.Kc3 b4+ 46.axb4+ axb4+ 47.Kd3! h4! 48.h3 b3! 49.Kc3 b2!, isn't an option. (A

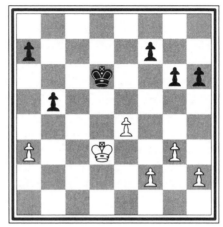

DIAGRAM 52.
Seirawan–Kasparov
Niksic, 1983

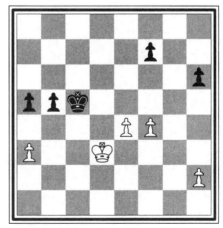

DIAGRAM 53.
Seirawan–Kasparov
Niksic, 1983

typical device, the passer is tossed away as a decoy.) With 50.Kxb2 Kd4 51.e5 Ke4 52.Kc3 Kxf4 53.Kd4 Kg3, Black picks up the h3-pawn, winning. This variation exposes the immediate impact of weakening the g3-square.

45.h4

It is important to stop the Black h-pawn from advancing but the cost is weakening the g3-square. What's next?

45...b4   46.a4

This allows Black to establish a protected passed pawn. This is better than the losing 46.axb4+ axb4 47.f5 f6, after which White's pawns fall one by one. By keeping a-pawns on the board, White also hopes for a saving chance to eat a runaway b-pawn and, while Black is snacking on the Kingside, to swallow up the a5-pawn as well. Your turn.

46...f6!

Black forces another concession. Did you realize what would happen after 46...b3, when the pawn advances? White would retain practical chances with 46...b3? 47.Kc3 b2 48.Kxb2 Kd4 49.Kb3 Kxe4 50.Kc4 Kxf4 51.Kb5 f5 52.Kxa5 Kg3 53.Kb6, after which both players make a Queen.

47.f5

White has no choice and must commit his center pawns. Dropping back with 47.Kd2 Kd4 is no fight, and 47.Ke3 Kc4 doesn't help either. Black faces another critical decision because his position has reached its maximum. What to do now?

47...Kc6!

Ring a bell? Triangulating, of course! Black wants to recreate the position, with White on move. As before, 47...b3? 48.Kc3 b2 49.Kxb2 Kd4 50.Kb3 Kxe4 51.Kc4 Kxf5 52.Kb5 Kg4 reaches the same Queen ending, when White has practical chances to save the game.

48.Kc4

White's hoping to keep an opposition. Your turn.

48...Kc7!   49.Kd3

The current position is illustrated in Diagram 54. As Black, you have to find

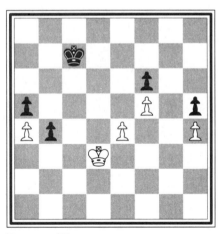

DIAGRAM 54.
Seirawan–Kasparov
Niksic, 1983

another precise move. (Pssst! I'll give you a little hint: Think about distant opposition...)

49...Kd7!!

Beautiful play, Kasparov! (That's you!) Black moves into a distant opposition and is able to achieve his goal.

50.Ke3

White plays his final trick, and now it's your turn.

50...Kc6!

Natural and strong. After 50...Kd6? 51.Kd4, Black wouldn't have made any progress.

51.Kd3

What would you have done against 51.Kd4? And what do you do now?

51...Kc5!

This achieves the same position as in Diagram 54, but this time it's White's turn to move. On 51.Kd4, were you prepared for 51...Kd6 52.Kc4 Ke5 53.Kd3 b3? If so, here's a hearty handclasp! It's important point to note that throughout all this maneuvering, White couldn't play e4-e5 because after ...f6xe5, Black's King would always be in the square of the f5-pawn.

52.Ke3

Okay, I lied; White still has one final, final trick. Your move!

52...b3!

So you're not falling for 52...Kc4? 53.e5!, when Black's King would step out of the square?

53.Kd3

What now? Be precise!

53...Kb4

Actually, 53...b2 also wins. Black realizes he can step out of the square, because his King will escort the b-pawn to coronation.

54.e5 Ka3!

White resigns. A flawless endgame by Garry and an indication of why he became FIDE Champion! This postmortem was a joint effort by Garry and me following the game. (After a highly competitive game of chess, one of the great pleasures is to share the lines of play that remained hidden during the game and analyze them with your opponent. The term *postmortem* is often especially appropriate!)

To further practice your endgame mastery, go over game collections of the world's great players, choose a side, and try to find the best lines of play. You won't be disappointed!

Solutions

QUIZ 1 (DIAGRAM 32): **3.Kd6!** With this move, White gains the opposition. After 3.Kc6 Kc8 4.b7+ Kb8, White only draws. If you tried 3.Kb5 Kc8 4.Ka6 Kb8 5.b7 to win, pat yourself on the back as well. This variation, 3...Kc8 4.Kc6 Kb8 5.b7 Ka7 6.Kc7, also wins.

QUIZ 2 (DIAGRAM 34): **1.Kg5!** This is the only winning move because White takes the opposition. Note that the move 1.Kg4 only draws because 1...Kg6 allows Black to take the opposition. Now the Kings mirror one another across the board: **1...Kf7 2.Kf5 Ke7 3.Ke5 Kd7 4.Kd5 Kc7 5.Kc5 Kb7 6.Kb5 Ka7 7.Kc6 Ka6 8.b4**, and White wins, as we've seen.

QUIZ 3 (DIAGRAM 35): If it is Black's move, the position is a draw. Black would play **1...Kf3**, stepping into the square. If it is White's move, **1.a4** wins because Black's King cannot step into the square. You can practice this visual exercise by randomly placing passed pawns away from the defending King to see whether or not the defender is in the square.

QUIZ 4 (DIAGRAM 41): **1.Kc3!** The immediate race, 1.g4 b5 2.g5 b4 3.g6 b3+ 4.Kc3 b2 5.g7 b1=Q 6.g8=Q+ Ka1, leads to a position that White can't win. With **1...Ka3 2.Kc4!**, White moves with finesse yet again. Once more, nothing is achieved by a pawn race. Then, with **2...Ka4 3.g4 b5+ 4.Kd3!!**, White makes a beautiful point. Black's King is still out of the square, whereas White's King threatens to rush back to the b1-square, blockading the pawn. Black has to waste time with his King to be able to push his pawn. After **4...Ka3 5.g5 b4 6.g6 b3 7.g7 b2 8.Kc2 Ka2 9.g8=Q+**, White checkmates on his next move. A lovely example of luring a King to a square and promoting with check.

QUIZ 5 (DIAGRAM 44): After 1.b6! axb6, the a-pawn breaks through with **2.c6 bxc6 3.a6**, and the a-pawn queens.

QUIZ 6 (DIAGRAM 48): After **57...f4**, 58.Kc3? would be a mistake because 58...f3 wins on the spot. Because of the hostile threat of ...e4-e3, White would have to abandon the c4-pawn, and **59.Kd2 Kxc4 60.Ke3 Kd5** leads to a simple win.

Queen and Pawn Endings

This chapter addresses two types of Queen endings: the basic Queen ending and the Queen vs. Queen ending. You will learn the principles of both, while keeping an eye out for specific patterns and tactics that will help you understand them.

In a basic Queen ending, the Queen fights to prevent a lone pawn from promoting. In Queen vs. Queen endings, in which the superior side is trying to advance a pawn for a second Queen, the strategy is far more complex. Key to both of these endings, as you shall learn, is the position of the Kings.

As a chess beginner, my favorite piece was the Queen. I delighted in my heroic campaigns, reveled in wiping out my opponent's pieces, and felt personally wronged when my Queen was captured.

As a game evolves, the pieces become increasingly powerful and increasingly valuable because they begin to *control more squares*. This is especially true of the long-range Bishops and Rooks. As a board becomes less cluttered with pawns and pieces, the firepower of the Queen really radiates.

Diagram 55 is the kind of position that I would delight in. Black's pieces are all wiped out with check!

1.Qe5+ Kd8   2.Qxb8+ Ke7

3.Qe5+ Kd8   4.Qxh8+ Kc7

5.Qxh2

DIAGRAM 55.

In terms of material, White has taken more than a Queen's worth! Such positions were especially enchanting to me; I thought the Queen was overwhelming, wonderful, certainly the twinkle of my eye! I gloated over all my captures, and was therefore confounded when it was shown to me that the Queen could be tripped up by a single lowly pawn.

Queen vs. b-, d-, e-, or g-Pawn

In Diagram 56, imagine that a pawn race has resulted in White's queening his pawn with check. Black is desperate to promote his pawn but has to spend time to move

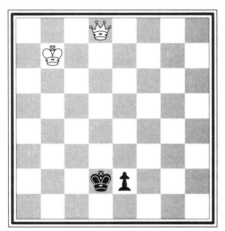

DIAGRAM 56.

his King out of check. How can White win the game? You should quickly recognize that White's only path to victory is to bring his King back to capture the e2-pawn and help deliver checkmate. The Queen cannot win it alone. Fortunately, the winning plan is simple.

1...Ke3

Black threatens to queen his pawn. White must prevent this. He plans to harass the Black King and force it to e1, the promotion square.

2.Qh4 Kd2   3.Qd4+ Kc2

4.Qe3 Kd1   5.Qd3+ Ke1

Black makes this sad but necessary move, as he has to protect the e-pawn. Without the threat of promotion, White can use the tempo to bring back his King. This procedure is repeated throughout the ensuing play.

6.Kc6 Kf2   7.Qd2 Kf1   8.Qf4+ Kg1   9.Qe3+ Kf1   10.Qf3+ Ke1

Once more, White gains time to bring his King closer.

11.Kd5 Kd2   12.Qf2 Kd1   13.Qd4+ Kc2   14.Qe3 Kd1

15.Qd3+ Ke1   16.Ke4!

White's King closes in on the victory.

16...Kf2   17.Qf3+ Ke1   18.Kd3

White captures the pawn and checkmates on the following move.

This pattern is repeated against a b-, d-, or g-pawn as well. The superior side will always be able to win a tempo to bring his King closer and to pick off the passer. Practice this pattern so that it is etched in your mind. Set up a random position with a b-, d-, or g-pawn ready to promote, and then convince yourself that the positions are winning. As for myself, it took no convincing at all. I was certain that the Queen would always win!

Queen vs. a- or h-Pawn

In Diagram 57, we see a similar situation as before, but now the pawn has shifted all the way over to the a-file. Early in my career I had a low regard for the h- and a-pawns; I thought they were the worst ones on the board! The reason for my disdain was that, unlike other pawns, they were limited and could capture in only one direction. Although, in general, the h- and a-pawns do have less value than other pawns, they redeem themselves in basic Queen endings. I learned this the hard way, when I found myself staring at the situation in Diagram 57. A draw! At first I could hardly believe my eyes. "What?" I cried out loud. Hadn't we seen this in Diagram 55, where the Queen wiped out Black's whole army? Despite my best efforts, I just couldn't win the position. My principal try was:

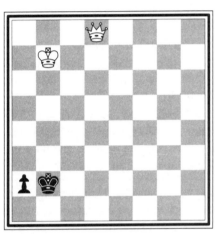

DIAGRAM 57.

1.Qd4+ Kb1   2.Qb4+ Kc2   3.Qa3 Kb1   4.Qb3+ Ka1!

Now I understood that my Queen was too powerful for its own good. In this situation, Black is stalemated, and White has no time to bring his King into play.

If White's King were a lot closer, say on the d2-square, the win would be a snap.

Set up the position with White's King on d2 and follow these moves:

1.Qd1+ Kb2   2.Qc1+ Kb3

3.Qa1

With the a2-pawn blockaded, White is quick to win it. The question is: Which squares does White's King have to be on for a winning position?

The winning zone is shown in Diagram 58. If White's King is on any of the squares inside this zone, the position is

DIAGRAM 58.

a win. As we can see, the d5-square is inside the zone, and White wins. The operation is simple:

1.Qf6+ Kb1

This is the only move because 1...Kc2 2.Qa1 wins on the spot.

2.Qf1+ Kb2   3.Qe2+ Kb1

Once more, 3...Kb3? allows 4.Qe5, with Qe5-a1 to follow.

4.Kc4! a1=Q   5.Kb3

White checkmates. (We saw this before, in Chapter Two, Diagram 39.)

If White's King is in the zone on, say, the e3-square, the win is also straightforward:

1.Qd2+ Kb1   2.Kd3 a1=Q   3.Qc2 Checkmate

Place the White King elsewhere in the zone, and figure out how White should win.

The winning zone of the h-pawn is mirrored on the other side of the board. This inability of the Queen to overcome a lousy a- or h-pawn was hard to believe.

QUIZ 1: Visualize the following position (do not set the position up on the board, but try to imagine the pattern of movements): White has a Queen on the e1-square. Black has a King on g2 and a pawn on h2 that is ready to queen. If White's King were on the e5-square, could White win?

Queen vs. c- or f-Pawn

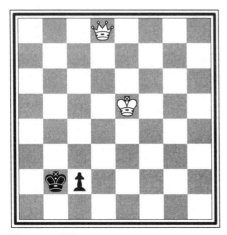

DIAGRAM 59.

Equally confusing to me was that both the c- and f-pawns could also withstand the power of the Queen. A typical situation is seen in Diagram 59. In this position, White's King is even closer than before. Despite this added advantage, the position is drawn.

1.Qb6+ Ka1!

Black avoids stepping onto c1, the promotion square, which would allow White time to draw his King closer to the c-pawn. Another bad move would be 1...Kc3? 2.Qd4+! Kb3 3.Qa1!, which successfully neutralizes Black's pawn.

2.Qd4+ Kb1   3.Qb4+ Ka1

4.Qc3+ Kb1   5.Qb3+

White has managed to maximize the potential of his Queen. Unfortunately, the Queen is too strong for its own good.

5...Ka1!

White is welcome to capture the c2-pawn with a stalemate, because he cannot strengthen his position any further. Once again, White is tripped up by the lack of a supporting King. Against a c-pawn, what is the winning zone? It is shown in Diagram 60.

As before, take the time to play out a few positions. Put the King inside the winning zone and challenge yourself to win the position.

DIAGRAM 60.

Queen and Pawn vs. Queen

As you know, with just a little help, a friendly pawn or even the misplaced pieces of the opponent are enough to allow the Queen checkmate. When not giving checkmate, the Queen can often save a position in which one player is behind in material by giving a perpetual check, thereby drawing the game. You will need to calculate specific positions to determine whether the position is won or drawn, but you will be aided by a number of general principles regarding Queen and pawn vs. Queen endings.

The reason Queen and pawn vs. Queen endings are notoriously difficult is that the defending side is often able to give a whole series of checks, driving the King around the empty board. While the superior side is trying to promote his passer, the twin tasks of escaping a perpetual check and promoting the pawn are quite difficult. Because of this difficulty, we will limit our discussion to those positions where the passed pawn is only one square away from queening. At one time, these endings were considered drawn because of the Queen's remarkable perpetual check-making ability. Today, with the advent of computers, new winning methods have been discovered, and these endings have been largely rewritten. Even wins featuring the "bad" a- and h-pawns have been worked out. We can't cover them all, so I'll just show a few examples of the recurring themes for the defender and attacker and encourage you to explore other possibilities.

In Diagram 61, we see a study by composers and endgame pioneers Josef Kling (1811–76) and Bernhard Horowitz (1808–85), which was first published in 1851. In the diagram, it is obvious that Black's King is misplaced. The best square for the defending King is directly in front of the passer, where he can hope to win the pawn. In a case like this, in which the King is blockading, the defender usually has no problem drawing the position. This brings up our first principle in these endings: *If the defending King is unable to stabilize itself in front of the passer, the best solution is to get the defending King as far away from the passer as possible.*

At first, this principle seems counter-intuitive, but Diagram 61 will help you understand it well. White wins with the quiet move:

1.Qb4!

One of the paradoxes of Queen endings is that the superior side is often better off making a quiet Queen move than trying a forceful series of checks. After 1.Qb4!, Black's King is frozen in place, and only his Queen can move. His Queen must maintain the pin against the b7-pawn, or the under-promotion b8=N+ will decide the outcome.

DIAGRAM 61.
Kling–Horowitz, 1851

1...Qh1!

Black takes the best defense to avoid a number of other attractive losses. Re-treating the Queen along the diagonal isn't easy: 1...Qd5 2.Qa4+ Kb6 3.Qb3+! Qxb3 4.b8=Q+ wins the Queen. It's the same with 1...Qf3 2.Qa4+ Kb6 3.Qb3+!, which wins. Another win is 1...Qg2 2.Qa3+! Kb6 3.Qb2+!, all because of a skewer tactic.

2.Qa3+ Kb6   3.Qb2+ Kc7

Black avoids the winning theme we've just witnessed, which would be 3...Ka6(?) 4.Qa2+ Kb6 5.Qb1+! Qxb1 6.b8=Q+, with another skewer.

4.Qh2+!! Qxh2   5.b8=Q+

Black's Queen is skewered yet again, this time on the diagonal.

Take another look at Diagram 61, and with the previous principle in mind, remove Black's King from the board. Now try to win the game against a friend, and you will discover that the pawn has no chance of queening. In Diagram 61, Black's King was in the way, and this fact tripped him up.

With the King out of the way, as in Diagram 62, the defender can exploit this new position to his advantage. The position in Diagram 62 was published by Giambatista Lolli (1698–1769) in 1763, 13 years before the United States became an independent nation! More than 200 years later, the analysis is still cor-

DIAGRAM 62.
G. Lolli, 1763

rect. Black draws by forcing White to queen his pawn:

1...Qh4+ 2.Qh7 Qd8+! 3.g8=Q

White achieves his aim of promoting his pawn to a Queen. But it's not enough because Black is able to establish a perpetual check.

3...Qf6+ 4.Qhg7 Qh4+

The game is drawn. Thus, you discover that if the King is far enough out of play, the defender can even allow the pawn to promote, provided that the newly hatched Queen can't break the perpetual check by *interposing with check*. For this reason, it is usually best if the defending King is out of play on the *edges* of the board.

In Diagram 63, we visit the last of these Queen and pawn vs. Queen endings. White's passer, the d-pawn, is one of the best he could have. Like other central pawns, it offers White's King good shielding opportunities. Black, for his part, is happy with the placement of his King, knowing it is out of the way.

DIAGRAM 63.

55

This placement, however, is not the salient feature of the position. The key factor is the *poor position of Black's Queen*. In general, the Queen makes a very poor blockade. Thus, the next principle is: *Whenever the defender's Queen is forced to blockade a passer on the promoting square, the game is lost.*

In the position in Diagram 63, Black will be unable to create any perpetual check opportunities because his *blockading Queen is limited in its movements*. As the defender in such endings, you have to fight to keep your Queen as active as possible. Resist using your Queen as a blockader.

1.Qd6+!

White's Queen takes up a powerful centralized position with a gain of tempo.

1...Ka2   2.Kf7!

White's King moves in such a way as to prevent Black's Queen from giving a single check.

2...Kb3   3.Qe6+ Kc2   4.Qe7

The blockading Queen is forced to move, and with that, the promoting pawn wins the game.

Queen with Many Pawns

Are you ready to learn how to deal with the most difficult Queen endings, those with multiple pawns? In such endings, the positions are so complex that you will have to calculate each position for its unique characteristics. Still, you can help your play by utilizing a few principles:

- *Queens are at their most powerful when centralized.*

- *The safety of the King is paramount.*

- *The most important pawn is a passer that is well advanced.*

- *It is important to be able to recognize perpetual check patterns.*

Before we tackle the difficult subject of Queen endings with a number of pawns, you should familiarize yourself with two very common perpetual check patterns. Diagrams 64 and 65 both show positions in which White's threat of promoting his passed pawn is unstoppable. Black's saving grace is a perpetual check.

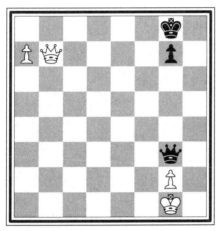

DIAGRAM 64.

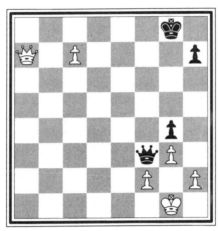

DIAGRAM 65.

In Diagram 64, the standard **1...Qe1+ 2.Kh2 Qh4+ 3.Kg1 Qe1+** perpetual check is the game saver.

Diagram 65 features another common perpetual check. Black saves his skin with **1...Qd1+ 2.Kg2 Qf3+ 3.Kg1 Qd1+**. If you remove both White's and Black's g-pawns, the drawing sequence is **1...Qd1+ 2.Kg2 Qg4+**. These two drawing patterns are common not only in endgame positions, but in middlegame positions, too.

For the next positions, you will be required to play White and answer a series of questions. As before, set up the position on your chessboard and cover all the moves but the one you are on with a blank sheet of paper.

In Diagram 66 (published by Nicolaas Cortlever, who was born in 1915 in Amsterdam and is still going strong), you are down two pawns. How do you play?

1.Qe7+

Of course. All other moves lose.

1...Qg5

A necessity, as 1...g5? 2.Qe1+ would win for White. Did you realize this? If so, well done. What do you do now?

DIAGRAM 66.
N. Cortlever, 1941

2.Qe4+! Qg4

QUIZ 2: Now what do you play?

The position in Diagram 67 is from an analysis published by Russian Grandmaster Yuri Averbach in 1962, and is a model of how to win such positions. Cover all the moves but the one you are on with a sheet of paper and play White. How would you play?

1.c7

Naturally, passed pawns must always be pushed!

1...Qd7

Black stops the pawn, hoping to save the game by perpetual check. What's next?

2.Qe4+!!

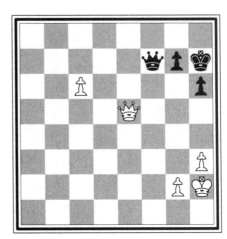

DIAGRAM 67.
Y. Averbach, 1962

Very nice. If you chose 2.Qc5 to force the defender to blockade with 2...Qc8, you made a good choice. However, it wasn't the best choice. In Queen endings, creating pawn weaknesses around the Kings by forcing the pawns to advance is of crucial importance. After 2.Qe4+!!, Black is forced to push his g-pawn forward. This makes Black's King that much more vulnerable to checks. After 2.Qc5 Qc8 3.Qd6 Qf5, again Black is poised to make a perpetual check.

2...g6

QUIZ 3: Explain why 2...Kh8 loses.

After 2...g6, how should you continue?

3.Qc2!

A powerful dual-purpose move. White is prepared to answer 3...Qd6+? with 4.g3, which wins while it also threatens to promote his pawn. Black must blockade.

3...Qc8

Your turn.

4.Qc5!

White immediately takes advantage of Black's loosened pawn shield.

4...h5

QUIZ 4: How would you have won after 4...g5? Find the most efficient method.

5.Qe7+

A nasty check. Black has only one move:

5...Kh6

Now is a key moment. What do you play?

6.h4!!

If you wanted to play 6.Qd8, how did you intend to answer 6...Qf5? Certainly not by 7.c8=Q?? Qe5+, which gives Black an escape with his perpetual check. The right choice confines Black's King, gives White's King a bit more breathing room, and forces Black's Queen to move.

6...Qh8

Being on a blockading square limits Black's options. The active try is 6...Qa6 7.Qf8+ Kh7 8.c8=Q, and it is too easy for White. Your turn.

7.Qe3+!

Black's King is chased back to a more vulnerable square.

7...Kh7

Your turn.

8.Qe6!

Naturally, White promotes his pawn.

8...Qd4

A last, gasping try for a perpetual check. Now what?

9.Qe7+

White takes advantage of move 7 to reposition his Queen.

9...Kh6 10.Qg5+ Kh7 11.c8=Q

And that wraps it up.

An Example from Linares

The position in Diagram 68 on the next page appears to have nothing to do with the chapter at hand. But it features a number of interesting turns. Diagram 68 is from a 1999 tournament game between the Bulgarian Grandmaster Veselin Topalov and the world's highest-rated player (at the time of this book's publication), Grandmaster Garry Kasparov. The game was played in Round 7 of the famous Linares tournament, held annually in Spain. The Linares tournament markets itself as the "Wimbledon of Chess" because year after year it features a round-robin of the world's highest-rated players.

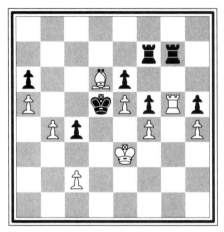

DIAGRAM 68.
Topalov–Kasparov
Linares, 1999, Round 7

The position in Diagram 68 was reached after Black's forty-third move. White, who is an exchange down (meaning a Rook for a Bishop or a Rook for a Knight), has erected a near fortress-like position, having closed all the files to keep Black's Rooks at bay. Looking closely at the position, we can discern that White's Rook is frozen. If he plays 44.Rxh5?? Rh7!, Black will trade Rooks and win the h-pawn, and the position will open to Black's advantage. White's King must remain near the center to prevent Black's King from encroaching. If it wanders too far to the Queenside, Black will trade Rooks on the g5-square, and the newly minted passer—either the h5-pawn, or the f5-pawn—would scurry to promotion. This situation obliges White's Bishop to move, a peculiar series of circumstances that allows Black's King to scoot around the board at will.

44.c3 Kc6

Unable to make progress in the center, Black takes another approach to penetrating White's fortress.

45.Kf3 Kb5 46.Bc5 Ka4
47.Bd4 Rd7 48.Ke3 Kb3
49.Ke2

The game has moved to the position shown in Diagram 69. Black has achieved his maximum and now needs a breakthrough.

49...Rxg5! 50.fxg5 Rxd4!
51.cxd4 c3 52.g6 c2
53.g7 c1=Q 54.g8=Q

DIAGRAM 69.
Topalov–Kasparov
Linares, 1999, Round 7

The game has now transformed into our topical Queen ending, as shown in Diagram 70. Time to take stock. How did Kasparov approach this ending? First and foremost, he counted the material and realized he was a pawn down. Not good, not good at all! However, he made a few other evaluations. Black's extremely active King is a key. It can create checkmating threats by combining the threat of capturing White's pawns with the idea of working with the Queen. The next trump is the passer. Which side has one? Of all the pawns on the board, Black's f5-pawn is the most dangerous. Thus, despite being a pawn down, Black has two key trumps: the better King, and the better passer. Is this enough to win? Follow the game to find out.

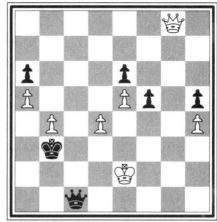

DIAGRAM 70.
Topalov–Kasparov
Linares, 1999, Round 7

54...Qc4+!

Another fine dual-purpose move. Kasparov defends his e6-pawn while playing to capture—with check—White's pawns.

55.Ke3 Kc3!

Black renews the threat to the d4-pawn, forcing White's Queen to take a defensive posture.

56.Qd8 Qd3+   57.Kf4 Qd2+!

A key move. White had hoped to escape with his King via the g5-square, not only to avoid Queen checks, but also to munch the h5-pawn, and so gain his own passer.

QUIZ 5: Why didn't Kasparov grab the d4-pawn with check and force the trade of Queens?

58.Kf3 Qd1+!

This fine move repositions the Queen. Black wants to push his f-pawn up the board to make a new Queen while creating checkmating threats. At the moment, White's King is blockading and has to be pushed aside.

59.Ke3

White couldn't step forward with his King, by playing 59.Kf4? because 59...Qg4+ 60.Ke3 f4+. (This is Black's point. Black's pawn marches forward with gain of tempo.) Then 61.Kf2 Qg3+ 62.Kf1 Qd3+ 63.Kg1 Qe3+ 64.Kf1 f3 wins the game because of the mating threat of 65...Qe2+ and 66.Qg2 checkmate.

59...Qg1+ 60.Ke2 Qg2+ 61.Ke3

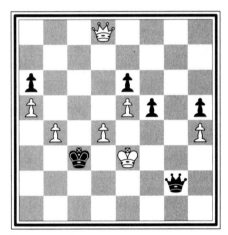

DIAGRAM 71.
Topalov–Kasparov
Linares, 1999, Round 7

The play has brought us to the position shown in Diagram 71, where Kasparov delivers a telling blow.

61...f4+!

Topalov resigns as he sees the lovely finale. He is forced to play 62.Kxf4 Kd3! (with the deadly threat of 63...Qg4 checkmate) 63.Qg5 Qf2, which produces an epaulet checkmate.

This game fragment contains an important lesson. When a King is able to make it *behind* enemy lines, quite often the enemy pawns act as a pawn shield! If you were to replay this fragment and extract a few pawns from the board—the d4- and b4-pawns, for instance—Black's King would be much more vulnerable to checks.

Of all the endings, I have found that Queen endings are the most difficult and complex. I encourage you to practice this ending, but I suggest that you do so in the context of a *whole* game. Merely replaying Queen ending positions will not give you an appreciation for the challenging and beautiful nature of this particular ending.

Solutions

QUIZ 1 (DIAGRAM 58): Yes, the position is clearly won. White plays **1.Qe2+ Kg1 2.Kf4 h1=Q 3.Kg3**, winning. If you were able to do this without looking at the board, you have a tremendous talent!

QUIZ 2 (DIAGRAM 66): If you chose **3.Qe7+** and claimed a perpetual check, excellent! Grabbing a draw two pawns down is a gift. If you are ambitious and realize White has a win, you are right! How? Amazingly, with **3.Qe3!**, Black is in zugzwang and is lost. This is because of the poor position of his King. Try to find a way out for yourself. Beautiful, no?

QUIZ 3 (DIAGRAM 67): White promotes after **2...Kh8 3.Qa8+ Kh7 4.c8=Q Qd6+ 5.g3 Qd2+ 6.Qg2!**, with a winning interposition.

QUIZ 4 (DIAGRAM 67): White forces the promotion of his pawn and protects his King by bringing his Queen to the b8-square: **4...g5 5.Qc2+! Kg7 6.Qb2+ Kh7 7.Qb8!**, winning. Note that after the c-pawn queens, the b8-Queen is ideally placed to protect the White King.

QUIZ 5 (DIAGRAM 70): Kasparov would have stumbled into a lost position after 57...Qxd4+?? 58.Qxd4+ Kxd4 59.b5! The pawn breakthrough that allows Topalov to win is **59...Kc5 60.bxa6 Kc6 61.Kg5**. Black will eat the h5-pawn while staying within the square of the f5-pawn. Thereafter, the h4-pawn will promote.

Rook Endings

Rook endings are common. In fact, among club, tournament, and correspondence players, Rook endings account for nearly half of all endings. For this reason, all tournament players (and potential tournament players) owe it to themselves to study Rook endings seriously.

This will be the longest and most important chapter in this book. Because periodically taking stock helps solidify understanding, midway-through the chapter we will recap the Rook ending principles that we have covered up to that point. The chapter is divided into eight types of Rook endings, featuring several key positions that are worth memorizing. In addition to showing you some great examples of Rook endings, I'll challenge you to play one side and answer a series of questions. Take these challenges seriously, as I did. Good luck, and have fun.

Rook vs. Pawn

The Extraordinary

The Rook moves in straight, humble lines: up and down, and side to side. In spite of its limitations, it has associated with it a wealth of beautiful endings. In general, the player with the Rook is trying to win; as you will see, however, this isn't always the case.

My own personal favorite—an ending that is certain to charm everyone who sees it—is shown in Diagram 72 on the next page. The position in this diagram has an intriguing history. It was published in the *Glasgow Weekly Citizen*, April 27, 1895, by Georges Barbier (1844–95). He was trying to recall a game from an 1875 match between a Mr. Fenton and a Mr. Potter, but he had done so incorrectly. The following week the position was corrected and declared drawn. After reading the article, Fernando Saavedra (1857–1922), a monk, discovered a single celebrated move that allowed White to win! As you play out this win, you will be enchanted by the number of tactics (in italics) that appear as if by magic. After all, there are only four pieces on the board!

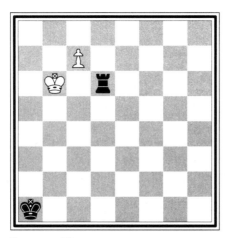

DIAGRAM 72.
F. Saavedra, 1895

1.Kb5

This move is self-evident. After 1.Ka7? or 1.Kb7?, Black plays 1...Rd7, resulting in an *absolute pin* of the c7-pawn and a subsequent capture and a draw. After 1.Kc5? Rd1!, Black is ready to play 2...Rc1+, *skewering* White on the c-file. Finally, 1.Ka5?? Rc6 flat out loses for White.

1...Rd5+ 2.Kb4

This is the only way to play for the win. Playing 2.Kb6 Rd6+ acquiesces to a draw by *perpetual check*.

2...Rd4+ 3.Kb3 Rd3+ 4.Kc2!

At last Black seems to have run out of luck. White has prevented the skewer on the c-file and is now ready to promote and win!

4...Rd4!!

What a lovely trap. The original solution, 5.c8=Q?, allows 5...Rc4+!! 6.Qxc4, for a *stalemate!* Surprise! So what can White do instead?

5.c8=R!!

A stunning *underpromotion* found by Fernando Saavedra—hence the name of the study. White sidesteps the stalemate trick and threatens checkmate on the a-file.

5...Ra4 6.Kb3!

Suddenly the threat of checkmate comes from a different direction. The hit against the a4-Rook creates a *double threat* because of the *echo checkmate* on the c1-square, which wins the game. Charming, no?

Sit back for a moment and consider the list of tactics featured in this ending: absolute pin, skewer, perpetual check, stalemate, underpromotion, double threat, and echo checkmate. That's quite an assortment!

The Ordinary

Having shared the extraordinary, I need to show you the ordinary. I hasten to point out that Rooks are usually stronger than passed pawns. Let's take a look at those positions in which the side with the Rook is trying to win.

The position in Diagram 73 is common enough. We can easily imagine that a Rook ending has taken place in which White has promoted his h-pawn and forced Black to capture, losing his Rook. Now it is Black's turn to try to advance his b-pawn to win back the Rook and draw the game. In approaching this position, follow these firm principles:

- *The King must escort the pawn to the promotion square.*

- *The pawn should not advance far from the reach of the escorting King.*

DIAGRAM 73.

- *The Rook should be behind the passed pawn.*

With these principles in mind, we can understand that if Black were to make the illegal move 1...b2? 2.Rb8, the advanced pawn would be lost. Right away we realize that the King and pawn must be linked with one another. Next we understand that h8 is the wrong square for the Rook. Clearly, the best square is b8, behind the b-pawn. We've already discerned a lot, but how should we go about calculating the position? Is the position in Diagram 73 a draw, or is it a win? To calculate correctly, don't think to yourself, "I go here, he goes there." Count tempi instead.

Take another glance at Diagram 73. To stop the pawn from queening, White will have to race back with his King to cover the promotion square—in this case, the b1-square. There are only two squares to run to: c2 and a2, which both cover the promotion square. We can discount the a2-square, as White's King is on the g-file. (If White's King were on the a-file, White would race toward the a2-square.) In short, we know that White's King has to get to the c2-square as quickly as possible. We count 1.Kf6, 2.Ke5, 3.Kd4, 4.Kd3, 5.Kc2. That's five moves, so we have to add another tempo for 6.Rb8, which also covers the b1-square. Thus in six moves, White wins.

Black must also count tempi. His King must cover the b1-square, and his pawn has to get there too! So he counts 1...b4, 2...Kc4, 3...b3, 4...Kc3, 5...b2, 6...Kc2. Counting the tempi ends in a draw!

Thus the crucial question is: Whose move is it? If it's White's move, he wins, but if it's Black's move, it's a draw. Train yourself to count tempi before doing concrete calculations. Only after you have counted tempi and determined the state of the position by normal play can you try to find a way to *win a tempo*. If you can win a tempo through tricky tactical play, you can turn the draw into a victory.

Now let's see the tempi that we have just counted unfold in actual moves. White wins with:

1.Kf6 b4   2.Ke5 Kc4   3.Ke4 b3   4.Rc8+ Kb4   5.Kd3 b2

6.Kc2 Ka3   7.Rb8

Black draws with:

1...b4   2.Kf6 Kc4   3.Ke5 b3   4.Ke4

Or he could try **4.Rc8+ Kd3**, aiming for the c2-square.

4...b2   5.Rb8 Kc3   6.Ke3 Kc2

Let's see another clear-cut example of counting tempi. In Diagram 74, White has the benefit of a good location for his Rook. While the ideal spot would be the

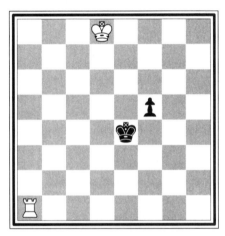

DIAGRAM 74.

f8-square, controlling the promotion square to start counting tempi is quite a plus! White needs six moves to get to either the e2- or g2-square with his King. Black needs five moves to set up his drawn position. With White to move, the sequence is clear. Because Black's King obstructs his path to the e2-square, he will head to the g2-square and win:

1.Ke7 f4   2.Kf6 f3   3.Kg5 f2

4.Kg4 Ke3   5.Kg3 Ke2   6.Kg2

Counting tempi gets close to the truth for most basic Rook ending positions, but it's not the *whole* truth. Often the superior side can win a crucial tempo and make a victory from a posi-tion that would be drawn according to the tempi count. This is usually done with a Rook check.

Diagram 75 features a position analyzed by the fifth World Champion, Machgielis (Max) Euwe (1901–81). Going by a strict tempi count, the game is a draw. If White can position his Rook behind the g–pawn with gain of tempo, he will win. Euwe shows us how to do it:

1.Rf6+!

Try to determine why 1.Kg6 is a mistake with which White could no longer win.

1...Ke3   2.Rg6 Kf4

White has favorably repositioned his Rook to its ideal post, behind the passer with a gain of tempo. Having earned that advantage, White's next concern is how to bring the King back into play. The discerning reader might have noticed that in Diagrams 73 and 74, the Kings came close to one another while jostling for the control of vital squares. In some positions, it is necessary to take a "creative" route. This tactic should spark a recollection of the crooked path, which we can see in action once again in the following:

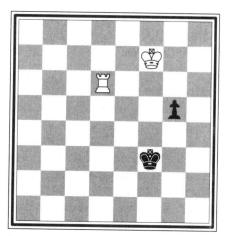

DIAGRAM 75.
M. Euwe, 1934

3.Kg7!

Strictly speaking, 3.Rg8 g4 4.Kg6 g3 5.Kh5 achieves the same position, but I prefer the choice he made.

3...g4   4.Kh6 g3   5.Kh5 Kf3   6.Kh4 g2   7.Kh3

Missing this tempo-winning Rook device is common, even in master games.

In the position in Diagram 76, White is on the move. He played **1.Kd6?**, and with **1...f5 2.Re2+ Kd4!**, Black stopped White's King from coming back to block the passer. The players then agreed to a draw. A pity. What did White miss?

1.Re2+!

White gains a crucial tempo. Black has two choices, but they both lose. He can play **1...Kd5 2.Rf2 Ke5 3.Kd7 f5 4.Ke7 f4 5.Rf1!** (White steps out of the way of ...Ke5-Ke4-Ke3 to avoid adding tempo.) **5...Ke4** (Otherwise, 5...Kf5 Kf7! gives Black the choice of how White's King approaches.) **6.Kf6 f3 7.Kg5 Ke3 8.Kg4 f2 9.Kg3**, and White wins. Or he can play **1...Kf3 2.Re1!** (threatening the skewer 3.Rf1+ and winning the f-pawn) **2...f5** (After 2...Kf2? 3.Re6 f5

DIAGRAM 76.
Díaz–Domínguez
Pinar del Rio, 1981

4.Rf6, White wins the pawn because it lacks protection.) **3.Kd6 f4 4.Ke5 Kf2 5.Ra1 f3 6.Kf4!**, and again White wins. Black is merely given the choice of which way White's King will cover the promotion square.

Cutting the King

I would like to return for a moment to a familiar position. Notice that Diagram 77 is quite similar to Diagram 73; I've just rearranged White's King and Rook and moved Black's King back one square. (By the way, this method of slightly altering the pieces of a given position is an excellent way to learn the secrets of endings.)

Black is on move and, after doing a tempi count, realizes that the position is drawn. Black plays **1...Kc5! 2.Kh7 b4 3.Kg6 Kc4 4.Kf5 b3 5.Ke4 b2 6.Rb7 Kc3** with an easy draw. White has a better try if Black plays 1...Kc5! 2.Rc7+ Kd4 3.Rb7 Kc4 4.Kg7 b4 5.Kf6 b3 6.Ke5 Kc3, but it isn't enough for victory.

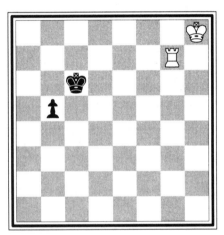

DIAGRAM 77.

The situation in Diagram 77 is a draw if Black plays correctly. But let's assume that his vigilance slips and that he thinks that he can do just as well by advancing his pawn:

1...b4??

Surprisingly, this is a losing move. Black is severely punished by not having the escorting King positioned with the passer, as the principles previously discussed dictate. White is now able to cut Black's King from the support of his pawn.

2.Rg5!

White wins on the spot. It doesn't matter how far White's King is from the promotion square, and counting tempi is no longer important. Black can't advance the pawn, because 2...b3 3.Rg3! b2 4.Rb3 wins the pawn and the game. This plan of cutting the King off from the passer is a common device for turning a draw into a win.

I began this section on Rook vs. pawn endings with an astoundingly deceptive position, a dirty trick for which I apologize. I'd like to make up for it by offering you a beautiful study by Grandmaster Pal Benko, America's most eminent problemist and endgame theoretician. Pal has delighted and confounded *Chess Life* magazine readers for the last 35 years. One of his pet studies, designed to torment

and instruct, is shown in Diagram 78. I use Pal's analysis below. It is White's turn to play and to win. How would you proceed?

Diagram 78 is a deceivingly simple position, with many hidden points. It is utterly misleading, and therein lies its charm. White's first move defies the laws of greed.

1.Rb7+!

A nasty check. Black now has to decide which pawn he should try to promote, and White will play accordingly. A starting move of 1.Rxc6? loses a critical tempo. After 1...a5, Black has no problems drawing. If you are thinking about

DIAGRAM 78.
P. Benko, 1980

capturing the pawn, you're not familiar with Benko's problems! He delights in showing this most natural choice to be a mistake.

1...Kc3   2.Kc7 a5   3.Ra7!

White gains a tempo by pulling back the Black King.

3...Kb4

Black can't put his faith in his c-pawn with 3...c5 4.Kc6! c4 5.Kc5 Kb3 6.Kd4! c3 7.Kd3, because Ra7-b7+ would surely follow, winning.

4.Kd6!!

Typical Benko, and right on the mark. There is a stalemate motif in the position, so White lets the c-pawn live. With the foolhardy 4.Kxc6? a4 5.Kd5 a3 6.Kd4 Kb3 7.Kd3 Kb2! 8.Kd2 a2 9.Rb7+ Ka1, Black is saved by the stalemate, and White's King can't come any closer. Now we see why the c-pawn is spared, a theme that is the key to the study.

4...a4   5.Ke5 a3   6.Kd4 Kb3   7.Kd3 Kb2   8.Kd2 a2   9.Rb7+ Ka3

Black has no choice. With 9...Ka1 10.Kc2 c5 11.Rd7, and thanks to the c-pawn, Black is checkmated next move.

10.Kc2! a1=N+

If Black queens the pawn, then 10...a1=Q? 11.Ra7+ skewers him.

11.Kc3 Ka2   12.Rb2+! Ka3   13.Rb6 Ka2   14.Rxc6 Kb1

15.Rh6 Ka2   16.Rb6!

This ends our discussion of basic Rook vs. pawn endings, but I encourage you to do more of your own investigating. Myriad positions illustrate how a Rook can cope with a passed pawn, and studying them will bring you much satisfaction. You now have the tools for understanding this type of ending. *Remember to count tempi.* Let's deal with the next challenge, Rook and pawn vs. Rook endings.

Rook and Pawn vs. Rook

Mastering Lucena

In Rook and pawn vs. Rook endings, there are three principles of play:

- ■ *The passed pawn must be supported by the King.*

- ■ *The defending King must be kept as far from the passer as possible. This is done by cutting off the enemy King with the Rook, either on the rank or file.*

- ■ *Both for attacker and defender, the Rook is best when placed behind the passer.*

Taking these principles to heart will serve us well.

In tournament circles, the position shown in Diagram 79 is arguably the best-known position in chess! This position's winning method was published by Luís

DIAGRAM 79.
L.R. Lucena, 1497

Ramírez Lucena 500 years ago, and it is as valid today as it was then. In Diagram 79, White will *build a bridge,* an effective strategy for all pawn positions (b-, c-, d-, e-, f-, and g-pawns) except those with the a- and h-pawns.

What do I mean by building a bridge? Consider the characteristics of the position. Black's King is cut off on the f-file and is unable to cover the promotion square. To win the game, White's King will have to move aside and promote the pawn, but the initial try is a dead end: With 1.Ke7? Re2+ 2.Kd6 Rd2+ 3.Kc6 Rc2+ 4.Kb6 Rd2 5.Kc7 Rc2+ 6.Kd8, White achieves nothing. Alternately, and to prevent Black from checking with his

Rook, White creates cover for his King by building a protective bridge between his King and his Rook:

1.Rf4! Rc1

Black waits because 1...Re2? 2.Rc4! would cover the c-file, preparing 3.Kc8 to promote the pawn.

2.Ke7

White threatens to promote the pawn. Black is therefore forced to give a series of checks.

2...Re1+   3.Kd6 Rd1+   4.Ke6

White drops the immediate threat to promote but is ready to play 5.Rf5 and 6.Rd5 to win. Black could play 4...Re1+, but then 5.Kd5! Rd1+ 6.Rd4 completes the bridge and wins the game. So play proceeds as follows: **4..Kg6** (setting the trap of 5.Rf5? Rxd7, winning the passer) **5.Rg4+!** (pushing Black's King further away from the d-pawn) **5...Kh5** (5...Kh7 6.Rg5! would lead to Rg5-d5) **6.Rg8!** (covering the d8-square. Black will soon run out of checks.) **6...Re1+ 7.Kd6 Rd1+ 8.Kc6 Rc1+ 9.Kb5 Rb1+ 10.Ka4**, and White zigzags his King back up the board. Eventually, d7-d8=Q will cost Black his Rook.

Mastering the Lucena position means the difference between drawing and winning. If you make the effort to learn its mechanics, it will be well worth it.

Another example is shown in Diagram 80. This diagram is similar to Diagram 79, and the procedure is identical. I've tried to help the defense by getting the Black King one file closer. It's Black's turn to move. He can't give up the h-file because 1...Re2? 2.Rh1 and Kg8-h8 will win at once.

1...Ke7   2.Re1+!

White's King needs room to be able to escape the g8-hatch. Black's King is pushed farther away from the passer.

2...Kd7

Black would lose even more quickly after 2...Kf6? 3.Kf8 or 2...Kd6? 3.Kf7 Rf1+ 4.Ke8 Rg2 5.Re7! Rg1 6.Rf7! because White would play Ke8-f8 and soon promote the pawn.

DIAGRAM 80.
L.R. Lucena, 1497

3.Re4!

White prepares to build his bridge. Once more, Black's Rook cannot give up the h-file.

3...Rh1 4.Kf7

With this, White threatens to promote and forces the following checks:

4...Rf1+ 5.Kg6 Rg1+ 6.Kf6 Rf1+ 7.Kg5 Rg1+ 8.Rg4!

The bridge is complete. White has stopped the series of checks and now has the joy of promoting a pawn.

Mastering Philidor

Diagram 81 illustrates the second-best-known Rook ending position. This classic device is a must for our bag of tricks. In this device, the defender is given the ideal situation: His King sits on the passed pawn's promotion square. To make a draw, it is crucial that the blockading King isn't forced away. Black has only one way to keep the position, as we can see in the diagram.

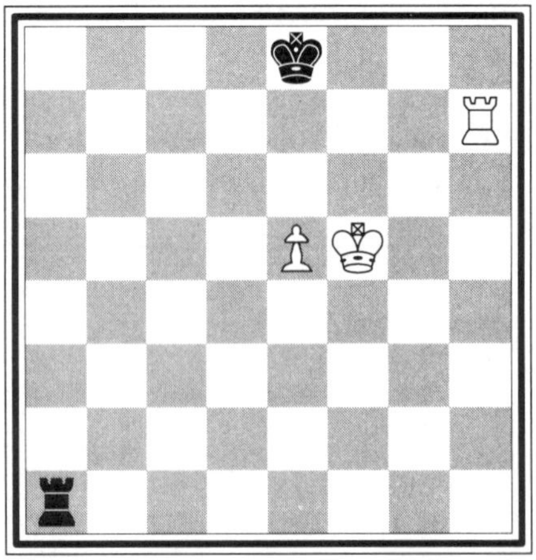

It was François-André Danican Philidor (1726–95), reputedly the best chess player of his time, who showed the world how to correctly defend these types of endings:

1...Ra6!

Black prevents White's King from advancing, planning to wait until White advances his pawn.

2.Rg7 Rb6 3.Ra7

White realizes that the intended 3.Rg6 Rxg6 4.Kxg6 Ke7 produces a drawn King and pawn ending.

DIAGRAM 81.
F.A.D. Philidor, 1777

3...Rc6 4.Rb7 Ra6 5.e6

Finally, White tires of the waiting game and commits his pawn forward. His threat is to advance his King with 6.Kf6 to win.

5...Ra1!

Well played! Now that the e6-square is no longer accessible, Black can check White's King from behind and draw the game.

6.Kf6 Rf1+   7.Ke5 Re1+

Play out the position against a friend and you'll realize that the draw is now easy.

The Philidor method of defense works against all pawns, meaning that the superior side cannot tolerate a blockading King.

Short Side vs. Long Side

Let's revisit Diagram 81 and assume Black is unfamiliar with Philidor's 1...Ra6! defense. Instead, Black makes a mistake with:

1...Rf1+?   2.Ke6!

Elated by his good fortune, White sets up a mating threat with his King and forces the blockading King to evacuate. Black's position has suddenly become precarious, and he has to play exactly to save the game.

2...Kf8!

The only move. After 2...Kd8 3.Rh8+ 4.Ke7, it's a win for White, as you'll discover shortly.

At this point, a discourse on the "short side" vs. the "long side" of the passer will be useful. When the blockading King is forced away from the promotion square—in this case, e8—it is best if the blockading King moves to the short side of the passer. In such a situation, the e-pawn almost bisects the board, but not quite. The short side is the Kingside. In the case of a passed d-pawn, the short side would be the Queenside. Why should the defending side move his King to the short side? The answer lies with the defensive Rook. When the blockading King is forced to flee the promotion square, the defending Rook has to give checks from the *side,* on the ranks of the board, instead of from *behind,* on the files. Remember this: *If the defender is unable to check from the side, the attacker will set up the Lucena position and win. The defender needs to check from the long side of the board, where the Rook will be more effective.*

Let's put this principle to practice:

3.Rh8+!

White's first order of business is to get Black's King as far away from the promotion square of the passer as possible.

3...Kg7   4.Re8

White protects his passer so that when the King moves, the passer can advance under the protecting influence of the Rook. We've now moved forward into the position shown in Diagram 82 at the top of the next page.

DIAGRAM 82.

4...Ra1!

This is the right defensive idea in such situations. Black is aiming for a series of checks on the ranks so that he can bring his King back to the promotion square.

5.Rd8

White's only chance is to block the expected checks with his Rook. If he tries 5.Kd7 Ra7+ 6.Kc6 Ra6+ 7.Kb7 Kf7!, it's an easy draw. After the text, White no longer protects his e-pawn with his Rook. Black shifts his defensive strategy once more.

5...Re1!

Black places the Rook behind the passer and awaits further development. White's King can't advance because of Black's attack on the passer.

6.Rd7+ Kf8   7.Rd8+ Kg7

White's checks have been ineffectual, and if he gives up control of the eighth rank, Black's King will scurry back to the e8-square.

8.Ra8

White wouldn't make progress after 8.Rd5 Kf8!, which would prevent Ke6-e7, freeing the e-pawn to advance. Now Black must fight to avoid the Lucena position, because after 9.Kd7 Kf7 10.Kd6 Re2 11.Ra5 Rd2+, it's a draw. However, White's move contains no threats, and Black keeps the position of his Rook and King.

8...Re2   9.Ra1 Kf8!   10.Rb1 Re3   11.Kd6 Rd3+   12.Ke6 Re3

White has made no progress, but he is wise to test the defensive ability of his opponent. He makes one last effort:

12.Rb8+ Kg7   13.Rb5 Kf8!   14.Kd6 Rd3+   15.Rd5 Rxd5+   16.Kxd5 Ke7

And it's a draw, an event we saw in Chapter Two.

Black's had an easy life so far. Let's make things much more difficult for him. In Diagram 83, shown on the next page, we have advanced the pawn a square, and it is now two moves away from promotion—a nice plus for White. On the other hand, we have also allowed Black to retain his advantage: his King on the short side and his Rook on the long side. But Black has an option, if he knows this principle: *The defender can draw when*

- *The defending King is only one file away from the pawn.*
- *The defending Rook is three files away from the pawn.*

In our example, Black's Rook is on the a-file, and the passer is on the e-file, with the b-, c-, and d-files between the Rook and passer. Thus, *the Rook is three files away.* Let's continue.

DIAGRAM 83.

In Diagram 83 we see that Black's first task is to harass White's King.

1...Ra7+   2.Rd7

Black's checks from the long side force this interposition. The "three file" principle is needed because, after 2.Kd6 Ra6+ 3.Kd7 Ra7+ 4.Kc6 Ra6+ 5.Kd5 Ra5+, we can see that White has not made progress. If the defensive Rook were only two files away, Black would lose a tempo with his Rook. For instance, in Diagram 83, if we allow that Black's Rook is on the b-file, 1...Rb7+ 2.Kd6 Rb6+ 3.Kd7 Rb7+ 4.Kc6 attacks the defending Rook, and White wins. If we continue this line with 4...Rb1 5.e7!, the pawn promotes. Thus, 4...Re7 5.Kd6 gains a tempo and wins. Remember, *the defender's Rook must be three files away from the passer.*

Continuing our analysis:

2...Ra8!

A crucial move. Black must prevent Ke7-e8, in which White would close in on the Lucena position.

3.Rd8

White allows Black to slip back after 3.Kd6+? Kf8 4.e7+ Kf7 5.Rd8 Ra6+, drawing.

3...Ra7+   4.Rd7 Ra8!   5.Rd6!

White's last move was a crafty one, one that puts enormous pressure on Black to find an exact defense.

Now set up your board to match Diagram 84 and try to figure out Black's best move. If you can find that answer, you should be able to identify the strengths and weaknesses of these three possible moves: 5...Rb8, 5...Ra7+, and 5...Kg6. Let's analyze each in turn.

■ The move 5...Rb8? is an immediate thumbs-down. It brings the Rook within two files of the e-pawn and loses: 6.Rd8! Rb7+ 7.Kd6 Rb6+ 8.Kd7! Rb7+ 9.Kc6 is White's win.

■ The trap behind 5.Rd6! is best revealed by the faux pas 5...Ra7+? 6.Ke8!, when the advance of the e-pawn becomes unstoppable. The usual 6...Kf6 runs into 7.e7+, which comes with check. If Black plays 6...Ra8+, then with 7.Rd8 Ra1 8.e7, White achieves the Lucena position and wins the game.

■ It looks like Black's only move is 5...Kg6! He'll have to wait for White to try to make progress.

5...Kg6! 6.Rd7

White returns to the previous positions.

Black has an easy task after 6.Kd7 Kf6! 7.e7+ Kf7 because of the threat of winning the e-pawn, which draws with this: ...Ra8-a7+. White can't prevent a draw with 6.Rd8 Ra7+ 7.Ke8 Kf6 or 7.Kf8 Kf6; in both cases, the e-pawn is soon lost.

6...Kg7

Black repeats the position, holding on to the opportunity to run back to the e8-square.

7.Rc7!

It is sensible for White to do his best to try to trick Black into making a mistake. The crucial thing for the defender is not to give up the a-file.

7...Ra1!

Now what? Well, a bad move would be 7...Rb8?? 8.Ra7, giving White a winning advantage. Note that the defender's Rook is no longer three files away from the passer.

8.Kd6+ Kf6!

Once again, this is the only saving move. If the King retreats, then 8...Kf8?? 9.Rc8+ Kg7 10.e7 wins on the spot.

9.Rf7+

This necessary move prevents Black from checking on the d-file and driving White's King away.

9...Kg6   10.Rf8

White is all set for his e-pawn to go home. Once more we see the benefits of checks on the long side:

10...Ra6+   11.Kd5 Ra5+   12.Kd4 Ra4+   13.Kc5 Ra5+

14.Kc4 Ra4+   15.Kb5 Re4

So, despite White's best efforts, he is unable to squeeze his passer home. Does this mean that if Black's Rook is only *two* files away from the passer, the position is won? The answer is usually yes, but there are exceptions. It depends on where the attacking Rook is.

Diagram 85 features an analysis published by Nikolay Dmitriyevich Grigoriev (1895–1938), considered one of the greatest endgame analysts of all time. In this position, White has been given one more advantage: control of the a-file. If it were White's play, he would start with 1.Rg1+, winning on the spot because setting up the Lucena position would be a snap. As it turns out, the a-file isn't ideal for White's Rook unless it is on the a7-square. According to Grigoriev, Black is just in time to secure a draw:

1...Rb7+   2.Kd6 Rb6+

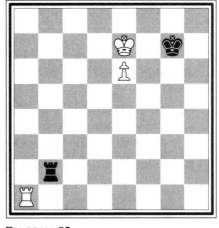

DIAGRAM 85.
N.D. Grigoriev, 1937

Black must avoid both 2...Kf8?? 3.Ra8+ and 2...Kf6?? 3.Rf1+ Kg7 4.e7, which win.

3.Kd7 Rb7+   4.Kd8 Rb8+

Black keeps up his harassment until White's King gives up the d-file.

5.Kc7 Rb2   6.Rf1

White stops Black's King from covering the promotion square.

6...Ra2!

Black switches to the a-file and is just in time to make a draw.

7.e7 Ra7+   8.Kd6 Ra6+   9.Kd5 Ra5+   10.Kc6 Ra6+   11.Kc5 Re6

Diagram 85 is a bit of an anomaly. Usually, when the defender's Rook isn't three files away, the game is lost.

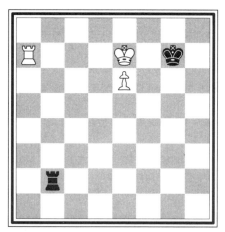

DIAGRAM 86.

In Diagram 86, we have connived to bring White to victory by steadily increasing his advantages. Black has no checks on the side, and although he is losing, he must find the sternest defense.

1...Rb8!

We've seen the win 1...Kg6 2.Ra8 Rb7+ 3.Kd6 Rb6+ 4.Kd7 Rb7+ 5.Kc6 Re7 6.Kd6 before. By choosing 1...Rb8!, Black does his best to avoid the Lucena position.

2.Kd6+!

It's the only way to Oz. Here's the logic: We've seen that 2.Ra1?? Rb7+ draws (Diagram 85), as do 2.Rd7? Ra8! (Diagram 84) and 2.Kd7 Kf8. Black now has three defensive possibilities: 2...Kf8, 2..Kg6, or 2...Kf6, which we'll refer to as variations A, B, and C. Let's take each one in turn:

- Variation A: **2...Kf8 3.Kd7! Re8** (3...Kg7 4.Ke7 transposes into variation C, and Black is trying to stop the rush of the passer.) **4.Ra1!** (preparing a check on the f-file) **4...Re7+ 5.Kd6 Rb7 6.Ra8+ Kg7 7.e7**, wins.

- Variation B: **2...Kg6 3.Ra1!** (A startling retreat. White's rationale is to be able to check the Black King or to support the passer from behind.) **3...Rb6+** (With 3...Rb2 4.e7 Rd2+ 5.Ke6 Re2+ 6.Kd7 Rd2+ 7.Ke8, White gains the Lucena position, and after 3...Kf6 4.e7 Rb6+ 5.Kd7 Rb7+ 6.Kd8 Rb8+ [6...Rxe7 7.Rf1+ wins] 7.Kc7 Re8 [7...Rh8 8.Kd7 wins] 8.Kd6!, the winning Ra1-f1+ will follow.) **4.Kd7 Rb7+ 5.Kc6 Rb8 6.Kc7! Rb2 7.Re1!** (The point behind White's retreat. The e-pawn is ready to rock.) **7...Rc2+ 8.Kd8 Rd2+ 9.Ke8**, and after **10.e7**, the Lucena position is achieved.

- Variation C: **2...Kf6 3.Kd7!** (White has to be very precise. He dodges 3.Rf7+? Kg6 4.Rf1 Ra8! 5.e7 Kg7, which draws, as we've seen in Diagram 84.) **3...Kg7** (After 3...Kg6, 4.Ra1 transposes into the win in variation B. Playing 3...Rh8 results in 4.e7 Kf7 5.Ra1, intending Ra1-f1+, which also wins. This last variation is a key point. Note how Black's Rook is tricked to the short side of the pawn.) **4.Ke7!** (Black is being badly squeezed.

White avoids another trap, 4.e7? Kf7!, and draws.) **4...Rb1** (Again 4...Kg6 5.Ra1 Rb7+ 6.Kd6 transposes into variation B. Black also avoids 4...Kg8 5.Ra1 or 4...Rc8 5.Ra1 Rc7+ 6.Kd8, with e6-e7 to follow, winning.) **5.Ra8!** The play's position is now as shown in Diagram 87. Black can't prevent Ke7-e8, in which the pawn advances and he is lost. His most logical choices cannot prevent his defeat. If he plays **5...Rb7+ 6.Kd6 Rb6+ 7.Kd7 Rb7+ 8.Kc6 Re7 9.Kd6 Rb7 10.e7**, White wins. Alternatively, with 5...Re1

6.Kd7 Rd1+ 7.Ke8 Rh1 8.Ra7+ Kf6 9.e7 Rh8+ 10.Kd7 Kf7 11.Ra1 Rb8 12.Rf1+, Black loses his Rook.

DIAGRAM 87.

These variations were very complex, requiring concentration throughout. It is precisely this type of study—reams of analysis—that cause such angst among chess students, myself included. Fear not and suffer not; just think of how wonderful it will be to steal a victory from a drawn position or turn a lost game into a draw! Apply yourself; you'll be glad you did.

Principles: A Recap

At this point you might be ready for a break. I know I am! Let me sum up some of the principles we've learned:

- ■ *In the Lucena position, building a bridge wins.*

- ■ *In the Philidor position, keeping the Rook on the sixth rank or third rank draws.*

- ■ *When the blockading King is forced away, go to the short side and move your Rook three files away from the passer.*

- ■ *When playing against a lone pawn, count the tempi.*

- ■ *Keep in mind the crooked path and how to win a tempo with a Rook check.*

Doesn't remembering these five principles sound a lot easier than memorizing reams of positions? Well, working with principles is *exactly* how I learned endings. I learned the concept, attached a name to it, and recalled it by its name. Now when someone says "Lucena," I think about building bridges.

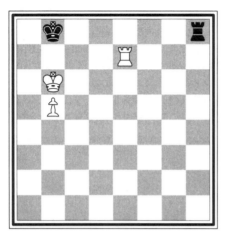

DIAGRAM 88.

The b- or g-Pawn

Unlike when fighting against a central pawn, a defender has less to worry about when fighting a b-pawn or g-pawn. For example, in Diagram 88, the defender is perfectly placed and has nothing to worry about. If it were Black's move, he would draw at once with 1...Rh6+ 2.Kc5 Rg6, following the advice of Philidor. Black waits for White to advance his pawn so that after 3.b6 Rg1!, Black can check from behind and draw easily.

Let's give White the chance to move first in Diagram 88.

1.Ka6 Rh6+   2.b6 Rh8

Black covers the threat of mate. White's Rook has no maneuvering room.

3.Rb7+ Ka8!

The only way to go wrong is with 3...Kc8?? 4.Ka7 Rh1 5.Rb8+ Kd7 6.Rg8 Ra1+ 7.Kb8, which allows White to flush out the blockading King. Then with b6-b7, he will achieve the Lucena position.

4.Ra7+ Kb8

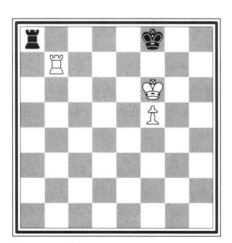

DIAGRAM 89.

White can't make further progress, because 5.b7?? Rh6+ will cost White his Rook and the game.

Now try another position by shifting the pawn over to the c- or f-file. The difference is immediate.

The c- or f-Pawn

The position in Diagram 89 is similar to that in Diagram 88, but the extra pawn on a file closer to the center makes all the difference. The defense could hold if Black had the move. He would play the Philidor defense with 1...Ra6+! 2.Ke5 Rc6, waiting for the pawn to advance with

3.f6 Rc1!, and drawing at once. However, because it is White's move in Diagram 89, the win is immediate.

1.Kg6! Kg8   2.f6 Rc8

Black has nothing better than this waiting move, and White wins.

QUIZ 1: If Black plays 2...Rf8, how can White win?

3.Rg7+ Kh8   4.Rh7+ Kg8   5.f7+ Kf8   6.Rh8+

In Diagrams 88 and 89, the defending King was in the ideal position, sitting on the promotion square. Sometimes life isn't so ideal, and the King is cut off. In the next section, we will explore positions where the defender has a tough life.

Cutting Off the King on the File

In Diagram 90, if Black's Rook and King could switch places, Black would have an easy draw utilizing Philidor's defense. As it is, Black's King is cut off from the c-file by White's Rook.

If it were Black's move, he would draw with:

1...Rd8!   2.Rxd8

Other moves allow Black's King to cross the d-file and cover the promotion square.

2...Kxd8   3.Kd4 Kc8!

Black draws, a scenario we also saw in Chapter Two.

DIAGRAM 90.

Remember, the aim for now is to make the defender's life difficult, not easy. Therefore, let's give White the move in Diagram 90. Think about the position in another way: If White's pawn were on the c7-square and the King were on the c6-square, winning would be a snap. This is the key to the position; White has to advance his pawn to gain victory.

1.Kb4!

There's the threat to advance the c-pawn.

1...Rb8+

Black has to give this check.

QUIZ 2: Can you see why 1...Rd8 would allow White to win?

2.Ka5 Rc8   3.Kb5 Rb8+   4.Ka6 Rc8

DIAGRAM 91.

Black is trying to hold up the advance of the passer. After 4...Rb2 5.c5! Ra2+ 6.Kb7 Rb2+ 7.Kc7, White will set up Lucena. In Diagram 91, Black is doing his best to hold on. White can make no further progress by advancing his King and must now utilize his Rook.

5.Rd4!

White keeps Black's King cut off from the d-file and is now ready to reposition his King and advance the passer. A grievous error is 5.Rc1?? Kd6, which allows Black's King to step toward the c-file and results in a draw.

5...Ke6

Black threatens to play 6...Ke5, which would harass White's Rook and cause a draw. (Diagram 90 shows that the position is drawn if Black's King is on the e6- or e5-square.)

6.Kb7! Rc5

This is a better choice, because 6...Ke5 7.Rd5+ wins Black's Rook. This little trick is so innocuous that most professional players hardly think about it as a tactic. But the endings are full of such *zwishenzugs*. (Zwishenzug is a German term for an "in-between" move that interrupts and thus changes the result of an otherwise logical sequence.) Great endgame players are, by necessity, great tacticians.

7.Kb6 Rc8   8.c5

White wins because Black is unable to prevent him from setting up the Lucena position.

Diagram 92 looks like Diagram 90, but there are crucial differences. In Diagram 90, Black's King is cut off on the long side of the passer. This time, the defender is in the right spot. The drawing method is quite easy:

DIAGRAM 92.

1.Kd4 Rh8!

84

Black immediately grabs the file that is furthest away from the passer, a technique known as *being on the long side of the law*.

2.c5 Rh4+

Black doggedly checks from the side for as long as he is able. Eventually White will have to step onto the b-file to seek refuge. When he does, Black's King will skip to the c-file, and the Philidor defense will save him.

3.Kd5 Rh5+ 4.Kc6 Rh6+ 5.Kb5 Kb7!

The Philidor position is in place.

Diagram 93 is also like Diagram 90, except for one thing: Black's King is cut off from the c-pawn by *two* files. This extra file means that Black's King will

have to spend an extra tempo getting back to the c-file, and that makes all the difference. The winning method is straightforward:

1.Kb4 Rb8+ 2.Ka5 Rc8

3.Kb5 Rb8+ 4.Ka6 Rc8

This move forces White's Rook to guard the c-pawn, as we saw in the discussion of Diagram 90.

5.Rc1!

This time White allows Black's King back in the game. White would also win after 5.Re4 Kf5 6.Rh4, but with a bit more difficulty.

DIAGRAM 93.

5...Ke7 6.Kb7 Rc5 7.Kb6 Rh5

He abandons the c-file, because the defense 7...Rc8 8.c5 Rb8+ 9.Kc7 Rb2 10.Re1+ Kf7 11.c6 is easily broken.

8.c5 Kd8

Black's King is dangerously close to covering the promotion square. It's time to push the defender away before it gets too comfortable.

9.Ra1

White had to avoid a reckless advance with 9.c6?? Rh2!, which would merely end with a draw. This constant vigilance in the endgame is crucial. Be as precise as possible in your play and in your analysis.

9...Rh2 10.Ra8+ Kd7 11.c6+ Kd6 12.Rd8+ Ke7 13.c7

The passer scores a victory for White.

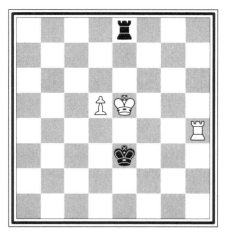

DIAGRAM 94.

Cutting Off the King on the Rank

When the defending King is cut off by a rank as in Diagram 94, the superior side should consider itself fortunate. In such cases, it is a game of King and pawn vs. Rook, and the Rook has no chance.

White's first order of business is getting out of check and preparing to escort the pawn.

1.Kd6 Rd8+   2.Ke6 Re8+

3.Kd7 Rg8

Black is helpless. Checks from the front or the side won't matter.

4.d6 Rg7+   5.Kc8 Rg8+

6.Kc7 Rg7+   7.d7

The pawn marches triumphantly down the board. This tactic of cutting off the defender's King by utilizing the rank is powerful and has snared many a victim.

Diagram 95 is from a famous position played in the 1970 FIDE Interzonal. Black has an easy draw with the direct 1...Rg8+ 2.Kf5 Rf8+ 3.Kg6 Rg8+ 4.Kf7 Rg4 5.Kf6 Kd4 6.Ra3 Ke4 7.Rb3 Rg8 because further progress isn't possible. Instead, Black stumbles ahead:

DIAGRAM 95.
Larsen–Taimanov
FIDE Interzonal
Palma de Mallorca, 1970

1...Kd4?

It's not a loss, but it is unfortunately a step in the wrong direction.

2.Ra3 Ke4?   3.g4

At the very least White is able to advance his pawn.

3...Rg8+!   4.Kh5 Rh8+

5.Kg5 Rg8+   6.Kh4 Ke5??

Incomprehensible! Black should first drive the White King away from its active square. The draw is assured after 6...Rh8+ 7.Kg3 Ke5 8.Ra6 Rh1! You are about to discover the joys of cutting on the rank. Feast your eyes on Diagram 96.

7.Ra6!

White cuts off the Black King's retreat. Presto! The game is now won for White.

7...Kf4

Equally futile is 7...Rh8+ 8.Kg5 Rg8+ 9.Kh5 Rh8+ 10.Rh6! Ra8 11.g5! Ra1 12.Rb6. White's pawn is all set for a coronation.

8.Rf6+ Ke5   9.g5

Taimanov now resigns. After 9...Rh8+ 10.Kg4 Rh1 11.Ra6! Rg1+ 12.Kh5 Rh1+ 13.Kg6 Rg1 14.Kh6 Rh1+ 15.Kg7, the pawn inexorably advances forward. This device of cutting along the rank is more commonly seen in a- or h-pawn endings.

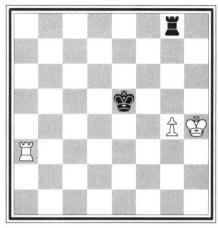

DIAGRAM 96.
Larsen–Taimanov
FIDE Interzonal
Palma de Mallorca, 1970

The a- or h-Pawn

You may have noticed that I haven't said much about endings with a Rook and an a- or h-pawn vs. a Rook. This special type of ending is generally easier for the defender to hold because, as in the case of the b- and g-pawns in Diagram 88, the superior side has no wiggle room.

Diagram 97 demonstrates just how difficult it is to win this superior ending. At first it appears that White should have no problems; after all, isn't this a Lucena position? No, it isn't, because White has no file other than the b-file to step into. Because White's King is stalemated, the only chance of rescue is to bring the White Rook to the b-file to release the King. However, note that Black's King is cut off four files (b, c, d, and e) away from the passer. This is how White wins:

1.Rc2 Ke7   2.Rc8 Kd6!

This is tougher than 2...Kd7 3.Rb8 Rh1 4.Kb7 Rb1+ 5.Ka6 Ra1+ 6.Kb6 Rb1+ 7.Kc5, which allows the White King to flee away from the Queenside.

3.Rb8 Rh1   4.Kb7 Rb1+   5.Kc8

There's no other escape route.

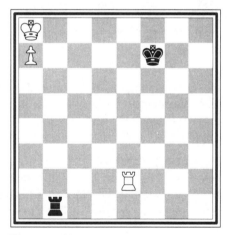

DIAGRAM 97.

5...Rc1+ 6.Kd8

It looks like White is winning. Black has run out of checks. But not out of tricks:

6...Rh1!

The rat threatens checkmate!

7.Rb6+ Kc5

We are now at the position in Diagram 98. How should White play? Take time to think about it before reading on.

Promoting to a Queen with 8.a8=Q?? Rh8+ allows a skewer. The attempt to interpose with 8.Re6? Ra1! 9.Re7 Kb6 only draws. Trying to get behind the passer

with 8.Ra6 Rh8+! 9.Ke7 Rh7+ 10.Kf8 (not 10.Kf6?? Rh6+!, which skewers the Rook) Rh8+ 11.Kg7 Ra8 12.Kf6 Kb5 13.Ra1 Kb6 also leads to a draw.

Did you find the answer? Here it is:

8.Rc6+!

The only way to win. The Rook is immune from capture as the pawn promotes with check and skewers Black's Rook!

8...Kb5

If Black plays 8...Kd5, White narrowly escapes with 9.Ra6! Rh8+ 10.Kc7 Rh7+ 11.Kb6 Rh6+ 12.Kb5.

9.Rc8! Rh8+   10.Kc7 Rh7+

DIAGRAM 98.

11.Kb8

Now White can rest comfortably.

This exciting example shows the difficulty of promoting an a-pawn. As we've seen, the defender's King has to be cut off far away from the passer. But sometimes even this advantage isn't enough.

Mastering Vancura

Diagram 99 is a study by the little-known Czech composer Josef Vancura (1898–1921), published three years after his death. As we can see, Black's King is out of action and must rely on his Rook to save the day.

1.Kb5

White couldn't have made a better move. After 1.a7 Ra6! 2.Kb5 Ra1 3.Kb6 Rb1+ 4.Kc7 Rc1+ 5.Kd7 Ra1, he would have no hope of winning.

1...Rf5+

Also a good move, and necessary. White was threatening to win with 2.Rc8. The King must not be allowed to protect the pawn and release the a8-Rook.

2.Kc6 Rf6+   3.Kd5

Clearly the White King cannot advance because of the endless series of checks on the f8-, f7-, and f6-squares.

3...Rf5+   4.Ke6 Rf6+   5.Ke5 Rb6

Black has run out of checks but continues to threaten the a6-pawn. Incidentally, he also sidesteps the threat of 6.Rg8+ and trading Rooks!

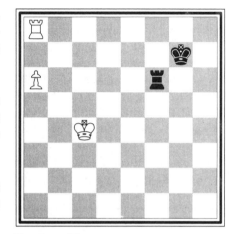

DIAGRAM 99.
J. Vancura, 1924

6.Kd5 Rf6!   7.Ra7+ Kg6   8.Ra8 Kg7

White can't make progress. Play out this position with a friend. Notice that the White King can't advance because of repetitive checks, the pawn can't advance because the defending Rook quickly gets behind the pawn, and the Rook is trapped. Make sure you understand exactly why the result is a draw.

Another position that takes time to appreciate is the one shown in Diagram 100, by the great German player Siegbert Tarrasch (1862–1934). He initially believed that the position was a win for White but later conceded his oversight. He based his original assessment on the following considerations: White intends to bring his King to the a7-square, release the captive a8-Rook, and win the game by promoting his pawn. Black's King is unable to enter the play because of a skewer threat.

DIAGRAM 100.
S. Tarrasch, 1908

Tarrasch envisioned this active defense: 1.Kf2 Kf7 2.Kf3 Kf7/e6? 3.a7! White is threatening to play either 4.Rh8 or 4.Re8+, to win. If the play continues with 3…Kd7 4.Rh8!, he sets up a winning skewer.

He also envisioned a passive defense, with White making a lengthy march with his King to the a7-square. Follow along with the moves to understand this idea: 1.Kf2 Kh7? 2.Ke2 Kg7? 3.Kd3 Ra4 4.Kc3 Kf7 5.Kb3 Ra1 6.Kb4 Rb1+ 7.Kc5 Rc1+ 8.Kb6 Rb1+ 9.Ka7 Ke7 10.Rb8! Rc1 11.Kb7 Rb1+ 12.Ka8 Ra1 13.a7 Kd7 14.Kb7 Rb1+ 15.Ka6 Ra1+ 16.Kb6 Rb1+ 17.Kc5, for a win.

However, Vancura's drawing method, published 16 years later, changed Tarrasch's assessment. Returning to Tarrasch's study, Black should play as follows:

1.Kf2 Ra5!   2.Ke3 Re5+!   3.Kd4 Re6!   4.Kd5 Rf6!

DIAGRAM 101.
D.L. Ponziani, 1782

And there it is, Vancura's position and a draw.

If it's White's move, he can try the following, which draws right away:

1.Kf3 Rf1+!   2.Ke4 Rf6!

Before leaving these awkward a- and h-pawns, let's look at two delightful studies that have a poetry all their own. The position in Diagram 101 was composed by Domenico Lorenzo Ponziani (1719–96). It has thrilled and delighted chess lovers for two centuries. From what you have learned, the position at first seems an innocent draw; after all, the defending King is so close! How can White possibly win? Give the position some careful thought before reading on.

The position has three salient features:

- ■ White's King is not cut off from the b-file.

- ■ If the c2-Rook shifts to the b-file, the result is an immediate draw.

- ■ Black's King is cut off on the rank, but if it were on the c8-square, then the result would be an immediate draw.

Here's the solution:

1.Kb8 Rb2+   2.Kc8 Ra2   3.Rg6+!

White's first step is to push Black all the way down the ranks!

3...Kc5

Black has no choice because the equally mundane 3...Kb5? 4.Kb7 and 3...Kd5? 4.Kb7 Rb2+ 5.Rb6! both lose—tactlessly.

4.Kb7 Rb2+   5.Kc7 Ra2   6.Rg5+!

The study begins to unfold. It would be a shame to play 6.Rc6+? Kd5 7.Kb7 Rxa7+ and get cracked on the head for not paying attention.

6...Kc4   7.Kb7 Rb2+   8.Kc6 Ra2   9.Rg4+ Kc3   10.Kb6 Rb2+

White's King must be checked to stop the threat of 11.Rg8 and the queening of the pawn on his next move.

11.Kc5 Ra2   12.Rg3+ Kc2   13.Rg2+! Kb3   14.Rxa2

There's the victory. Sweet, no?

Diagram 102 is a composition by Alexei Alexeyevich Troitzky (1866–1942), who is widely regarded as the founder of the modern art of study composition. Black appears to have an easy draw in this situation because White's King will have no cover if it tries to run to the Queen-side. It turns out that White can rely on Black's King for shelter.

1.Kf4

White introduces the threat of check and queening the pawn.

1...Kf2

Black hides behind White's King. But which side is doing the other a favor?

2.Ke4 Ke2

Black has to remain in lockstep. It's a win if he plays 2...Ra4+ 3.Kd5 Ra5+ 4.Kc6 Ra6+ 5.Kb7.

3.Kd4 Kd2   4.Kc5 Kc3

DIAGRAM 102.
A.A. Troitzky, 1896

DIAGRAM 103.
A.A. Troitzky, 1896

The position is now as shown in Diagram 103, where a new ambush awaits Black.

5.Rc8!!

Splendid! White sets up a discovered check, which forces a fatal double attack.

5...Rxa7   6.Kb6+!

A lovely finish. White wins Black's Rook.

For now, I'll bring this discussion of Rook and pawn vs. Rook endings to a close. However, I heartily encourage you to further your studies. There are volumes of books on endings from which to choose. I highly recommend works by Yuri Averbach, Vassily Smyslov, Henrikh Moiseyevich Kasparyan, André Cheron, and Pal Benko, to mention but a few.

Rook and Pawn vs. Rook and Pawn

In a hard-fought game, both sides often wind up with pawns. In this case, the advantage of the superior side—perhaps a more active Rook or King, or a further advanced passer—is subtler. Most of these endings are drawn unless you know that they, like other Rook endings, have their tricks.

The Ordinary

The position in Diagram 104 occurred in the nineteenth game of the 1929 World Championship match between Alexander Alekhine (1892–1946) and Efim Bogoljubow (1889–1952). The characteristics of the position are very much in White's favor: His Rook is behind his passer, his passer is further advanced, and his King is more active. Meanwhile Black's King is standing in the way of his pawn. Despite all White's advantages, however, Black—with flawless play—manages to draw the game! Black sees that he can't prevent White's passer from promoting, which means he will be forced to give up his Rook. But then Black will be left with an f-pawn that he hopes will cost White his Rook, and the game will be drawn. Both players realize that the outcome will be decided in a simple race. Will White's King be able to get back in time to cover the f1-promotion square? How should Black play?

1...Kg4??

A groaner. This colossal blunder costs Black the game at once, proving that even at the World Championship level, basic mistakes occur. In such positions, the defending side must use its King to restrict the enemy King from approaching. As I indicated earlier, White's King must race back to either the e2- or g2-square. Because White's King is on the c-file, it is unlikely that the g2-square will be White's choice. Indeed, his only chance is to gather speed and run to the e2-square. Black should therefore *prevent this approach*. We count tempi after that last move: 1...f5, 2...f4, 3...f3, 4..Kg3, 5...f2, 6...Kg2, 7...f1=Q to win

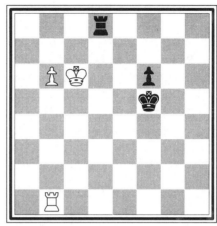

DIAGRAM 104.
Alekhine–Bogoljubow
Weisbaden, 1929

the Rook. White's King will make it to the e2-square in four moves, after which the win is straightforward.

2.b7 f5

Now what? Nothing is gained from 2...Rb8 3.Kc7 Rxb7+ 4.Kxb7, as White is five tempi from the e2-square, while Black still needs seven tempi.

3.b8=Q Rxb8 4.Rxb8 f4 5.Kd5 f3 6.Ke4 f2 7.Rf8 Kg3 8.Ke3

White wins the passer and the game.

I'm not sure if this example is encouraging or not! It's nice to know that even the best players err, but if *they* make such basic mistakes, what chance do *we* have to get it right? Easy: Only fools learn from experience; clever people learn from the experience of others!

Look again at Diagram 104, and let's see how Black should have played:

1...Ke4!

Black's paying attention now and chooses a far more logical approach. He gets out of the way of the f-pawn and blocks White's King from rushing back to the e2-square.

2.b7

This time, White won't win with this move. (In a moment, we'll revisit this position to see another attempt by White.)

2...f5 3.b8=Q Rxb8 4.Rxb8 f4 5.Rb4+

93

The standard method to get the Rook behind the passer is 5.Re8+ Kd4 6.Rf8 Ke3 7.Kd5 f3, which results in a draw because White's King cannot approach the e2-square. Therefore, White tries a different tack.

5...Ke3   6.Kd5 f3   7.Rb3+ Ke2

Black must avoid giving White the win by 7...Kf4? 8.Kd4 f2 9.Ra1 Kf3 10.Kd3 Kg2 11.Ke2, in which White covers the promotion square.

8.Ke4 f2   9.Rb2+ Ke1   10.Ke3

Our analysis of the Alekhine–Bogoljubow game brings us to the position in Diagram 105. In view of the double threat of Rb2-b1 checkmate and Rb2xf2, Black's surrender seems inevitable. However, Black can use one last tactic to save himself:

10...f1=N+!

Underpromoting to a Knight does the trick—a delightful resource when you're trying to draw, but a painful one when you're trying to win! Now a new duel takes place: A lone Rook and a Knight will fight it out. A draw will be the result, but only if the defender keeps his Knight close to his King. In Chapter Eight, we will look at this in more detail. For now, accept the fact that this ending is drawn! White was close, but not close enough.

Now let's take a last look at Diagram 104 with another try for White in mind:

1...Ke4!   2.Re1+

DIAGRAM 105.
Alekhine–Bogoljubow
Weisbaden, 1929

White wants to pick up a tempo by repositioning his Rook in front of the f-pawn. The drawback is that his King will have to trundle all the way up to the b8-square to win the Black Rook.

2...Kf4   3.Rf1+ Ke5!

Black continues to use his King to block White's path to the e2-square, and 3...Kg5 would allow White's King to race back and win the game. Play out that continuation to confirm it for yourself.

4.b7 f5   5.Kc7 Rf8   6.b8=Q Rxb8   7.Kxb8 f4   8.Kc7

Black's King is well placed to block White's King. It will be too late to rescue his Rook.

8...Ke4   9.Kd6 f3

Black draws without even needing an underpromotion to save himself.

Now let's look at an example in which the defender puts up sterling resistance. The position in Diagram 106 is from a tournament game between the legendary Estonian player Paul Keres (1916–75) and Vladas Ionovich Mikenas (1910–92).

The position favors White. He has just advanced his passer, which is now one square away from promotion, but Black's pawn needs four moves to do the same. White's King has a clear advantage, too: It covers the d8-promotion square, but Black's King needs four moves to cover the g1-square. In short, White has the upper hand. Only with incredible precision can Black save this draw.

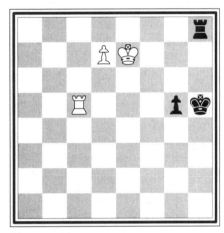

DIAGRAM 106.
Keres–Mikenas, 1937

1...Kg4!

As you know, Black is far behind in a race that will see the White King run to the f2-square. (Remember the crooked path?) Black plans to block White's approach to the g1-square while covering it himself. The natural choice, 1...Kh4? 2.Rc8! Rh7+ 3.Ke6 Rxd7 4.Rxd7 g4 5.Ke6 g3 6.Kf5! g2 7.Kf4!, would mean a win for White.

2.Kf6

White realizes that 2.Rc8 Rh7+ 3.Ke6 Rxd7 4.Kxd7 Kf4! will fall short. Note how Black's King prevents White's King from approaching the f2-square. Then 5.Ke6 g4 6.Rc4+ Kf3 7.Kf5 g3 8.Rc3+ Kf2 9.Kf4 g2 10.Rc2+ Kf1 11.Kf3 g1=N+! leads to the theoretical draw of Rook vs. Knight, which is covered in Chapter Eight. The purpose of choosing 2.Kf6 is to set a trap.

2...Rf8+!

Aha! Black's not falling for it. He narrowly escapes 2...Rh6+?? 3.Ke5 Rh8 4.Rc8 and a win for White.

3.Ke6 Rd8

The threat of 4.Rc8 had to be answered. Black is now ready to sacrifice his Rook for the passer.

4.Rd5

Recognizing the futility of 4.Rc8 Rxd7 5.Kxd7 Kf4!, White transposes to this move and tries one last trick.

4...Kf4!

Black continues with his plan of restraining White's King and is ready to launch his g-pawn up the board.

5.Rf5+

White can always win the Rook with 5.Ke7 Rxd7+ 6.Kxd7, but 6...g4 will equalize the game.

5...Kg4   6.Rf7

White's intention is to cut off Black's King in the forlorn hope that his own King can rush back to cover the promotion square. The plan fails because it takes too much time.

6...Kh3!   7.Kf5

This depressing choice is an admission that 7.Ke7 Rxd7+ 8.Kxd7 g4 9.Ke6 g3 10.Rh7+ Kg2 11.Ke5 Kf3! is just too slow for White to win.

7...g4   8.Kf4 g3   9.Kf3

White's King has returned in time, and the threat of checkmate (Rg7-h7) in one move should not be overlooked. The problem for White is that Black's King now has time to scurry back to cover the d-pawn.

9...Kh4!

With this, the players agree to a draw. One possible line would be 10.Rg7 Kh5 11.Kxg3 Kh6 12.Re7 Kg6 13.Kf4 Kf6 14.Rh7 Ke6, followed by capturing the d7-pawn.

These two examples demonstrate that when the game is reduced in material, a positional advantage—a further advanced passer or a more active King or Rook—often needs to be significant to tip the balance. Otherwise, the game will be a draw.

The Extraordinary

The positions in Diagram 105 and 106 are aptly described as "ordinary" because even the best play results in a draw. There are, however, some lovely examples in which a *balanced-looking* position contains a charm all its own.

Consider the position in Diagram 107, a study created by Dr. Emmanuel Lasker (1868–1941), the second World Chess Champion. On the surface, things appear quite balanced. The material is even, both players have a passer that is one move from promotion, and both players have ideal Rook placements, with the Rooks behind the passers. Now White's sole positional advantage is the superior King. White's King covers the promotion square, while Black's King is misplaced. Nevertheless, if Black could play ...Ka5-b6, he could draw at once, because the threat of ...Rc2xc7 would trade pawns. White, therefore, takes advantage of Black's King by applying an instructive maneuver:

1.Kb7

The sequence 1.Kd8 Rd2+ 2.Ke8 Rc2 3.Kd8 Rd2+ 4.Rd7 Rxd7+ 5.Kxd7 h1=Q 6.c8=Q Qh3+ ends with a draw.

DIAGRAM 107.
E. Lasker, 1890

1...Rb2+   2.Ka7 Rc2   3.Rh5+!

Black sees the first sign that something is amiss as his King is driven backward.

3...Ka4

There's no other move because 3...Kb4? 4.Kb7 wins at once, when Black is denied a check on the b-file.

4.Kb7 Rb2+   5.Ka6 Rc2   6.Rh4+

We are beginning to see the same type of maneuver as the one Ponziani demonstrated in Diagram 101.

6...Ka3   7.Kb6

This threat to capture the h2-pawn forces Black into another check.

7...Rb2+   8.Ka5 Rc2   9.Rh3+ Ka2   10.Rxh2!

With this, Black is pushed into an absolute pin and cannot retaliate by capturing White's passer.

10...Rxh2   11.c8=Q

The play has brought us to a Queen vs. Rook ending, which is covered in Chapter Nine, and White wins.

The extraordinary example we've just looked at is also quite practical, as is the one demonstrated by the position in Diagram 108, shown on the next page. Again, at first glance the position doesn't seem extraordinary. White has two significant

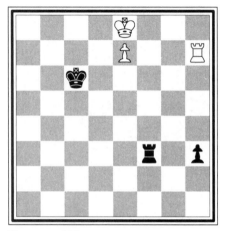

DIAGRAM 108.

pluses: the better King, and a pawn only one square away from promoting. He can carry out Ponziani's method of pushing back Black's King, but he has to use a neat twist at the end to score the win.

1.Kd8 Rd3+ 2.Kc8 Re3 3.Rh6+
With this, White begins unfolding Ponziani's method.

3...Kc5!
This is the best defense. The weaker choice, 3...Kd5?? 4.Kd7, permits the promotion of White's e-pawn, while 3...Kb5? 4.Kd7 Rd3+ 5.Rd6! h2 (better than 5...Rxd6+ because of 6.Kxd6 h2 7.e8=Q+) 6.e8=Q h1=Q 7.Rxd3 leaves White a Rook ahead, prepared to move his King with check. Thus the b5-square is ruled out for Black's King, because if he steps onto the deadly e8-a4 diagonal, White is able to promote with check.

4.Kd7 Rd3+ 5.Kc7 Re3 6.Rh5+!
Black's King is being pushed backward, and he must choose his move wisely.

6...Kb4!
This is smart, because stepping onto the d-file allows 6...Kd4? 7.Kd7 to win, whereas 6...Kc4 7.Kd7 Rd3+ 8.Kc6 Re3 9.Rh4+ Kc3 10.Rxh3 forces Black to the third rank and into a pin. Then 10...Rxh3 11.e8=Q achieves a Queen vs. Rook position, a forced win for the Queen.

7.Kd7 Rd3+ 8.Kc6 Re3
Black knows better than to fall for 8...Rc3+? 9.Kb6 Re3 10.Rh4+ Kb3 11.Rxh3, which pins Black's Rook and promotes the e-pawn. White seems to have hit a wall, as Diagram 109 shows, because he can't make further progress using Lasker's method of pushing Black's King up the board to the fatal third rank. Now comes the twist.

9.Rh4+! Ka5
Clever! He avoids the third rank and the pin, 9...Kb3? 10.Rxh3, which would win on the spot.

10.Kd6
White protects the e-pawn and threatens to capture the h3-pawn.

10...Rd3+

The trap—10...Kb6—leads to 11.Rh8! Rd3+ 12.Ke6 Re3+ 13.Kf6 Rf3+ 14.Kg5, and a win for White. If Black had played 10...Kb6, White would have had to avoid 11.Rxh3? Rxh3! 12.e8=Q Rd3+ 13.Ke7 Re3+, which results in a draw because of the skewer of White's newly promoted Queen.

11.Kc5 Re3

After 11...Rc3+ 12.Kd4 Rc8 13.Kd5, White would march his King to the f7-square to both cover the promotion square and win Black's Rook.

12.Rxh3!!

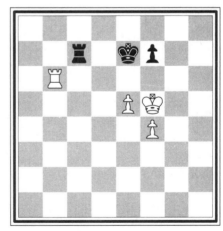

DIAGRAM 109.

White delivers a winning thunderbolt! Now White can checkmate the poor Black King after 12...Rxe7 with 13.Ra3.

Rook and Duo vs. Rook and Pawn

Although struggles between single passers are intense and require precise calculation, more often than not, the duel isn't between passers at all. Usually one player has the material advantage of an extra pawn on one side of the board and is trying to create a passer, while the other player is doing his utmost to save a difficult position. In such cases, principles of play, as well as precise calculation, are important.

The position featured in Diagram 110 shows a typical ending. The presence of an extra pair of pawns, in this case the f-pawns, gives the superior side an opportunity to drive the material advantage home. Just consider what an easy life Black would have if the f-pawns were traded!

DIAGRAM 110.
Moscow, 1956

This is a good time to examine some playing principles for Rook endings in which the pawns are on the same side of the board. The following principles should be our guide to these extra pawn endings.

- *The defender should try to trade pawns.*

- *The attacker should avoid pawn trades.*

- *In general, the attacker should try to trade Rooks and force a King and pawn ending.*

- *The attacker should advance his pawns as far as possible to create threats, and these pawn advances must be supported by the King.*

The position in Diagram 110 was taken from a game played but never completed in Moscow in 1956. The game was adjudicated, and the judges had to make a decision. Is the game won or drawn? Work on the answer by yourself. Later we'll return to this position and review the play.

In the meantime, consider the position in Diagram 111. In general, positions in which a passer has yet to be created offer the defender excellent drawing opportunities. This isn't the case in Diagram 111. White has moved his pawns up the board, and they control a lot of squares, hemming in Black's King. Furthermore, White's King is doing a marvelous job of supporting their advance. Black's position is almost like a fortress, but White can break down the defenses by attacking the g7-pawn. How?

1.Kh5!

White's King is really pressing the limits of his advantage. He's dreaming of further progress by Kh5-g6, which is possible if Black's King is driven away.

1...Rc7

Black marks time. He has two active defenses, which both fail. The first is 1...Ra1 (hoping to check White's King from behind) 2.Rb7+! (taking the opportunity to drive back Black's King) 2...Kf8 3.Kg6 Ra6+ 4.f6 gxf6 5.gxf6 Ra8 6.Rh7, and White wins, as we saw in Diagram 89. The second is 1...g6+ 2.Kh6! (The capture 2.fxg6+ Kg7! 3.Rf4 Ra1! would allow Black to use the Philidor defense to

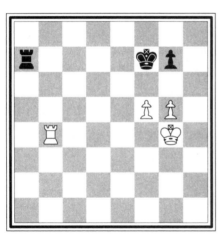

DIAGRAM 111.
Chekhover–Kasakevich, 1949

draw.) 2...gxf5 3.g6+ Kf6 4.Rb6+! Ke5 5.g7 Ra8 6.Rg6! (saving an important tempo over 6.Kh7, as Black is forced to blockade the promotion square) 6...Rg8 7.Kh7 Ra8 8.g8=Q Rxg8 9.Rxg8 f4 10.Kg6 f3 11.Kg5 Ke4 12.Kg4 f2 13.Rf8 Ke3 14.Kg3. White catches the passer in time and wins. As we can see, it doesn't take much to tip the balance between a win and a draw.

In principle, a move such as ...g7-g6 should be played only to force the trade of pawns, and not to open the door to an attacking King or to the establishment of a protected passed pawn.

2.Rb8 Ra7

This isn't the best defense. Black should have played 2...Rc6 to make White's life more difficult. We will return to this better option shortly.

3.g6+

This is the crucial nuance. Black's King is not left in peace as it proudly guards the g7-pawn.

3...Kf6

After 3...Ke7, 4.Rg8 Kf6 would transpose to the game. On the other hand, after 3...Ke7, 4.Rg8 Kd6 5.Rxg7 Rxg7 6.f6 Ra7 7.g7 Ra8 8.f7 would witness the crowning of a new White Queen. This sacrifice of the Rook to establish two connected passed pawns that are close to promoting is a motif that we will explore later in this chapter.

4.Rf8+ Ke5

The game has evolved into the position featured in Diagram 112. Get ready for White's classic breakthrough:

5.f6!!

This type of breakthrough is key to winning this category of Rook endings. The defending King, as you have seen, is forced away, and the breakthrough then creates a passer. In Diagram 112, White has to be careful to avoid the temptation of winning a pawn with 5.Rf7? Ra1! 6.Rxg7?? Kf4!, because then Black wins with an unpreventable checkmate. Now that would be a painful defeat!

5...gxf6 6.Kh6

If you're smart, you'll figure out why White's King crept up the board.

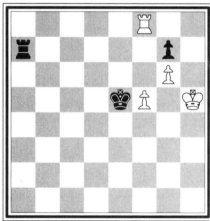

DIAGRAM 112.
Chekhover–Kasakevich, 1949

6...Ra1

Black is unable to stop the advance of White's g-pawn, so he hopes to spoil matters with checks from behind. It's futile to try 6...f5 7.g7 Rxg7 8.Kxg7 f4, because White's Rook is ideally placed. White would then play 9.Kg6 Ke4 10.Kg5 f3 11.Kg4, slurping up the f-pawn.

7.g7 Rh1+   8.Kg6 Rg1+   9.Kf7

Black resigns.

The finish might have been 9...f5 10.g8=Q Rxg8 11.Kxg8 f4 12.Kg7 Ke4 13.Kg6 f3 14.Kg5 Ke3 15.Kg4 f2 16.Kg3, but White wins as before. At least this variation brings Black closer to gaining his draw.

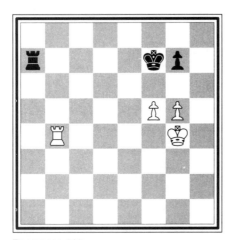

DIAGRAM 113.
Chekhover–Kasakevich, 1949

Let's revisit this ending from the position in Diagram 113 to see how to improve Black's play. This time, instead of following the moves played in the game, we will improve on Black's play with our analysis.

1.Kh5 Rc7   2.Rb8 Rc6!

This is a better defense than the 2...Ra7 that was played in the game.

3.g6+ Ke7   4.Rg8 Kf6

5.Rf8+ Ke5   6.f6!!

This is the same breakthrough sacrifice that we've seen before, and it is White's only winning method.

6...Rxf6   7.Rf7!

The point of White's sacrifice. He will capture the g7-pawn and push his g-pawn home.

7...Ke6

The alternate, 7...Rf5+ 8.Kg4 Rf6 9.Kg5 Ra6 10.Rxg7, wins, as we'll see.

8.Rxg7 Rf1   9.Ra7!

Black's King is cut from the seventh rank.

9...Rh1+   10.Kg5 Rg1+   11.Kh6 Rh1+   12.Kg7 Rg1

13.Kh7 Rh1+   14.Kg8 Kf6   15.g7

White achieves the Lucena position and wins.

This example should alert you to the type of position to avoid. If the attacker can advance his pawns and King far up the board, the breakthrough sacrifice will beat the defense.

Let us now revisit the position adjudicated in Diagram 110. The same position is shown in Diagram 114. Based on the example we've just discussed, how would you judge the position?

White was awarded a win because if he plays Kf4-g5 and f4-f5, he will break through as we have just witnessed. Fair enough. But as Grandmaster Grigory Levenfish (1889–1961) pointed out, the position is drawn if White is prevented from advancing the f-pawn.

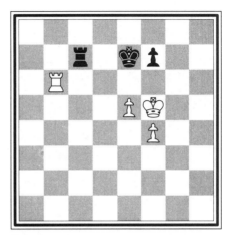

DIAGRAM 114.

1.Kg5 Rc5!

The only defense. Black must prevent White from pushing his f-pawn forward. It is likely that the judges based their verdicts on the other active defense: 1...Rc1? 2.Rb7+ Kf8 (Weaker is 2...Ke6? 3.f5+ Kxe5 4.Re7+! Kd6 5.Rxf7, which wins.) 3.f5 Rh1 4.Ra7! (An important finesse. White waits a turn for Black to move his Rook up the h-file.) 4...Rh2 5.Ra8+ Ke7 6.f6+ Kd7 7.Rf8 Rh7 (With the Black Rook on the h2-square instead of on the h1-square, the checks fail, and after 7...Rg2+ 8.Kf4 Rf2+ 9.Ke3, the f7-pawn falls.) 8.Kf5 Rh5+ (Black loses quickly if he moves his King, because 8...Kc7 9.e6! fxe6+ 10.Kxe6, or even 10.Kg6, wins.) 9.Ke4 Rh7 10.Kd5 Kc7 11.Re8! Kd7 12.Re7+ Kd8 13.Kd6 Kc8 14.e6. With this defense, White wins.

2.Kh6

White tries to penetrate with his King. A direct try with 2.Rb7+ Kf8! (not 2...Ke6?? 3.f5+ Kxe5 4.Re7+ Kd6 5.Rxf7, which results in victory) 3.f5 Rxe5 4.Kf6 Re1 5.Rxf7+ Kg8 6.Rg7+ Kh8 7.Ra7 Rf1! produces a draw, as we have seen previously.

2...Rc1! 3.Rb7+ Kf8! 4.f5

The course of our analysis brings us to the position in Diagram 115, shown on the next page. White seems to have realized his goal and is ready for his patented breakthrough. However, Black's purpose in holding up f4-f5 is now apparent: White's King has been separated from his pawns. Black can exploit this circumstance to save the position.

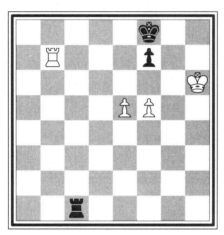

DIAGRAM 115.

4...Rg1!

This is the key defense and the saving move. White's King is cut off from the action.

5.Rb8+ Ke7   6.f6+ Ke6

7.Re8+ Kf5   8.Kh7

The last try. The breakthrough 8.e6 Kxf6 no longer works. Neither does 8.Re7 Rg2 9.Rxf7 Kxe5 10.Rg7 Rf2 (or 10.Rf8 Ke6) 11.f7 Ke6 12.Kg6 Rf6+ 13.Kh7 Rxf7, which produces a draw.

8...Rg2   9.Re7

The position still sparkles with traps. Black has to be extremely vigilant. After 9.Rg8 Ra2 10.Kg7 Kxe5 11.Kxf7 Kf5! (with the threat of ...Ra2-a7+ winning the f6-pawn) 12.Rf8 Ra7+ (or 12.Re8 Ra6) 13.Kg8 Kg6 14.f7 Rb7 15.Ra8 Rxf7 16.Ra6+ Rf6, a draw is the reward for the tenacious defender.

9...Rg5!!

Black steps carefully. On the g5-square, Black envisions that he will be able to play ...Kf5xe5xf6, capturing both White pawns while protecting the Black Rook. To see the danger, play out 9...Rg1?? 10.Rxf7 Kxe5 11.Rg7! Rh1+ 12.Kg6 Rg1+ 13.Kf7 Rf1 14.Rg5+ and watch White win.

10.Rxf7

If White tries 10.Kh8 Rg1! 11.Rxf7 Kxe5 12.Rg7 Rh8+ 13.Kg8 Kxf6, the result is a draw because Kh7-g6 is denied.

10...Kxe5   11.Kh6

The move 11.Rg7 Kxf6 would reveal Black's point. On the g5-square, the Rook would be protected by Black's King.

11...Rg8   12.Rg7 Rf8   13.f7 Kf6!

Black draws. This is an impressive piece of analysis by Grandmaster Levenfish; unfortunately for the defending player, he wasn't one of the judges who adjudicated the game!

At the beginning of this section, I deliberately chose examples in which the defender's pawn was on its original square. This position allowed the attacker to squeeze the defender and thereby create winning threats. Normally, the defender has an easier time if his pawn is advanced by one square. Of course, the pawn must not be in danger of being captured! Let's continue to look at positions in which the attacker has a number of strengths to complement his material advantage.

The position in Diagram 116 is from a game played by Vasily Smyslov and Paul Keres in 1949, with the colors reversed. Along with the material advantage of an extra pawn, White has three other positional pluses: he has a protected passed f-pawn, which is well advanced; he has a more active King; and Black's h6-pawn is a lesser pawn than, say, a more centralized g- or f-pawn. White would have no chance of success if, for instance, his King were sitting on the g3-square and Black's were on the g5-square. Despite the advantages, the game is drawn because White's King has no room to maneuver; it can't march up the h-file.

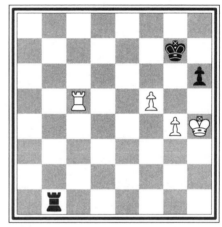

DIAGRAM 116.
Keres–Smyslov
USSR Championship
Moscow, 1949

1.Rc7+ Kf6!

Black must prevent White's King from penetrating. A loss is in store if he plays 1...Kg8??, because 2.Kh5 Rb6 3.Re7 Ra6 4.Re6 Rxe6 5.fxe6 Kg7 6.e7 Kf7 7.Kxh6 wins.

2.Rc6+

Nothing is gained from 2.Rh7 Rh1+ 3.Kg3 Rg1+ 4.Kf3 Rh1 5.Kg2 Rh4 6.Kg3 Rh1, in which White can't improve his position.

2...Kg7   3.Rg6+ Kh7   4.Re6 Kg7!

An important point: Black avoids 5.Re7+ Kg8, which would force his King to retreat.

5.Kg3

White gives up his attempts to squeeze up the h-file.

5...Rf1

Black is cutting the King off the f-file.

6.Re7+ Kf6   7.Rh7 Rh1   8.Kg2 Rh4   9.Kf3 Rh1

White hasn't made any progress.

DIAGRAM 117.

10.Rh8 Kg7   11.Rd8 Rf1+
12.Kg2 Rf4   13.Rd7+Kf6
14.Rd6+ Kg7   15.Kg3
A draw was agreed.

In the course of play, as we've just seen, White had problems centralizing his King. The astute reader (you!) might wonder whether White could have won if he had gained that extra plus. The answer is no.

In Diagram 117, White's prospects have improved considerably. However, even here White's various attempts all fall short. Normally, the superior side would like to trade Rooks, hoping that the extra pawn will carry the day. Let's look at some possible plays:

■ With 1.Rd7+ Rxd7 2.Kxd7 Kf6! 3.Kd6 h5! 4.gxh5 Kxf5, the result is a simple draw.

■ With 1.f6+ Kg6 2.Rb6 Rf7! 3.Ke5 Rf8 4.Re6 Rf7, White can't make progress.

■ With 1.Rb6 Rc7 2.Rb8 (intending Rb8-e8-e7+) 2...Rc6+ 3.Ke7 Rc7+ 4.Ke8 Rf7!, Black intends to draw using ...h6-h5.

DIAGRAM 118.

These examples demonstrate that the attacker has greater chances if his King has room to maneuver.

In Diagram 118, I've moved the position over one file. The attacker can win only if his King can penetrate Black's camp. White has the same telling advantages as in Diagram 116, except that instead of having only the g6-square to step onto, White has *both* the f6- and h6-squares as springboards. If Black were on move, he would play 1...Rg1+. Then after 2.Kf3 Rf1+ 3.Ke3 Re1+ 4.Kf2 Re4 5.Kf3 Re1, he would likely draw. However, we are going to give White the move.

1.Rb7+! Ke6

As we've previously seen, the King retreat 1...Kf8 2.Kg5 Ra6 3.Rd7 with Rd7-d6 to follow would cost Black the game immediately.

2.Kg5 Rg1+ 3.Kh6!

The crucial resource. This penetration is decisive, but White still has to overcome some formidable resistance.

3...Rg4! 4.Rb6+ Ke7 5.Rf6

It would be a tragic mistake to play 5.Rxg6?? Rxf4, which gives Black an easy draw.

5...Kd7

As we can see in Diagram 119, White has made terrific progress and is on the verge of winning. What would you do if you were White? Be careful now. Here is a hint: Think of the opposition.

6.Kh7!

White's fighting for the opposition. He hits a roadblock if he plays 6.Kg7 Ke7 7.e6 Rh4! 8.Kxg6 Rg4+ 9.Kf5 Rxf4+!, which is good enough to draw but not to win.

6...Ke8 7.Kg8! Ke7

The other defense is 7...Rg1 8.Kg7 Rg4 9.Rf7! Rg1 (After 9...Kd8, 10.Kf8 prepares the rush of the e-pawn.) 10.Kf6! Rg4 11.Ke6. White squirms to victory.

8.Kg7!

White has achieved the opposition, and Black is forced to give way.

8...Ke8 9.Rf7 Kd8

After 9...Rg1 10.Kf6 Rg4 11.Ke6, White's King on the e6-square is decisive.

10.Kf8 Rh5 11.e6 Rh8+

12.Kg7 Re8

Now White has his choice of wins: either 13.Rf8 to trade Rooks, or 13.Rd7+ Kc8 14.Kf7 to win the g6-pawn.

I hope that by presenting these examples, I have shown you how tough it is to win endings that involve unequal combinations of Rooks and pawns.

DIAGRAM 119.

Rook and Trio vs. Rook and Duo

Another extremely common ending in tournament play is a Rook and three pawns vs. a Rook and two pawns, all on the same side of the board. In general, the defender has a rather easy time holding the position provided he doesn't allow the attacker to advance his pawns too far.

Diagram 120 shows a position quite typical of this type of Rook ending. White has an extra pawn, a Rook controlling the absolute seventh, a more active King, and no chances to win! The game is a simple draw. In positions such as these, the defender should play ...h7-h5 to keep White's Kingside restrained. The game might continue as follows:

1...h5! 2.Kh3 Ra4 3.f3

DIAGRAM 120.

White tries to advance his pawns.

3...Ra4 4.g4

White achieves some measure of glory, but it isn't enough.

4...hxg4+ 5.fxg4 Ra3+

With this move, Black both separates White's King from his pawns and cuts the King on the third rank.

6.Kg2 Rb3

Black marks time. White's only option is to try to activate his King by bringing his Rook back to the f3-square.

7.Rd2 Kg7

Black takes the opportunity to get off the last rank.

8.Rf2 Rb3 9.Rf3 Rb4 10.Kg3

White is trying hard, and we must admire his effort.

10...Ra4 11.Re3 Kf7 12.Kf3 Kf6 13.Re4

White's efforts are entirely understandable. He has pushed his pawns and is trying to activate his King.

13...Ra3+ 14.Kf4

Black has several ways to draw the position:

- With **14...g5+ 15.hxg5+ Kg7 16.Re7+ Kg6 17.Re6+ Kg7 18.g6 Ra5**, he gains an easy draw.

- With **14...Ra6 15.Rb4 Rc6 16.Ke4 Ra6 17.Kd5 Ra5+ 18.Kc6 Ra1**, White's King marches far from the action. Black will happily attack the h-pawn from behind.

- Probably the only way Black can make his own life difficult is to let White's King penetrate with **14...Rh3? 15.Ra4 Rxh4 16.Ra6+ Kf7 17.Kg5**, after which White has managed to activate his King.

Despite the tendency of endings with Rook and three pawns vs. Rook and two pawns to result in a draw, the defender can be tripped up fairly easily if the attacker's pawns are well advanced.

The position in Diagram 121 is a classic (the colors have been reversed). The sixth World Champion, Mikhail Moiseyevich Botvinnik (1911–95), has been nursing a series of advantages: an extra pawn, active pieces, and, most crucially, advanced Kingside pawns. Because White has the ability to penetrate to both the e6- and g6-squares, even with the move Black is unable to hold the position.

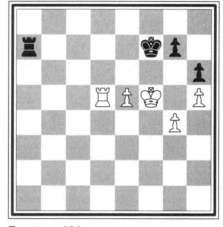

1...Ke7

Black's first task is to prevent 2.Rd7+ Rxd7 3.e6+ Ke7 4.exd7 Kxd7 5.Kg6 and a winning King and pawn ending.

DIAGRAM 121.
Botvinnik–Najdorf, 1956

2.e6

White sets up the threat of trading Rooks. Black has to cede the seventh rank.

2...Ra4

White's penetration after 2...Ra6 3.Rd7+ Kf8 4.Kg6! Rxe6+ 5.Kh7 Re4 6.Rxg7 would be decisive. Then after Rg7-g6 and Kh7xh6, the h6-pawn would fall, and White's two-pawn material advantage would win.

3.g5!

A fine sacrifice. White intends to penetrate with his King through the g6-square. He doesn't want to be troubled with a Rook check on the g-file.

3...hxg5   4.Rd7+ Kf8   5.Rf7+ Kg8

After 5...Ke8 6.Rxg7, White's h-pawn is ready to march home.

6.Kg6!

This was the point of White's temporary pawn sacrifice. White is now ready to harvest Black's pawns. Black doesn't have the salvation of a check on the g-file.

6...g4   7.h6

White finishes in flamboyant style. I'm not a big believer in winning beautifully, preferring the simple win to the aesthetic. However, when a beautiful win does occur, it's wonderful! Most of your victories will be of the mundane garden variety. Cherish them. Sometimes when you set up an opponent for an elegant flourish, your calculations can include a nasty oversight. The mundane but powerful play

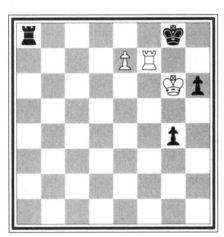

DIAGRAM 122.
Botvinnik–Najdorf, 1956

7.Rxg7+ Kh8 (7...Kf8 8.h6 g3 9.e7+ Ke8 10.h7 Rh4 11.Kf6 Rh6+ 12.Rg6 also wins.) 8.e7 Ra8 9.h6 g3 10.h7 g2 11.Rg8+ Rxg8+ 12.hxg8=Q+ Kxg8 13.e8=Q is checkmate and a professional finish.

7...gxh6

Black prevents 8.h7+ Kh8 9.Rf8 and checkmate. The other defense, 7...Ra8 8.hxg7 g3 9.e7 Ra6+ 10.Rf6 Rxf6+ 11.Kxf6 g2 12.e8=Q+, is checkmate next move.

8.e7 Ra8

The game has evolved to the position in Diagram 122.

QUIZ 4: White has sacrificed two pawns since Diagram 121. What was White's winning idea?

I have rarely been successful against the British Grandmaster Jonathan Speelman. The position in Diagram 123 is from one of our tournament games. I had hardly any hope of winning this position because tournament practice confirms that Black should draw. However, Jonathan, the author of several high-quality endgame books, committed a number of instructive mistakes, and the result of the game came as a great surprise to both of us.

One of the nice benefits of Black's position is the g5-pawns, so I feel I have no choice but to swap a pair of pawns:

1.h4 gxh4+ 2.Kxh4 Kh7?!

An entirely understandable mistake. Black is anxious to activate his King, but the defender shouldn't be thinking about this. Instead, Black should be asking himself, "What can White do?" All White can do is try to advance his Kingside pawns, so Black should make this advance as difficult as possible. The best move was 2...Rb1! 3.f4 (not the unfortunate 3.Kh5 Rb5+ 4.Kg6?? Rg5, resulting in checkmate) 3...Rg1, which leaves White searching for a way to improve his position.

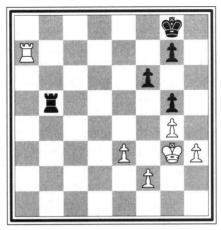

DIAGRAM 123.
Seirawan–Speelman
London, 1984

3.f4 Kh6?!

Black is still on the wrong track. Activating the King is not a priority. Better is 3...Rb1, as mentioned before.

4.Ra6

White not only prevents Black's threat of ...g7-g5+, but also introduces his own chances for g4-g5+ and a push forward.

4...Rb1?

Although Black has slipped in his ability to restrain White's advance, in reality his position is perfectly fine. After 4...Kh7! 5.Kg3 Rb1, Black should draw. By insisting on keeping an active King, Black falls into trouble.

5.g5+! Kg6 6.e4!

By now the alarm bells are beginning to go off. White has managed to advance his pawns to the position shown in Diagram 124, and already the winning threat of e4-e5 has appeared.

DIAGRAM 124.
Seirawan–Speelman
London, 1984

6...Rb4?

This move looks good because the fourth rank features some juicy targets. Nevertheless, this mistake is decisive. Playing 6...Rh1+ 7.Kg3 Kf7 8.Ra7+ Kf8 9.gxf6 gxf6 10.Kg4 Rf1 11.Kf5 Rf2 should lead to a defensive idea of 12.Ra6 Kg7 13.Rxf6 Rxf4+ 14.Kxf4 Kxf6, with a drawn King and pawn ending.

7.f5+ Kh7

White squeezes up the board and is winning after 7...Kf7 8.Ra7+ Kf8 9.Kh5 Rxe4 10.Kg6 Rg4 11.Rf7+ Ke8 12.Rxg7 Rxg5+ 13.Kxf6. The finish could be 13...Rh5 14.Rg8+ Kd7 15.Kg6 Rh1 16.f6 Rg1+ 17.Kf7 with the Lucena position to follow.

8.Re6 fxg5+   9.Kxg5

At this point, White has achieved tremendous success. His e-pawn is passed, his King is active, and, most importantly, he is closing in on the position shown earlier in Diagram 118, which is a winning position.

9...Rb1   10.Re8 Rg1+   11.Kf4 Ra1

Black could continue to check with 11...Rf1+ 12.Ke5, but he can't prevent an eventual e4-e5, which would make White's King more active. For example, 12...Ra1 13.Ke6 Ra6+ 14.Kf7 Rf6+ 15.Ke7 Ra6 (or 15...Kh6 16.Rh8+ Kg5 17.Rh7) 16.e5 is a winning position.

12.e5 Re1   13.Rc8 Re2   14.e6!

Now there is no stopping the e-pawn.

14...Re1

White expected 14...g6 15.Kg5 gxf5 16.Kf6! f4 17.Rc3 Kg8 18.e7, with the cruel intention of using Rc3-c8+ and e7-e8 to win Black's Rook.

15.Rd8 Re2   16.Rd4! g6   17.Re4!

The point. The principle that *Rooks belong behind passed pawns* is as valid as ever.

17...Rxe4+

After 17...Rf2+, 18.Kg3 Rxf5 19.e7 would win.

18.Kxe4 gxf5+

At the time this game was played, adjournments were common after five hours of play. The arbiter had just given me an envelope in which to "seal" my move. While I was double-checking that 19.Ke5 Kg7 20.Kd6 Kf8 21.Kd7 was indeed a winning play, Jonathan resigned.

If an endgame specialist like Grandmaster Speelman can lose these endings, the message is clear: So can you! Practice your skills to make sure that you are comfortable defending, and skilled with the extra pawn.

The Outside Passed Pawn

In another common Rook ending, both players have an equal number of pawns on one side of the board, and one player has a passed pawn on the other side. The position in Diagram 125 is a fine example of a cut and dried win.

DIAGRAM 125.

What is it about Diagram 125 that makes White's task so easy? First, he has an extra pawn. This is a very good thing. In time, you will love to count pawns in your favor as well. Second, Black's pawns are doubled, which means that the f4-Rook is unassailable. With the f2-pawn firmly protected by the f4-Rook, White will be able to march his King over to the Queenside and escort the a-pawn to promotion. Black will be unable to create any counterplay on the Kingside. Third, Black's King is stuck either on the e6- or g6-square protecting the f-pawns. This means that Black's King can't trundle over to the Queenside to prevent White's plan. Overwhelming advantages such as these aren't very common. Let's help the defender.

The position in Diagram 126 provides a false illusion. The initial impression is that White has the same winning advantages as he does in the position in Diagram 125, with the added advantage that his Rook is posted behind his passed pawn. But this position will result in a draw. Why? The difference is the defender's ability to create counterplay. In Diagram 126, Black's King is ideally posted for counterplay purposes. He will draw White's King far away from the Kingside before sacrificing his Rook. The

DIAGRAM 126.
Marshall–Duras
San Sebastian, 1912

following analysis is provided by my good friend and fine teacher, International Master Nikolay Minev.

1.Kc3

White heads to the Queenside to win Black's Rook. There is nuance worth noting here. White doesn't make the obvious 1.Kc4? move. Why? Because Black would be able to sacrifice the Rook immediately with 1...Rxa4+!, and then 2.Rxa4 Kxg2 3.Kd3 h3 4.Ke2 h2 results in a draw. White's crafty point is that now 1...Rxa4? 2.Rxa4 Kxg2 3.Rxh4 snares the h4-pawn.

1...Rf5

Black is not just marking time; he has a trick in mind.

2.a5!

White avoids 2.Kb4 Rf2! 3.Rxf2 Kxf2 4.a5 Kxg2 5.a6 h3 6.a7 h2 7.a8=Q+ Kg1, which draws as we saw in Chapter Two.

2...Rf8!

In the actual game, Duras miscalculated and played 2...Rxa5? 3.Rxa5 Kxg2. Then Marshall promptly returned the favor by playing 4.Kd2??. He had the opportunity to win a tempo and the game with 4.Rg5+! Kf3 5.Rh5 Kg3 6.Kd2 h3 7.Ke2 Kg2 (7...h2 8.Kf1) 8.Rg5+ Kh1 9.Kf2 h2 10.Kg3! Kg1 11.Kh3 Kh1 12.Rd5. However, after 4.Kd2?? h3 5.Ke2 h2 6.Rg5+ Kh1!, the players agreed to a draw. We'll continue to follow Minev's analysis, which shows the proper way for Black to draw.

3.a6 Rc8+ 4.Kd4 Ra8 5.a7

White has played wonderfully, having advanced his pawn far up the board. It seems as though he is winning easily.

5...Kh2!

Well played! Black waits for White's King to advance toward the a-pawn. A loss awaits 5...Rd8+ 6.Kc5 Rg8 7.Rb2 Ra8 8.Kb6 because Black's Rook will be captured by White's King. In this way, White will keep his g2-pawn protected.

6.Kc5

The only other option is 6.g4+ Kg3 7.g5 h3 8.g6 h2 9.Rxh2 Kxh2 10.g7 Kg3 11.Kc5 Kg4 12.Kb6 Rg8!, which produces a draw. Harmless is 6.Ke4 Kg3 7.Kf5 Rf8+, with Black keeping up a series of checks to drive White's King back to the Queenside. Now Black reveals why he has been waiting.

6...Rxa7!

Just in time! If White is allowed to play Kc5-b6, he will win. Now White's King has been drawn far enough away from the Kingside, and Black achieves a draw.

7.Rxa7 Kxg2 8.Rg7+!

White is playing to win a tempo, the motif that Marshall missed. Unfortunately, it isn't enough for White to win.

8...Kf3   9.Rh7 Kg3   10.Kd4 h3   11.Ke3 Kg2!

Accuracy is required at all times in the ending. Black has to dodge 11...h2?? 12.Rg7+ Kh3 13.Kf2! h1=N+ 14.Kf3 Kh2 15.Rg8, which puts him in *zugzwang* and causes him to lose. (Zugzwang, a German term meaning *compulsion to move,* involves making an undesirable move because it is illegal to pass.)

12.Rg7+ Kf1!

Dangers lurk everywhere! Creeping into the corner would be a grave mistake because 12...Kh1? 13.Kf3 h2 14.Kg3! wins.

13.Rf7+ Kg1!

Black avoids other ways to go wrong, such as 13...Kg2 14.Rf2+ Kg3! (the trap being 14...Kg1? 15.Kf3 h2 16.Rg2+! Kh1 17.Ra2, with mate next move) 15.Rf8 Kg2! and a draw. The other trap is 15...h2? 16.Rg8+ Kh3 17.Kf2!, with a win for White.

14.Ke2

Playing 14.Kf3 h2 15.Rg7+ Kf1! also draws.

14...h2   15.Rg7+ Kh1

Black has earned his hard-fought draw.

The defender must create counterplay on the opposite side from the passer to save the game. If the defender is unable to create counterplay, the passer will normally win the game.

The position in Diagram 127 is a classic taken from the 1927 World Championship match held in Buenos Aires between José Raúl Capablanca, the defending Champion, and his challenger, Alexander Alekhine. Along with having an extra pawn, White has the additional advantage that his Rook is behind the passed a5-pawn. Unable to make counterplay on the Kingside, Black's King will shadow White's King as he tries to press his a-pawn home. White has to play precisely to achieve victory.

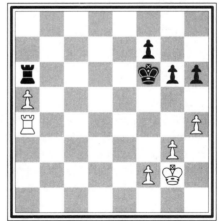

**DIAGRAM 127.
Alekhine–Capablanca
Buenos Aires, 1927**

1.Kf3 Ke5   2.Ke3 h5!

Black is setting up the Kingside to avoid a space disadvantage. If allowed, White would aim to play g3-g4-g5 to gain space.

3.Kd3 Kd5   4.Kc3 Kc5

Black prevents the Kc3-b4-b5 threat to his Rook.

5.Ra2!

Very nice. White has hit a temporary roadblock, so he takes advantage of his Rook's superior placement to lose a tempo and place Black in zugzwang. (This ability to move a Rook from behind a passer and to lose a tempo is one reason that the Rook's placement is so beneficial.) Black has a near fortress, but the requirement to move will force him to weaken his position by moving one of his ideally placed pieces. Note that Black's blockading Rook can't make a passing move. If the Rook retreats, the a5-pawn will advance.

5...Kb5

Much weaker would be 5...Kd5? 6.Kb4 Kc6 7.Kc4, which permits White's King to advance. Black's idea is to blockade the a-pawn with his King to release his Rook.

6.Kd4!

Now that Black's King is committed to the Queenside, White's King swings over to the Kingside. Naturally the invitation to capture the a5-pawn and transpose to a lost King and pawn ending is declined.

6...Rd6+   7.Ke5 Re6+   8.Kf4 Ka6

Black's King takes up the blockading assignment, but White's King now penetrates the Kingside.

9.Kg5! Re5+   10.Kh6 Rf5

Black opts for an active defense with his Rook. After 10...Re7 11.Kg7 Rc7 12.Ra3!, followed by Ra3-f3, White wins easily because Black's Kingside pawns will fall like dominoes.

11.f4?

This sad error prolongs the game because White loses the option Ra2-a3-f3. The straightforward 11.Kg7 Rf3 12.Kg8! (marking time) 12...Rf6 (12...f5 13.Kg7 f4 14.Kxg6 fxg3 15.fxg3 Rxag3+ 16.Kxh5 wins a second pawn and the game.) 13.f4 Rf5 14.Kg7 would have been the preferred path, because it puts Black once again in zugzwang, and his position falls apart.

11...Rc5!

Recognizing that he can't keep his position because of White's plan of Kh6-g7, Black quickly shifts his Rook to another defensive position.

12.Ra3

White prevents ...Rc5-c3 with counter-play against the g3-pawn.

12...Rc7 13.Kg7 Rd7 14.f5?!

Right idea, but wrong execution. White should have played 14.Kf6! Rc7 15.f5 gxf5 16.Kxf5 Rc6 17.Kg5 Rc5+ 18.Kf6 Rc7 19.Kg7!, planning to play Ra3-f3, which wins Black's Kingside.

14...gxf5 15.Kh6

As you can see in Diagram 128, Alekhine's idea is to pick up the h5-pawn and run his own h-pawn up the board. Capablanca finds his only chance to stay in the game:

15...f4! 16.gxf4 Rd5

17.Kg7 Rf5!

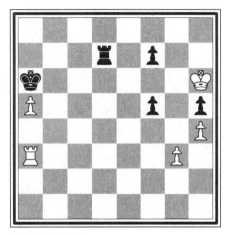

DIAGRAM 128.
Alekhine–Capablanca
Buenos Aires, 1927

This time, the passive defense 17...Rd7 fails for a new reason: After 18.f5 Rc7 19.f6, a plan of Ra3-e7 will win.

18.Ra4 Kb5 19.Re4 Ka6

The a5-pawn leads a charmed life. If Black had tried 19...Kxa5 20.Re5+ Rxe5 21.fxe5, he would have landed himself in Loserville.

20.Kh6!

White's previous slack performance forces him to find another way to win the position.

20...Rxa5

With 20...Kb7, White's h-pawn becomes too strong after 21.Re5 Rxf4 22.Kg5 Rf1 23.Rf5!.

21.Re5! Ra1 22.Kxh5 Rg1 23. Rg5 Rh1 24.Rf5 Kb6

25.Rxf7 Kc6 26.Re7

And Black hangs it up.

This Alekhine–Capablanca classic ending is an important one to commit to memory. But after studying a position like this one, you can hone your ending prowess by altering the positional factors a little bit to see how the changes affect the outcome. Let's try it.

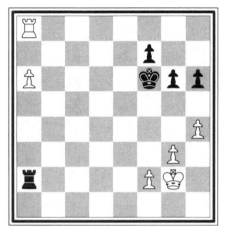

DIAGRAM 129.

In Diagram 129, I've switched the position of the Rooks, giving the defender much brighter prospects. The position in Diagram 129 is a far cry from the one in Diagram 125. In this new position, Black has clear counterplay against White's Kingside. When White's King tries to rush over to the Queenside, his Kingside pawns will be left vulnerable. This factor will allow the defender just enough counterplay to force a draw.

1.Kf3 h5   2.Ke3 Kf5

While White heads to the Queenside, Black's King takes the opportunity to sneak into the Kingside.

3.f3

A necessary precaution to keep Black's King at bay for a short while.

3...Ra3+   4.Kd4 Rxf3   5.Rf8

White presents a double threat of rushing the a-pawn and picking up the f7-pawn.

5...Ra3!

Black must avoid losing with this choice: 5...Rxg3? 6.a7 Ra6 7.a8=Q Rxa8 8.Rxa8 Kg4 9.Ke4 Kxh4 10.Kf4 g5+ 11.Kf5 g4 12.Kf4 Kh3 13.Rg8, when Black's pawns will all fall.

6.Rxf7+ Kg4   7.Rf6 Kxg3   8.Rxg6+ Kxh4

Black has managed to win a pawn, evening the force count. He can now cruise to a draw by pushing his h-pawn.

9.Kc5 Kh3   10.Kb6 h4   11.Rg5!

A standard trap. White's idea is to swing his Rook across to the a-file.

11...Rxa6+

Black sacrifices his Rook at once. He could go with 11...Kh2 12.Ra5 Rxa5 (12...Rb3+ 13.Kc7 Rc3+ 14.Kd7 Rd3+ 15.Ke7 Re3+ 16.Kf7 Rc3 17.a7 Rc8 only helps White because his King has been driven to the Kingside.) 13.Kxa5 h3 14.a7 Kg1 15.a8=Q h2, producing a draw like the one you saw in Chapter Two. Instead he chooses 11...Rxa6+, reasoning that he would rather leave his opponent with a Rook than a Queen!

12.Kxa6 Kh2   13.Kb5 h3   14.Kc4 Kh1   15.Kd3 h2

And there's the draw.

From this example, you learn the importance of the defender's counterplay. If the attacker can prevent counterplay, as we saw in Diagram 125, the position is usually won.

The position in Diagram 130 shows another typical example of these endings with an outside passer. Kingside is locked up, limiting Black's Kingside counterplay. On the other hand, White's King can't wander to the Queenside because of the vulnerable g3-pawn. The key factor is the f5-pawn, which will provide White with a winning target. Let's look at how White goes about winning the position.

1.a7!

The consequences of this move are immense. White will not be able to queen his a-pawn by charging over with his King because Black's Rook will be

DIAGRAM 130.

able to chase White's King away. On the plus side, this move stops Black's King from moving toward the Queenside because of a skewer. Furthermore, Black's Rook can't capture the g3-pawn because of the power of the passer. Let's see how play now proceeds.

1...Kh7 2.Kf1 Kg7 3.Ke1 Kh7 4.Kd1 Kg7 5.Kc1 Kh7 6.Kb1 Ra5

Step one accomplished. White's King is released from the first rank and can charge up the board.

7.Kb2 Kg7 8.Kb3 Kh7

9.Kb4 Ra1 10.Kc5 Kg7

The play brings us to the position in Diagram 131. White can't make progress on the Queenside with 11.Kb6 Rb1+! (not allowing White's Rook to escape) 12.Kc7 Ra1 13.Kb7 Rb1+ 14.Kc8 Rc1+ 15.Kd7 Ra1 because White's King gets chased away. A different approach is called for.

11.Kd5!

DIAGRAM 131.

Note this important change of direction. White heads for the vulnerable f5-pawn, for without this target, the position is drawn.

    11...Ra2 12.Ke5 Ra5+ 13.Ke6 Ra6+

Black is squeezed and must shed the f5-pawn. After 13...Kh7 14.Kf6, the f5-pawn would also fall.

    14.Kxf5 Rf5+ 15.Ke6 Ra6+ 16.Ke7 Ra5 17.f5!

White wins because either the f-pawn or the a-pawn is decisive.

QUIZ 5: If the g4-pawn is placed back on the g6-square in Diagram 130, this winning method would no longer be available. How would you evaluate the new position?

Rook vs. Connected Passed Pawns

While the Saavedra position mentioned at the beginning of the chapter (Diagram 72) is a charmer, we know that the Rook is usually far superior to a mere pawn. Surprisingly, the Rook has tremendous problems when fighting two connected

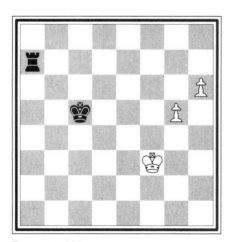

DIAGRAM 132.

passed pawns. When both pawns are just two moves away from promotion, they can often defeat a Rook by themselves. When I was first learning endings, this came as a bit of a shock.

If it is White's turn to move in Diagram 132, he wins with:

    1.g6 Ra6 2.g7 Rg6 3.h7

Here, White will queen, and in the resulting position, the Queen will out-duel Black's Rook.

Because the threat of pushing the g-pawn is so strong, let's give Black the move:

    1...Rh7

Black attempts to prevent the g-pawn from advancing. If he plays 1...Kd5, then 2.g6 Ke6 3.h7! Ra8 4.g7 Kf7 5.h8=Q wins.

    2.Kg4!

White rushes to support his h6-pawn so that he can push his g-pawn forward.

    2...Kd5 3.Kh5 Ke6 4.g6 Ra7 5.h7 Ra1!

This makes sense, as Black is hoping for a skewer on the h-file. Naturally, 5...Ra8 6.g7 Kf7 7.h8=Q is an easy win. The current position is shown in Diagram 133.

6.Kg4!!

A dandy of a move. White correctly perceives that he doesn't need his King's help to win the game. The pawns can carry the day on their own. In fact, White's King is in the way, and Black could use this factor to save the game. For instance, 6.Kh6? Kf5! 7.Kg7 Rh1 8.Kf7 Rh2 ends nicely with a draw. Another failure is 6.g7? Kf5! (threatening checkmate) 7.Kh4 Kf4! 8.Kh3 Kf3

DIAGRAM 133.

9.Kh2 Ra2+ 10.Kg1 Ra1+ 11.Kh2 Ra2+ 12.Kh3 Ra1, which ends in a draw. In many studies, the player with the Rook must rely on similar tactics to either save or win the game.

6...Rg1+   7.Kf3 Rh1   8.g7

Sincere thanks to International Master Minev for this lovely example.

The position in Diagram 134 appears to be a slam-dunk win for Black. He has only to play ...a3-a2 to claim victory. White's only chance is to try to take advantage of the Black King's unfortunate position.

1.Kf5!

You were probably expecting that move, weren't you? White is setting up a checkmate, as we saw in the previous example.

1...Kh4

After 1...Kh6 2.Kf6, White would shadow the Black King and force a transposition back to the main line.

2.Kf4 Kh3   3.Kf3 Kh2

DIAGRAM 134.
J. Kling and B. Horowitz, 1851

121

At last Black has escaped the mating threats, but—surprise, surprise—he still can't advance his a-pawn because the b-pawn would then be captured with check.

4.Ke3 Kg2

This is Black's only chance. After 4...Kh3 5.Kf3!, he ends up in the same position as before. And 4...Kg3 5.Rg1+ Kh4 (5...Kh2 6.Rb1! draws) 6.Kf4 Kh3 7.Kf3 Kh4 (Black must avoid 7...Kh2?? 8.Rb1! so that he doesn't have to tolerate White's smirking at his zugzwang) 8.Kf4 draws.

5.Kd3 Kf3

At last Black is ready to advance his a-pawn.

6.Kc3 a2   7.Kxb2 axb1=Q+   8.Kxb1

And the game is a draw.

What I find particularly charming about this study is its beginnings. Who would have guessed, from Diagram 134, that White would find time to bring his King back to the Queenside? Many practice and study examples plumb the intricacies of a Rook vs. connected passed pawns, and I encourage you to study them.

Stalemate as an Offensive Weapon

Stalemate is a resource most often associated with the defense of a position, as in a Queen vs. an a- or h-pawn ending, for example. But in Rook endings, the attacker often takes advantage of a stalemate to force a victory. This nice device is worth knowing about.

In Diagram 135, it is easy to imagine that a race in a Rook ending has rewarded White with an extra Rook. But Black is quick to regain the lost Rook:

1...Kb2

Black threatens to queen. If it weren't for the a7-pawn, White would win with 2.Kd4 a1=Q 3.Rxa1 Kxa1 4.Ke5, after which White's King would march triumphantly to mop up the Kingside. The presence of the a7-pawn means that any King and pawn ending would be lost for White.

DIAGRAM 135.

2.Rf2+ Kb1   3.Rf1+ Kb2

White could repeat the position by perpetual check and make a draw. Instead, he has a fine maneuver for victory.

4.Ra1!!

A lovely move, and Black is presented with the opportunity to capture the Rook for nothing. Black refuses the capture for awhile, but will eventually be forced to accept the gift.

4...a6

The immediate 4...Kxa1 5.Kc2 a6 6.Kc1 a5 7.Kc2 will transpose into our main line.

5.Kd2 a5   6.Kd1 a4   7.Kd2 a3   8.Kd1 Kxa1

At last, Black accepts White's offer. After 8...Kb3 9.Kc1, White will capture the a-pawns.

9.Kc2

Black is now in stalemate! He is forced to move his Kingside pawns.

9...h5   10.gxh6 g5   11.h7 g4   12.h8=Q Checkmate

Studying this device of using stalemate offensively will show you numerous examples of beautiful endgames. I urge you to ferret them out by doing some research in other endgame books. In particular, search for studies by Genrikh Kasparyan, Alexei Alexeyevich Troitzky, and my favorite, Grandmaster Pal Benko.

You're Me, Age Sixteen

Although a lot of material seems to have been presented in this chapter on Rook endings, it is light reading compared with the volumes of books written about them. As you advance and become a stronger player, further study of these endings will become mandatory—and more satisfying! For now, I hope you've enjoyed how rich these endings are. I'll close this chapter with two examples from my own practice.

The position in Diagram 136 on the next page is a fragment from a very important game in my young career. It was the 1976 American Open, held in Santa Monica, California. I was a sixteen-year-old playing Black against the powerful Southern California International Master David Strauss. It was the last round of the tournament, and a victory would give either player a share of first prize.

For this exercise, set up the position shown in Diagram 136, cover the book with a piece of paper, read White's moves and the commentary, and play the Black side

DIAGRAM 136.
Strauss–Seirawan
American Open, 1976

of the position before reading Black's moves. I will present quiz questions throughout the exercise, starting with this one:

QUIZ 6: Before starting play, try to articulate to yourself the positional factors of this particular position. After you think that you have listed as many as you can, compare your list with mine.

Strauss begins with a dubious move:

1.Kg3?

A step in the wrong direction. White is greedily appraising Black's Kingside *pawn islands* and decides to play for a race of Kingside vs. Queenside pawns. (A pawn island is a group of pawns of one color separated by at least one file from any other pawns of the same color.) White should have played 1.Ke3 Kd5 2.Kd3, with Kc5 3.Ra4 producing reasonable drawing chances. Keep in mind, however, that this is a last-round game, in which both players are going for the win. Your turn.

1...Kd5!

Natural, and quite strong. Black has to energize his Queenside prospects.

2.Kf4

White is coming to munch the Kingside pawns. What are you going to do about it?

2...Kc4!

Nothing! After 2...Ke6? 3.g4, Black has wasted tempi, giving White a clear advantage.

3.g4

Now White is gearing up for the race.

QUIZ 7: How would you meet 3.Ra3? Calculate as far as you think appropriate.

Black now has a fine choice: 3...Kxc3 or 3...Kb5. What should you do?

3...Kxc3

My friends would laugh at such a question. They would say, "With Yaz, there is no choice. He'd take the pawn!" And they would be quite right, too. Now Black has gained connected passed pawns.

4.h4!

White is not only geared up, he's going in style! What should you do now?

4...b5!

Although this means the loss of the Kingside pawns, the players are in a race, and Black can't hesitate. After 4...Kc4? 5.Kf5 Kb5 6.Ra1 a5 7.Kxf6, the outcome of the game would be unclear.

5.Rxf6

White grabs pawns and unleashes his own passers. How should you advance the pawns?

5...b4

If Black took 5...a5 instead, it wouldn't make much difference. I prefer this move because the a7-pawn covers the b6-square, and that might make it awkward for White's Rook to get behind the b-pawn.

6.Rc6+!

Now *that's* an annoying check. Your turn.

6...Kb2!

If you didn't want to step in front of the b-pawn, good for you! Neither did I! My concern was being driven from the Queenside with 6...Kd3 7.Rd6+ Ke2 8.Rxh6 b3 9.Rh7 Rb8 (to stop Rh7-b7) 10.Rxa7 b2 11.Ra2, when White can sacrifice his Rook. There was no way that I wanted to figure out how to stop White's pawns.

7.Rxh6

Your turn.

7...a5!

You get no points for any move other than this one. Black is ahead in the race, and the only way to keep the lead is to keep running.

8.Re6

White has to get the Rook back into play and out of the way of the pawns.

QUIZ 8: How would you respond to 8.Rb6?

8...a4!

Black has to push the right pawn. After all, it is the a-pawn that has a clear path to promotion.

9.h5

Your turn.

9...a3

Sound the battle cry!

10.Re2+

The righteous b-pawn queens with 10.h6 a2 11.Re2+ Ka3! 12.Rxa2+ Kxa2 13.g5 b3.

10...Kc1

Black simply steps aside for the b-pawn. (10...Kc3 would also do the trick.)

11.g5

White's pawns are far too slow. Your turn.

11...b3

Triumph! The alternative, 11...a2, would also have won, but I like running with both pawns. At this moment in the match, David resigned and was the first to congratulate me on the tournament victory. Years later, David told me that I responded, "Thank you, Mr. Strauss. I enjoyed our game tremendously and look forward to playing you again!" David didn't know whether I was being facetious. I assured him that my comment was genuine.

The next exercise is from my game with Hungarian Grandmaster Lajos Portisch, played in Niksic, Yugoslavia, in 1983. It had been a long, hard-fought game in one of the strongest tournaments of the year. Lajos had been grimly hanging on in a difficult ending. Just as you did in the previous example, set up the position indicated in Diagram 137, but this time play White's position.

QUIZ 9: Before beginning the exercise, articulate the positional factors and compare them to those in the Solutions section at the end of the chapter.

DIAGRAM 137.
Seirawan–Portisch
Niksic, 1983

No peeking! Begin.

1.a4!

Passed pawns must be pushed! The way for White to utilize his advantage is to make the passer a dangerous threat.

1...Kh7

Black's Rook is on the ideal square, and the pawns cannot move without being captured, so Black passes with his King. Now what?

2.a5

This was a gimme. My applause after your first move was a give-away.

2...Kg7

As before, Black awaits White's plan. Your turn.

3.a6

Another easy one. Now the choices will get more difficult.

3...Ra1

Black decides that he can't keep his Rook on the second rank. What do you do now?

QUIZ 10: How would you have answered 3...Kh7?

4.Kg4!

A natural enough move.

QUIZ 11: Why did you reject 4.g3?

4...Ra2

Black is doing his best to get Kingside counterplay. Your turn.

5.Kf5

You chose a natural invasion square. A terrible mistake would have been 5.g3?? Rxh2 6.a7 Ra2 7.gxh4 gxh4 8.Kxh4 Ra1, with a draw. As you might remember from Diagram 130, the f6-pawn is not vulnerable. However, Lajos pointed out after the game that White had a much more powerful move with 5.Kh5! Kf7 (not 5...Rxg2 6.Ra7+ Kf8 7.Rb7! Rxh2 8.a7 Ra2 9.Rb8+ Ke7 10.a8=Q Rxa8 11.Rxa8, which wins) 6.Kh6! Rxg2 7.a7 Ra2 8.Rh8! Rxa7 9.Rh7+, skewering Black's Rook. If *you* played 5.Kh5, well done! Too bad you're stuck with having to play with my inaccuracy.

5...Rxg2

Fast food on the Kingside. How should you follow up?

6.Ra7+

This drives Black from the protection of the f6-pawn. Oops, that was a clue. No credit for the next move.

6...Kh6   7.Kxf6 Rxh2

White has broken through with his King. What should you play now?

8.Ra8!

White sets up a mating threat that Black must address.

8...Kh7

Forced. Now what?

9.Kxg5

Make me proud: Did you take the pawn?

9...h3

Your turn.

10.Kg4!

Don't get carried away. That powerful passed h-pawn deserves your complete attention.

10...Rf2

QUIZ 12: How would you handle 10...Rh1?

11.Kxh3

Capturing the pawn seemed the simplest way to me. Lajos felt that 11.a7 h2 12.Rh8+ Kxh8 13.a8=Q+ was better. I was aware of the winning procedure discussed for Diagram 130, though, and was satisfied with my choice.

11...Rxf3+   12.Kg2 Ra3

Now what?

13.a7!

At this point, Black resigned because there was no way to prevent White's King from moving to the Queenside and up the board, and eventually worming its way to the e6-square. This would force a zugzwang and the loss of the e5-pawn. Then, after winning the e5-pawn, White's e4-pawn would win the game. Easy as ABC, right? It certainly was!

Skill with Rook endgames is crucial to chess mastery. I hope this chapter serves to inspire you to continue your studies in this rich field. You can count on one thing: The journey will be inspirational.

Solutions

QUIZ 1 (DIAGRAM 89): After **2...Rf8**, a series of checks clinch the game: **3.Rg7+ Kh8 4.Rh7+ Kg8 5.f7+ Rxf7 6.Rxf7 Kh8 7.Rf8** Checkmate.

QUIZ 2 (DIAGRAM 90): Trying to get back with the King by playing **1...Rd8? 2.Rxd8 Kxd8 3.Kb5!** wins for White.

QUIZ 3 (DIAGRAM 97): White can't escape with 5.Ka6 because 5...Ra1+ 6.Kb6 Rb1+ 7.Ka5 Ra1+ 8.Kb4? Rxa7 wins the passer.

QUIZ 4 (DIAGRAM 122): **9.Rf6! Re8** (After 9...g3 10.Rd6, checkmate follows.) **10.Rd6!** Then there is no defense against Rd6-d8, with checkmate to follow.

QUIZ 5 (DIAGRAM 131): The position is a draw. If White tries to bring his King to the Queenside with 1.Kf1 Ra3 2.Kf2 Kh7, White can't advance his King without losing the g3-pawn and, quite likely, the f4-pawn as well. White will be forced to play a6-a7, which means that his King can't hide on the a7-square.

QUIZ 6 (DIAGRAM 136): Both players have majorities on opposite sides, but it is Black who has a passer: the a7-pawn. Black has the slightly more active King. White's Rook, although well placed, is not stable and will be forced to move. This being the case, the a8-Rook is in perfect position to protect the a-pawn while advancing. Based on these considerations, Black has the advantage.

QUIZ 7 (DIAGRAM 136): The a3-Rook, while providing fine defensive service to the c3-pawn, is vulnerable to an attack by **3.Ra3 a5! 4.Kxf6 a4 5.f4 Kd3! 6.f5 Kc2 7.c4** (to save the Rook) **Kb2 8.Re3 a3**, which wins.

QUIZ 8 (DIAGRAM 136): The simplest response is **8...b3 9.h5 a4 10.h6 a3 11.h7 a2 12.Ra6 Rh8! 13.Kg6 a1=Q**, which wins.

QUIZ 9 (DIAGRAM 137): White's a-pawn is an extra passer. The Kingside structure, while balanced, has a weakness in White's favor: the weak f5-square. Black's King is stuck on an inactive circuit, playing a completely defensive role. Although better placed, White's King will have to abandon the Kingside pawns to press his advantage. The position of the Rooks is heavily in Black's favor because his Rook is behind the passer.

QUIZ 10 (DIAGRAM 137): The simple **4.g3!** is the right way to release White's King from its defensive duties.

QUIZ 11 (DIAGRAM 137): There was no reason to reject 4.g3. It is just that activating the King is even stronger!

QUIZ 12 (DIAGRAM 137): Black's move is actually a mistake because **11.a7 Ra1** (**11...h2 12.Rh8+ Kxh8 13.a8=Q+** allows White to promote with check.) **12.Kxh3** wins a pawn over the game.

Bishop Endings

Bishop endings are quite straightforward. Although Bishops, like Rooks, are far-ranging pieces, Bishop endings have fewer tricks to them than Rook endings. The positions tend to be cut and dried: They are either won or drawn, without the tactics associated with Rook endings. They do, however, tend to involve a lot of subtle play. This chapter covers four types of Bishop endings. The first deals with a "wrong Bishop" that can't help promote a pawn. The second demonstrates how effectively a Bishop defends against passed pawns. The third involves a Bishop and pawn vs. a Bishop, and the fourth addresses Bishops of opposite color. Before moving on to these sections, let's examine the four basic principles of Bishop endings:

- *Bishops are powerful, long-ranging pieces that work very well in open positions.*

- *Because they are limited to exactly 32 squares, or half the board, Bishops are unable to break blockades that are on the wrong squares. That is, a light-squared Bishop won't do well against a dark-squared blockade.*

- *For the previous reasons, it's an advantage to have two Bishops on an open board.*

- *Bishops are effective against connected passers; in fact, they're often more effective than Rooks.*

The Wrong Bishop

Club players and grandmasters have repeatedly been tripped up by the "wrong Bishop" position seen in Diagram 138 on the next page. When I first saw it, I was amazed. If a player could not win the position with a pawn and a Bishop to the good, surely this game of chess is a draw.

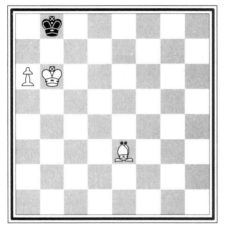

DIAGRAM 138.

As we can see in Diagram 138, the Bishop doesn't control the a8-promotion square. White has the wrong Bishop and the game is completely drawn. White might attempt 1.Bf4+ Ka8! (Naturally, 1...Kc8?? 2.a7 would allow White to win.) 2.Bg3, with a stalemate and a draw. As long as Black stays put in the a8-corner, he can't lose.

Another amazing position featuring a misplaced Bishop is shown in Diagram 139. In this position, the Bishop is completely useless, and the game is drawn. If the Bishop were on the d6-square, for example, the position would be a simple win. A sample line of play might run: 1.Kb5 Ka8! 2.Bb8 (This is not a difficult choice, as either 2.Ka6 or 2.Kc6 is instant stalemate.) 2...Kxb8 3.Kc6 Kc8, which draws. Or: 3.Ka6 Ka8, for a draw that we saw in Chapter Two.

Stalemates are common. Diagram 140 shows that regardless of whose move it is, this position is drawn. If it were Black's turn, he would quickly play 1...Kg8 and head for the stalemating corner. If it were White's turn, he would play 1.Kd6 Ke8 2.Bf7+ Kf8! 3.Kc7 Ke7 4.Bc4 Kf8, and Black couldn't be budged.

DIAGRAM 139.

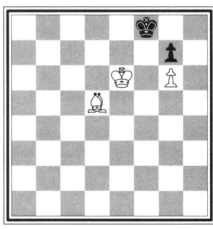

DIAGRAM 140.

These examples feature Bishops at their worst. Perhaps you think that I'm treating the Bishops unfairly. Not so! While writing this book, I played a challenge match in Bermuda. As the highest-rated American Grandmaster, I faced the highest-rated United Kingdom Grandmaster, Michael Adams. Our combative match ended in a 5–5 tie. But adjacent to our games, an international event was taking place, and I watched the position shown in Diagram 141 unfold before my eyes.

After a hard, five-hour battle, the young Israeli International Master Alik Gershon was ready to realize his advantage against the Icelandic Grandmaster Throstur Thorhallsson. The simple win was 1.Kg5 h3 (1...g3 2.h3!) 2.g3, after which Kg5-h4 and Be4-f5 would mean that Black would lose both his pawns and the game. Alik, certainly aware of the wrong-colored Bishop, discovered a simpler win:

1.h3? gxh3 2.gxh3 Ba6!

Black isn't helped by 2...Bf1 3.Kg4, which would win the h-pawn.

3.Kg5 Bxb7 4.Bxb7

Black moves according to Alik's plan. (After 4...Kxb7 5.Kxh4, Alik had confidently calculated a winning King and pawn ending. His opponent's next move, shown in Diagram 142, was a shock.)

4...Kd7!

This snaps White to attention! Black refuses to recapture the Bishop and, instead, hightails it for the h8-square, where he manages to make a draw. Books can be filled with lamentable tales of players left holding the wrong Bishop. Let this be a warning to you!

DIAGRAM 141.
Gershon–Thorhallsson
Bermuda, 1999

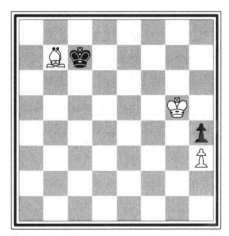

DIAGRAM 142.
Gershon–Thorhallsson
Bermuda, 1999

Bishop vs. Passed Pawn(s)

The Bishop's long-range powers make it very effective in combating passed pawns. The position in Diagram 143 is an easy one for Black to handle.

DIAGRAM 143.

Despite the fact that the Kings are far from White's passed pawns, the Bishop holds them at bay:

1.b6

Obviously, 1.a6 Bc5 would have been even more comfortable for Black.

1...Bc5   2.b7 Ba7   3.a6 Ke5

With the Bishop holding up the pawns' advance, the Black King comes back to snatch up the passers.

A Bishop might have difficulties when dealing with passed pawns that are far apart from one another. The position in Diagram 144 is an easy draw for Black, but if we move the pawns and Bishop up the board one square, as in Diagram 145, the position is won. White plays either 1.a7 or 1.e7, after which the other passer promotes. My colleagues say that this is a case in which the "bridesmaids" are too far apart.

DIAGRAM 144.

DIAGRAM 145.

Bishop and Pawn vs. Bishop

In general, most Bishop and pawn vs. Bishop endings are drawn. It is not enough that the superior side has an extra pawn; he must also control the promotion square with his King. Diagram 146 illustrates such an ending.

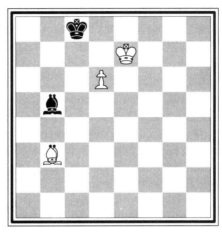

This position has the requisite advantages for White. He controls the queening square, and his pawn has only to travel through the d7-square, after which Black won't be able to sacrifice his Bishop and win. White has only to drive Black's Bishop off the a4-e8 diagonal to win.

DIAGRAM 146.

1.Bf7

This move leads to the simple threat of Bf7-e8, pushing away Black's Bishop. After this is done, the d-pawn will march triumphantly to its coronation.

1...Bd7

After 1...Ba4 2.Be8, the d-pawn becomes unstoppable.

2.Be6 Bxe6   3.Kxe6 Kd8   4.d7 Kc7   5.Ke7

Oftentimes, driving the defender away from the critical diagonal isn't easy. As we can see in Diagram 147, White faces an important question: Where should he move his King?

1.Kg8!

This is the right decision, because after 1.Ke8 Bd6 2.Bf8 Bf4 3.Bb4 Bh6!, White succeeds in pushing the defender from the a3-f8 diagonal, but the new h6-f8 diagonal serves him well. Then after 4.Bc3 Kd6 5.Bd2 Bg7 6.Bb4+ Ke6 7.Bf8 Bc3 8.Bh6 Bb4, the win is no longer possible. Realize that Black's critical diagonals, a3-f8 and h6-f8, are not equal: The h6-f8 diagonal is significantly shorter. As a general principle,

DIAGRAM 147.

the attacking King must move to the defender's shorter diagonal. We will see in the next few moves how this makes a difference.

1...Kf5

Black tries to prevent the threat posed by 2.Bf8 Be3 3.Ba3 Bh6 4.Bb2 with 4...Bg7 and a win to follow.

2.Bf8 Be3   3.Ba3 Bh6   4.Bc1

The defender's Bishop is stuck because White's King controls its movements. This is why White's King moved to the shorter diagonal. The result would be the same even if Black's King had played 1...Kg6 2.Bf8 Be3 3.Ba3 Bh6 4.Bc1 Bg7 5.Bd2!, which places Black in zugzwang. You can see the importance of the short diagonal. The h6-f8 diagonal is only three squares long, yet it is fatal.

In Diagram 148, the defense is successful because the critical diagonals— h5-e8 and a2-g8—are more than three squares long.

1...Be8   2.Bc2 Kg5!

Black prevents 3.Bg6 and keeps the draw.

3.Bb3 Bh5   4.Bf7 Bd1   5.Bg6 Bb3

It's another draw. When Black is chased off one diagonal, he promptly jumps on the other one to sacrifice his Bishop for the pawn.

Bishop endings can possess a lovely subtlety. The position in Diagram 149 is a study by Luigi Clenturini (1820–1900), first published in 1847. White's winning procedure seems easy enough. He must chase the defending Bishop from the b8-square. The only way to do this is to challenge Black's control from the

DIAGRAM 148.

DIAGRAM 149.
L. Clenturini, 1847

b8-square. If White can play 1.Bb8 Bg1 2.Bg3 Ba7 3.Bf2, he wins. How can White get his Bishop to the b8-square? The direct 1.Bh4 Kb6! 2.Bf2+ Ka6! stops him from playing Bf2-a7-b8. Continuing with 3.Bh4 Kb6 4.Bd8+ Kc6, the position is only repeated. Greater subtlety is required to maneuver through this situation.

Suppose it is Black's move. See what happens if he tries any of these plays:

■ 1...Bg3

■ 1...Bf4

■ 1...Be5

All fail, as they invite 2.Bh4, 2.Bg5, and 2.Bf6, respectively, allowing White to transfer his Bishop to the g1-a7 diagonal with tempo. This allows White to move his Bishop to the a7-square before it can be stopped by Black's King. If it is Black's move, his only option is 1...Bd6! 2.Be7 Bh2!, after which White's Bishop is still denied a quick access to the a7-square.

The only "safe squares" for Black's Bishop are the d6- and h2-squares. If it is White's move, he can use this advantage to create a zugzwang.

1.Bh4 Kb6   2.Bf2+ Ka   3.Bc5!

Here is the key move. Black's Bishop is denied access to the d6-square and is forced to a less favorable square.

3...Bg3

White has lured Black's Bishop to a vulnerable square. To his credit, Black didn't try 3...Kb5 4.Ba7 Ka6 5.Bb8! Bg1 6.Bg3 Ba7 7.Bf2, with which White will win.

4.Be7!

Now White threatens to challenge the diagonal from the c7-square. Black's King has to block this threat.

4...Kb5   5.Bd8 Kc6

Black reaches the original position, but with a crucial difference: Black's Bishop is now vulnerable to a tempo winner.

6.Bh4!

Had Black played 3...Bf4, then 6.Bg5 would be a winner; if he'd tried 3...Be5, then 6.Bf6 would do the same trick.

6...Bh2   7.Bf2 Bf4   8.Ba7 Bh2   9.Bb8 Bg1   10.Bg3 Ba7   11.Bf2

This winning play is a fine example of the subtlety of the Bishop ending. Remember the principle: *The attacking King should move to the shorter diagonal.* In the previous example, the critical diagonals are the h2-b8 diagonal and the a7-b8 diagonal. Had White's King been on the a8-square, then winning would have been no problem because White's King is on the side of the short diagonal.

Bishops of Opposite Color

We have just seen four examples of how difficult it is to win positions with Bishops of the same color. In positions with Bishops of opposite color, the defender has such great drawing chances that the attacker cannot expect to win the game with an advantage of only one pawn. In general, a two-pawn advantage is required. Sometimes further positional advantages are necessary, such as an active King or poorly placed defensive pieces.

In the position in Diagram 150, published in 1916 by Switzerland's Moriz Henneberger, White has the advantage of two connected passed pawns. But it isn't enough. He must activate his King to support their advance. White has to win using his d-pawn, because the more immediate 1.c6+?? Kc7 would create a dark-squared blockade that can't be broken. However, trying to advance with 1.d6?? Bxd6 allows Black to sacrifice his Bishop for both pawns, producing an easy draw. Therefore, White has to advance his King to support the march of the d-pawn. This means that Black's King must be checked away.

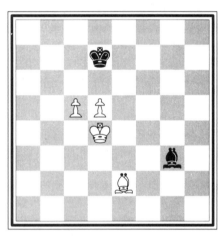

DIAGRAM 150.
M. Henneberger, 1916

1.Bb5+!

Here White follows an important principle: *The attacking Bishop must control as many squares in front of the pawns as possible.* Thus, while 1.Bg4+ appears to push Black's King aside, in fact it does not, and 1...Kc7 2.Ke4 (to advance to the e6-square and support the d-pawn) 2...Bf2! 3.d6+ Kc6 4.d7 Kc7 5.c6 Bh4 results in a dark-squared blockade and an immediate draw.

1...Ke7

This move offers the most resistance. Black can't retreat by 1...Kd8? 2.d6 because White would advance with his King and push the c-pawn forward. Also, 1...Kc7 2.Ke4! Bh2 (If Black tries 2...Bf2 3.d6+ Kd8 4.c6, the pawns advance.) 3.Kf5 Bg3 4.Ke6 Bf4 5.d6+ Kc8 6.c6 wins.

2.Ba4

White's Bishop steps aside to make room for White's King. Because it can't step to the e6-square, the next best thing is for the King to head to the c6-square.

2...Bf4   3.Kc4 Bg3

Black marks time, because he is unable to prevent White's King from penetrating. If he tries 3...Kd8 4.d6, he allows the d-pawn to advance, and 3...Bc7 4.Kb5 Kd7 5.Ka6+ Ke7 6.Kb7 Bg3 7.Kc6 will transpose.

4.Kb5 Kd7   5.Kb6+ Ke7   6.Kc6

White has reached his goal and is ready to advance the passers.

6...Bf4   7.d6+ Ke6   8.Bb3+ Ke5   9.Kd7

White wins, as the c-pawn is now unstoppable.

Is it fair to conclude, from this one example, that positions of opposite-colored Bishops are lost against connected passers? Not at all! The only reason that Black lost the position in Diagram 150 is because his Bishop was misplaced. Had Black's Bishop been on the e7- or f8-squares eyeing the c5-pawn, the game would have been drawn. Why? Because the defender's Bishop both stops the d-pawn from advancing and attacks White's c5-pawn. In this way, White's King is forced to protect the c5-pawn. If White plays 1.Bb5+ Kc7, Black just plays his Bishop back and forth between the e7- and f8-squares. This sparks a defensive idea: If the defender's Bishop can attack one of the pawns so that he can play back and forth along a diagonal, the game is drawn. Thus, if you advance the pawn as shown in Diagram 151, the defender is lost.

In Diagram 151, Black's Bishop is on its ideal square, and Black has constructed a fortress. His only problem is that his pieces can't move from their ideal squares.

1.Kc5!

This leaves Black in zugzwang. Any move he makes will cost him the game. If the Bishop could step backward on the diagonal, he would draw.

DIAGRAM 151.

DIAGRAM 152.

Why are endings with Bishops of opposite color notoriously difficult to win? The position in Diagram 152 offers a clear clue. As we can see, White is three connected passed pawns ahead, but he has no way to win the position. If White tries to bring his King to the b5-square, Black plays ...Kd8-c7 and stops further penetration. If White tries moving his King to the f5-square, Black responds with ...Kd8-e7, stopping him there. In the meantime, Black can simply pass with his Bishop. You see, then, that when there is a blockade, the attacker needs much more than a material advantage to win.

In the next section, we'll look at some practical examples from my tournament play. Pay special attention to the tremendous accuracy required in these endings. A single slip is all that is needed to turn a hard-earned draw into a loss.

Eureka! in Quebec

The position illustrated in Diagram 153 is from the fifth round of the game I played with Norman Weinstein in the 1977 Quebec Open. After an exhausting six-hour session, the game was adjourned. Norman sealed his move, and I went home to analyze the position.

Despite my fatigue following the game, I analyzed the position for several hours and gave the position up as drawn. My analysis started with 1.Bxb4—the expected sealed move—and 1...Bxb3—a natural recapture. Eventually, I realized that my two Kingside passers would cost White his Bishop. Although I was happy about this insight, the new position had its own problem. I'd be left with the wrong Bishop. After convincing myself that there were no swindles, I took a relaxing, hot bath. While soaking in the suds, Eureka! I had a sudden epiphany that the position was won. I rushed to my chess set to confirm my realization. It was Norman's bad luck that he had had to seal his move, and when the game was resumed, it became clear why:

1.Bxb4

As expected. Now comes the surprise...
Black must not capture the b3-pawn!

1...h4! 2.Bd2 h3

3.Kg1 Kg3 4.Be1+ Kf3 5.Bd2

This sensible move is designed to prevent 5...Ke2 and a rush of the f-pawn.

5...Bf5! 6.b4 Bc8!

Black thus prevents a Queenside breakthrough and prepares to win White's Bishop.

7.Kh2 Ke4! 8.Bc1 Bd7! 9.Kg1

A regrettable retreat. White's choices weren't palatable, because playing 9.Bd2 would have put the Bishop on a vulnerable square, causing 9...f3 10.Kg3 Kd3! 11.Be1 Ke2 to win. The other option,

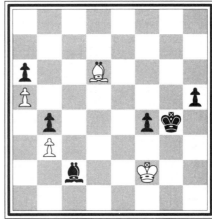

DIAGRAM 153.
Weinstein–Seirawan
Quebec, 1977

9.b5 axb5 10.a6 b4 11.a7 Bc6 12.Kxh3 f3 13.Kg3 Kd3 14.Kf2 Kc2 15.Ba3 b2, would also have won.

9...f3 10.Bg5 Kd3 11.Bf4 Ke2 12.Bg3

Norman is being cooperative thus far, all according to my homework analysis. It is time to win the Bishop.

12...f2+ 13.Bxf2 h2+

14.Kg2 h1=Q+

With a shrug and a smile, Norman now resigns. Why? Take a look at the position shown in Diagram 154. My analysis had concluded:

15.Kxh1 Kxf2 16.Kh2 Bc8

17.Kh1 Bb7+ 18.Kh2 Bg2!

This places White in stalemate. The b-pawn—my burst of inspiration—is the cause of White's downfall. He is forced to transfer the a6-pawn into a winning b5-pawn:

19.b5 axb5 20.a6 b4

21.a7 b3 22.a8=Q Bxa8

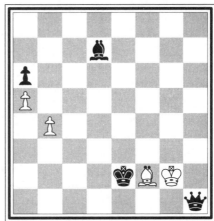

DIAGRAM 154.
Weinstein–Seirawan
Quebec, 1977

A nice win. Lady Fortune had smiled upon me back there in that bathtub. During the heat of battle, I would certainly have captured the b3-pawn, given half a chance.

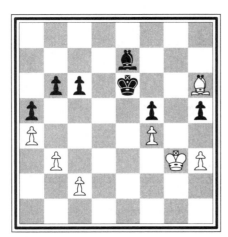

DIAGRAM 155.
Larsen–Polugaevsky
Le Havre, 1967

The position in Diagram 155 was taken from the book *Grandmaster Preparation* (Pergemon Press, Oxford, 1981), a wonderful collection of best games by Russian Grandmaster Lev Polugaevsky. His annotations continue to have a powerful impact on me.

The position shown in Diagram 155 occurred six moves after Polugaevsky and Bent Larsen resumed an adjourned game. Let's analyze the fundamentals of the position. It is hard to believe that with equal material, either player could lose, but which side is in better standing? The Queenside structure favors White because Black's b6- and a5-pawns are vulnerable to an attack of White's Bishop. However, White's f4-pawn, for similar reasons, also presents a potential weakness. White's King has a plan of activating itself by Bh6-g5, with Kg3-h4 to follow. It's Black's move. How should he play? A line like 1...Kf7 2.Bg5 Bc5 3.Bd8 Bd4 4.Kf3 (because 4.Kh4 Kg6 threatens ...5...Bf2 Checkmate!) 4...Ke6 5.Ke2 Kd7 6.Bg5 must surely be a draw. But should Black play for victory? Black has the attractive possibility of routing his King through the center and attacking White's f4-pawn. In this case, White's King will munch the h5-pawn. Then which passer—the f5-pawn or the h3-pawn—is stronger?

1...Kd5!

Black boldly plays for the win, and correctly so! In all endings, piece centralization is important, but that isn't the crucial issue here. At this point, the position calls for precise calculation. Black can and should envision that his own passer, the f5-pawn, is stronger than the h3-pawn. The pawn is stronger because it is advanced one square closer to promotion. In *Informant #1* (Chess Informator, 1966), the text was wrongly analyzed as a mistake. (Every six months, the *Informant* chess books compile the best of the grandmaster games.)

2.Bg5

Larsen has no choice and must continue his plan of targeting the h5-pawn. If he tries to seize the defensive with 2.Kf3 Kc5! 3.Ke3 Kb4 4.Kd3 b5! 5.axb5 axb5 6.Bg7 a4 7.bxa4 bxa4, Black's passed a4-pawn is more dangerous than White's passed c2-pawn.

2...Bd6!

Black targets the f4-pawn. In his adjournment analysis, Larsen had expected 2...Bc5 (to protect the b6-pawn) 3.Kh4 Kd4 4.Kxh5 Kc3, a position he thought held equal chances to the text. However, Larsen was wrong. As Polugaevsky points out in *Grandmaster Preparation*, "The 'h' pawn is considerably more important than all of the Queenside pawns." Indeed, after continuing with 5.Kg6 Kxc2 6.h4 Kxb3 7.h5 Bf8 8.Kf7!, the h-pawn will promote.

3.Bd8?

This dubious step is essentially the losing move. White should have played 3.Kf3 b5! when Black had the superior position because of his active King.

3...Ke4! 4.Bxb6 Bxf4+ 5.Kh4 Bd2! 6.Kxh5

The players have now reached the position shown in Diagram 156. Black's plan has been a fine success. As is obvious, Black's f5-passer is more dangerous than the h3-pawn. It is further advanced, and White's King blocks the progress of his h-pawn. In fact, only White's Bishop can prevent its promotion. With this general situation in mind, it is time for specific analysis. However, now another overlooked factor takes hold: psychology. When analyzing a position or preparing a variation, it's often easy to misread an essential human trait and competitor's tool: confidence. Never forget that a game of chess is a contest between two people who pick up "tells," or bodily signals, from one another. You'll

DIAGRAM 156.
Larsen–Polugaevsky
Le Havre, 1967

find yourself asking, "If my position is so good, why is my opponent playing so confidently? Why is he not nervous?" Grandmaster Polugaevsky describes this psychological assay in reference to this round with Larsen:

> This paradoxical decision [trading Kingside pawns] taken by Larsen on the resumption of the game affected me psychologically. I simply couldn't believe that the resulting position was favorable for White; but on the other hand, I had not carried through my adjournment analysis to the end. And I was further influenced by the feeling that Larsen was confidently following an already familiar path, along which he had accurately noted all the pitfalls, whereas I was having to act "spontaneously."

This is it! This is the kicker. At every level of chess play, players gamble. It's that simple. A puzzle is sometimes—but not always—a bluff; it can also be a matter of setting problems before your opponent. You test your opponent with psychological subtleties. If your opponent answers all the tests correctly, you probably will lose. However, if you can confront your opponent with tests that he is uncomfortable with, the gamble might very well pay off. Grandmaster Bent Larsen is one of the best chess gamblers I have ever seen. Let's see how the game continued.

6...f4??

A calculated move, but a decisive mistake! This kind of error is arguably the most common. Let me explain. Black has lost a pawn. He hasn't blundered the pawn—it was a deliberate sacrifice. However, Black is extremely conscious of his missing pawn. It is a natural human response to show immediate compensation. But there is no reason to rush, because careful thought is needed. Only White's Bishop could stop the f-pawn's charge. If Black can prevent White's King from retreating, the game is won; that is, by 6...Kf3! 7.h4 f4 8.Kg6 Be3 9.Bxa5 Ke2 10.Bc7 f3 11.Bg3 Bf4, Black wins. (Apparently 6...Kf3 was missed by Larsen in his adjournment analysis and by Polugaevsky at the board.)

It is remarkable that such a natural move as pushing a passed pawn could be a decisive mistake. Now it is Larsen's turn to show that he has a winning position. The path to victory is very narrow indeed, and Larsen's ensuing play is magnificent.

7.Kg4 Be1

Black prepares to push the f-pawn home. Attempting 7...f3? 8.Kg3 Be3 9.Bxa5 f2 10.Kg2 would be a painful realization that Black has mistakenly allowed White's King to get back in time.

8.h4 f3   9.Kh3!!

It is this retreat by way of the crooked path that wins the game. By aiming for the g2-square with his King, the f3-passer is effectively controlled. Meanwhile, White has his h4-passer and—yes—an extra Queenside pawn!

9...Kf4 10.Bc5!

This places Black in zugzwang. After 10...f2 11.Kg2 f1=Q+ 12.Kxf2 Bxh4 13.Bb6, Black loses a second pawn on the Queenside, and the game. If Black's Bishop retreats with 10...Bc3 11.Kh2 Bg7 12.Bf2, White will bring his King to the f1-square, fully neutralizing the f-pawn. Thereafter, the retreat Bf2-e1 and b3-b4 will create a winning passed a4-pawn.

10...Kf5

This is the only move, but Black's King isn't effective on this square. Even worse would be 10...Ke4 11.h5 Kf5 12.Be3!, in which the h-pawn becomes quite powerful.

11.Be7!

White aggresses with a dual threat. He wants to play Kh3-h2-g1-f1, stopping the f-pawn once and for all. At the same time, he is prepared to advance his h-pawn to prevent ...Kf5-g5, which would win the pawn. Black is unable to cope with both of these threats.

11...Ke4

Black wants to stop White's King from getting back to the f1-square. Now Black's vigilance over the h-pawn has subsided.

12.h5!

White puts his trump to good use. He avoids 12.Kh2? Ke3 13.Kg1? Ke2, which merely helps Black. Now Black is forced to respond to White's threat of running his h-pawn up the board.

12...Bd2

Black had to stop the h-pawn from advancing by avoiding 12...Ke3 13.Bc5+! Ke2 (because 13...Kd2 14.h6 Kxc2 15.Bd4 allows the h-pawn to carry the day) 14.h6 f2 15.Bxf2 Bxf2 16.h7 Bd4 17.b4! axb4 18.a5 Kd2 19.a6 Kxc2 20.a7, which would again put White's bridesmaids too far apart. White promotes and wins.

13.Bc5!

Beautifully played. Black's King is prevented from advancing, and, once more, White reintroduces the threat of bringing his King to the f1-square.

13...Be3 14.Bf8!

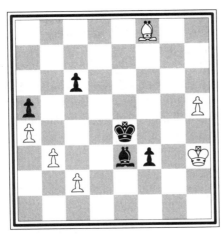

DIAGRAM 157.
Larsen–Polugaevsky
Le Havre, 1967

White's point is now clear. He is ready to support the advance of his h-pawn, while Black can't advance with his King. The current position is shown in Diagram 157.

14...Bd4

Black moves the Bishop to control the h8-square and allow his King to advance. A weaker option was 14...Kf5? 15.h6 Kg6 16.Kg3 f2 17.Kg2, with a winning position for White.

15.Bh6!!

Once more, White stops Black's King from advancing and threatens Kh3-g3 to better neutralize the f-pawn. This can't be allowed. Missing the target, Grandmaster Polugaevsky points out that "...15.h6? Ke3 16.Bg7 Bxg7 17.hxg7 f2 would allow a draw."

15...Be5   16.Bd2!!

"Four brilliant moves by the White Bishop, and Black's position has become hopeless. The a5-pawn is doomed."

16...Bf4

Black continues to fight for control of the e3-square. Despite the high price, there is no other option.

17.Bxa5 Ke3   18.Be1!

Here he is able to cover the f2-square from another diagonal. A bad move would have been 18.Bb6+? Ke2 19.a5 Be3!, blocking White's Bishop from covering the f2-square.

18...Ke2   19.Kg4!!

"This shows the extent to which Larsen's analysis went further than my careless analysis. Despite all of White's previous successes, it is only this move that leads to a win. Incidentally, it was made instantly..." (Another quote from Grandmaster Polugaevsky.) To Polugaevsky's analysis, I would add that 19.Bh4 Bg5 20.Bg3 Bf4 would have been Black's drawing idea.

19...Bh6

After the trade 19...Kxe1 20.Kxf3, White's bridesmaids, the a-pawn and h-pawn, are too far apart.

20.Bh4

The purpose of White's nineteenth move is clear: Now White's King protects the g5-square, making ...Bf4-g5 impossible.

20...Bd2

Black is desperately trying to hold up the advance of the a4-pawn.

21.Bg3

A slight quibble here. Simpler would have been 21.b4 Bxb4 (or else 22.b5 wins) 22.h6 Bc3 23.h7, allowing the a-pawn to advance next.

21...c5

Black's Bishop can't move, because it would release either the a-pawn or the h-pawn. Black's King can't move, so 21...c5 was the best choice. White's next move places Black in zugzwang.

22.c4! f2   23.Bxf2 Kxf2   24.h6! Ke3

The point of c2-c4 is clear. After 24...Bxh6 25.a5!, that demure a-pawn bridesmaid is unstoppable.

25.h7 Bc3   26.a5

This win concludes an amazing example of a Bishop ending! It is because of such daring that Grandmaster Bent Larsen has been a chess lover's hero for decades. Needless to say, *Grandmaster Preparation* is a wonderful book, but it has been out of print for some time. If you can find a used copy, grab it right away!

Test Your Skills

Diagram 158 on the next page is a composition by Gioacchino Greco (1600–34), sometimes known as "Il Calabrese." In his May 1999 *Chess Life* column, Grandmaster Andrew Soltis refers to Greco as the "first chess professional." While the legacy that Greco has left us is important, I suspect that chess, with its 1400-year history, had many professionals before Greco. Just think of all the caliphs and pirates that must have wagered their treasures on the outcome of a game. Certainly one professional that Soltis overlooked is Abu-Bakr Muhammad ben Yahya as-Suli (854–946). The *Oxford Companion to Chess* (Oxford University Press, 1996) refers to this early pioneer as:

> ...the strongest player of his time, composer, and author of the first book describing a systematic way of playing Shatranj [an early form of chess]. For more than 600 years the highest praise an Arab could bestow on a chess player was to say that he played like Yahya as-Suli...

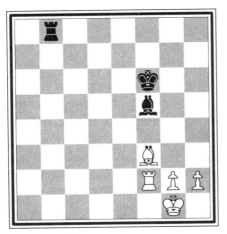

DIAGRAM 158.
G. Greco, circa 1620

It seems only reasonable to call as-Suli—who was renowned for 600 years—an early chess professional. The history of chess is astonishing in its scope; I love poring through books to read about the fascinating past of this old game.

But I digress... on with testing your skills!

QUIZ 1: In Diagram 158, White is ready to exploit a nearly certain win with his two extra pawns. How can Black foil White's ambitions?

QUIZ 2: In Diagram 159, how would you evaluate the position? Can White win the game?

QUIZ 3: What is the correct result for the position in Diagram 160?
(Be very careful; White has the wrong Bishop here.)

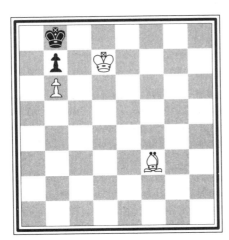

DIAGRAM 159.

DIAGRAM 160.
Paulsen–Metger
Nuremberg, 1888

QUIZ 4: Can White possibly win the position in Diagram 161?

Of course, this position is a draw based on the material on the board. But the position is a crafty study.

DIAGRAM 161.
B. Horowitz, 1884

Solutions

QUIZ 1 (DIAGRAM 158): This is a 480-year-old classic! Our predecessors certainly knew about the wrong Bishop. The move **1...Rb1+! 2.Rf1 Rxf1+ 3.Kxf1 Bh3!!** forces a wrong Bishop position, regardless of how White plays, because of **...Bh3xg2**, which draws.

QUIZ 2 (DIAGRAM 159): The evaluation is clear: White is better! But if Black plays correctly, the game is drawn. White's best try is **1.Kd8 Ka8 2.Bc6**, after which he hopes for **2...bxc6?? 3.Kc7!**, which wins. Black can keep the position by playing **2...Kb8 3.Kd7 bxc6! 4.Kxc6 Kc8**, with a draw, as we saw in Chapter Two.

QUIZ 3 (DIAGRAM 160): The actual game saw **1.Kc4? b5! 2.axb6+** (Otherwise Black's King makes it to the a8-corner.) **2...Kb7 3.Kb5 Ka8 4.Bb8 Kxb8 5.Kc6 Kc8**, and the players agreed to a draw. The crucial point is that White cannot allow Black to advance his b-pawn with tempo. The beautiful feint **1.Kd4!!** is a winner. White's King takes a circuitous route to get to the Queenside by playing **Kd5-d4-c3-b4-b5**, for a win. A poor choice is **1.Ke6? b5! 2.a6 b4**, when White's Bishop is forced to allow Black's King to reach the a8-corner. Then Black has at least three winning choices:

- ■ **1...b5 2.a6!! Kc6** (Black's King will not be allowed to get to the corner.) **3.Kc3 Kd6 4.Kb4 Kc6 5.Ka5**!

- ■ **1...b6 2.a6! Kc6 3.Kc4 Kd6 4.Kb4! Kc6** (4...Kc7 5.Kb5 Kc8 6.Kxc6 wins.) **5.Bb8! b5 6.Ba7! Kc7 7.Kxb5**.

- ■ **1...Kc6 2.Bb6!** (2.Kc3? b6! 3.a6 Kb5 draws.) **2...Kd6** (Because 2...Kb5 catches the King offside, 3.Kd5! Ka6 4.Kd6 Kb5 5.Kc7 Ka6 6.Kb8 wins.) **3.Kc4 Kc6 4.Kb4 Kd6 5.Kb5 Kd7 6.Bf2** (covering the b8-square from a more mobile diagonal) **6...Kc8 7.Bg3 Kd7 8.Kb6 Kc8 9.Bf4**.

QUIZ 4 (DIAGRAM 161): White crafts a lovely win based on the poor position of Black's forces: **1.Bf2+ Kh5 2.g4+ Kh6 3.Kf6 Kh7** (3…Bh7?? 4.Be3 Checkmate) **4.g5 Kh8 5.Bd4 Kh7** (Another checkmate is delivered after 5…Bh7 6.Kxf7.) **6.Ba1 Kh8 7.g6! fxg6 8.Kxg6**, delivering a remarkable checkmate. In chess studies, the final position is considered "pure" because all the pieces are necessary to produce checkmate.

Knight Endings

The Knight is perhaps the most difficult piece to master. In this chapter, I'll introduce a training technique called the *hopping game* that will help you get a firm rein on your horses. You'll get an overview of the principles behind Knight endings, and then you'll delve into the mysteries of play in two kinds of Knight endings: Knight vs. pawns and Knight vs. Knight. A few samples from tournament practice and some quizzes will round out the chapter.

The Knights, with their hopping and forking techniques, have given novice players fits for generations. The Knight movements are indeed difficult to grasp, and literally hundreds of games need to be played before you get a good handle on a Knight's role and its nuances. The hopping game, an excellent training tool that has been used by chess coaches the world over, was introduced to me when I was a beginner. I immediately fell in love with this game, recognizing that I had a powerful tool at my disposal, and I have used it ever since.

The Hopping Game

The essence of the hopping game is to learn to move the Knight to a destination in as few moves as possible. To begin the game, clear the board of pieces and put the Knight on a corner square. In Diagram 162, I've put the Knight on the a1-square and designated the h8-square as the destination square. Your task is to move the Knight to the h8-square as efficiently as you can. Try this now.

That exercise was simple enough. Now repeat the process, this time using a different path. Don't allow the Knight to land on any of the squares it previ-

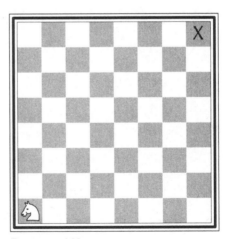

DIAGRAM 162.
Move the Knight to h8.

ously took—you can mark them with pawns to keep track. Again, it seems pretty clear that the f7- and g6- squares can be used only once, so after finding two unique paths, that challenge ends. But it isn't the end of the hopping game, whose challenges seem infinite!

Looking again at Diagram 162, the next challenge is to make the g8-square the destination square and to move the Knight to the starting b1-square. As a student doing this exercise, I knew that I'd have to find three unique paths from start to finish, because only the e7-, f6-, and h6-squares allow a Knight jump. You'll discover, as I did, that as the destination square gets closer to the center, the number of paths grows. For instance, the e5-destination square is accessible from eight different squares! Can a Knight travel from the c3-square along eight unique paths to get to e5? Believe me, I started leaving trails of white and black pawns all over the board trying to find out!

These tests were rigorous and continuous. My early chess teachers were well aware of the difficulty of mastering the Knight movements, so my hopping tests also became more difficult. Soon, Black pawns were scattered randomly around the board, and I was instructed to find a path to the destination square without hopping to a square controlled by a Black pawn.

The position in Diagram 163 presented a typical challenge. I'd approach it as if it were a maze. I'd look at the e8 destination square first and then try to work my way backward to the starting position. I'd see that my only point of entry was through the g7-square, and that it could be reached from the f5-square, and that f5 could be accessed from the d4-square, and then—bingo!—I'd have my solution. As my skills increased, so did the number of pawns appearing on the board!

As my ability to recognize the patterns of the Knight's hops improved, I created more challenging exercises, making the hopping game increasingly difficult. A favorite exercise was to try to capture all of Black's pawns in the fewest possible moves. Diagram 164 was fairly typical of the test. I quickly realized that Knights like to feast on structures that are advanced. For instance, in Diagram 164, White, playing a line like

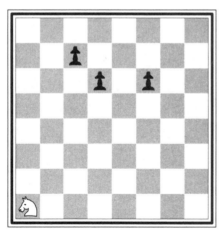

DIAGRAM 163.
Move the Knight to e8.

Nf4-h5-xg7-e8-xf6, will munch the King-side pawns quite efficiently. Capturing the Queenside pawns will require an additional move.

As I continued to make progress, my teachers became ruthless. Ever more pawns were placed on the board, and the process of trying to make the captures in the fewest moves became quite difficult. These hopping exams were a main part of my chess-learning diet, and it is a true testament to the tough and able guidance of my early teachers that I learned to use my Knights effectively. Until the hopping game was introduced, I'd delight in trading Knights or trading a Bishop for a Knight as quickly as possible. I saw these pieces as a curse!

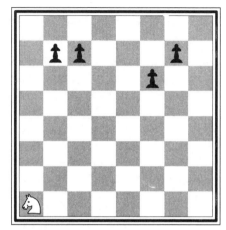

DIAGRAM 164.
Capture the pawns in as few moves as possible.

There are many variations to the hopping game. Another old favorite is to put the Knight on the a1-square and four Black pawns on the c3-, c6-, f3-, and f6-squares. In this variation of the game, the Knight's objective is to go around the board and land on all the squares that are not protected by Black's pawns. White is not allowed to capture the Black pawns. Using a stopwatch is a good tool. Eventually I was able to complete this game in about two minutes. Hopping exams tested my creativity and my teachers', a challenge we all relished.

What makes the Knight such a difficult piece to fathom? Its crooked movements certainly account for its surprising moves, and Knights have their own special characteristics that the following principles highlight:

■ *Knights are short-ranging pieces that are most effective in the midst of the battle.*

■ *Knights are least effective at the edges of the board, where they control the fewest squares.*

■ *Centralized, Knights can attack or defend up to eight squares.*

■ *While they are excellent blockers of passed pawns, Knights hate to blockade a- and h-pawns.*

■ *Knights operate best in closed positions.*

My Kingdom for a Pass

Knights are endowed with remarkable abilities. They are the only pieces that can jump over others, and they can move to every square on the board while doing it. Yet for all their powers, they can't make a pass. They can't take a stutter step. They can't lose a tempo for you. If you put a Knight on the a1-square, as in Diagram 162, and move it to all three corners of the board and then back to the a1-square, you will make an even-numbered journey of moves. In both 1.Na1-b3, 2.Nb3-a1 and 1.Na1-b3, 2.Nb3-c1, 3.Nc1-d3, 4.Nd3-e1, 5.Ne1-c2, 6.Nc2-a1, White makes an even number of moves—two and six—to get to the a1-corner. This inability to pass or lose a tempo is an important limitation. As you have seen in other endings, at times you want to create a situation that forces your opponent to make a move. Picture a Rook ending. If your Rook is behind a passer and you're pushing your way up the board, you can sometimes pass with a Rook move and not damage your position in any way. Meanwhile, your opponent is forced to move.

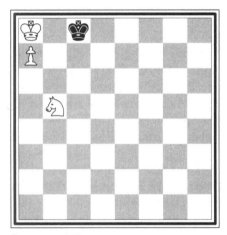

DIAGRAM 165.

The position in Diagram 165 shows how this inability to lose a tempo is the difference between winning and drawing. White, a pawn and a Knight to the good, has just one problem: a hemmed-in King. If Black allows the White King to escape from the corner, he loses. If it is Black's move, he is forced to play 1...Kd8 or 1...Kd7, after which he loses to 2.Kb7, and the pawn queens. But if it's White's move, the game is a draw! After 1.Nd6+ Kc7, White would like Black to move. After 2.Ne8+ Kc8, it's obvious that Black intends to shuttle his King between the c8- and c7-squares, and although White's Knight might snort in fury and rampage around the board, there is nothing that White can do to prevent a repetition and a draw.

In Chapter Five, I discussed two examples of a wrong Bishop. Does that mean the Knights are better because I've listed only one drawback of the Knight? Not at all; for all its prowess, the Knight does have a shortcoming when it is up against an a- or an h-pawn. Examine Diagram 166. Black's King is entrenched in the corner, and White's King can't approach because of the threat of stalemate. The position is drawn. The problem for White is that the a-pawn has advanced one square too far. If the a7-pawn were on the a6-square, White would win easily.

DIAGRAM 166.

Knight vs. Passed Pawn

Knights can handle the burden of stopping passers, but their ability to do this depends on how far the passer has advanced, and which type of passed pawn is advancing. In the previous chapters, the a- and h-pawns have patiently tolerated their fair share of ridicule for not being centralized and for being able to capture in only one direction. What is the secret to their composure? These two pawns know that in Knight endings, they simply shine. For a change, the pawns are in the limelight, and these far outside passers give the Knight a whole new dynamic of trouble. If a Knight is forced to blockade a passed a-pawn, it is drawn away from the center of battle, rendering it less effective. Because the Knight has a shorter range of squares to which it can move, it has a much harder time than other pieces in keeping a passer under control.

In Diagram 167, the Knight can just hold out on its own:

1.Kb6 Nc8+   2.Kc7 Na7

3.Kb7 Nb5   4.Kb6

White has forced the Knight to give up its guard of the a7-square.

4...Nd6!

Black manages to hang on, hoping that 5.a7 Nc8+ 6.Kb7 Nxa7 will save the day. From this position, I used to like playing 5.Kc6 Nc8 6.Kc7 Na7 7.Kb7 Nb5 8.Kc6.

DIAGRAM 167.

White's King uses the c6-, c7-, b7-, and b6-squares, while the Black Knight circles around the King. This fascinated me; I imagined a kind of ring-around-the-rosy childhood game. The position is drawn.

DIAGRAM 168.

DIAGRAM 169.

It is only with an a-pawn or h-pawn that the Knight is helpless. In Diagram 168 the pawn is advanced a square, and that square makes all the difference. After 1.Kc6 Kg7 2.Kb7 Kf7 3.Kxa8 Ke7 4.Kb7, the pawn promotes and wins. In Diagram 169, the a-pawn has been transformed into a b-pawn, and the position is drawn after 1.Kc7 Na6+ 2.Kb6 Nb8 3.Ka7 Nd7.

The position in Diagram 170 is a real brainteaser. The solution to this study by Nikolay Dmitriyevich Grigoriev, introduced in Chapter Four, is as profound as it is elegant. White's Knight has to stop the h-pawn, and White's King is unable to lend a hand. How will the Knight do this? Work your way backward, remembering that the Knight can't resist by covering the h1-square. White will therefore have to block the pawn on the h2-square. Because of Black's well-placed King, the

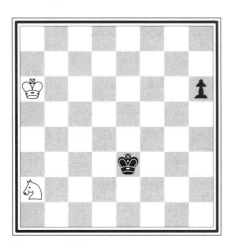

DIAGRAM 170.
N.D. Grigoriev, 1932

Knight must aspire to the g4- or f1-square to stop the pawn. It seems impossible to get to the f1-square, so White must try to reach the g4-square.

1.Nb4!

White avoids the tempting 1.Nc3 h5 2.Nd5+ Kf3!, a fine move, in which Black's King places itself in *diagonal* opposition to the White Knight. This position—one well known to chess masters—now means that it will take the Knight three moves to check Black's King again. Continuing the line with 3.Nc7 h4 4.Ne6 Kg4! recreates the same circumstance of diagonal opposition. Black prevents Ne6-g5+ and advances his pawn. Now with 5.Nc5 h3 6.Ne4 h2!, Black wins when White fails to stop the pawn from reaching the h2-square.

1...h5   2.Nc6!

Black avoids 2.Nd5+ Kf3!, which is the position we just discussed. White makes a beeline to the g4-square. Failure awaits 2.Nc2+? Ke4! (the same diagonal opposition we've just seen) 3.Ne1 h4 4.Ng2 h3, awarding the win to Black. This tactical circumstance of a Knight on g2 vs. a pawn on h3, which will come up again later in the chapter, is worth remembering.

2...Ke4!

Black steps into the Knight's diagonal opposition. After 2...h4? 3.Ne5, White is safe when his Knight makes it to the g4-square. The tactical point is that with 3...Kf4 4.Ng6+, Black's King walks into a Knight fork. It now appears that White's Knight is cut off from entering the Kingside. Now we'll see the real beauty of the study.

3.Na5!!

This is a move that was beyond the limits of my early chess understanding. Indeed, the only way to understand this move is by recalling the critical defensive g4- and f1-squares. White's Knight is denied the g4-square when 3.Nd8 h4 4.Ne6 Kf5! 5.Nd4+ Kg4 6.Nc2 Kf4! wins, so a new approach is required. White makes tracks for the f1-square.

3...h4

Here is a most challenging play. If Black's King tries to stop the Knight by 3...Kd5 4.Nb3!, the Knight makes it to the f1-square via the d2-square. If Black's King tries 3...Kd4 4.Nc6+!, the play is sufficient to bring about a draw.

4.Nc4!

White reaches the ideal square and threatens to make it to the f1-square with tempo. Note that 4.Nb3? Ke3! would deny White his goal.

4...Kf3

Black plays his best chance because the alternative, 4...h3 5.Nd2+ Ke3 6.Nf1+, recreates the draw that we've seen before.

5.Ne5+!

White continues to find the best choice in a maze of traps. A loss awaits 5.Nd2+? Ke2 6.Ne4 h3 7.Ng3+ Kf2, winning for Black.

5...Kg3

Black's King guards the g4-square.

6.Nc4!

Back to the ideal square.

6...h3

If Black tries to stop the Knight with 6...Kf4 7.Nd2, aiming for the f1-square, or with 6...Kf2 7.Ne5, aiming for the g4-square, both would draw.

7.Ne3!

Like a grasshopper on caffeine, the Knight finally reaches its goal in this amazing hopping example and makes a draw.

Let's turn our attention now to those positions in which a player possesses an extra Knight.

Knight and Pawn vs. Pawn

Having an extra Knight is no guarantee of victory, even when both players have a pawn. In general, whenever a player is an extra piece ahead, his is usually a win-

DIAGRAM 171.
N.D. Grigoriev, 1933

ning position. But as you've seen, the defender has resources. The position shown in Diagram 171, another enjoyable study by Nikolay Dmitriyevich Grigoriev, is fairly common to Knight endings. White has a problem winning because his Knight is far out of play, stopping Black's a-pawn. If White's h-pawn were a g-pawn, he would easily win. He could promptly march the g-pawn up the board, use his Knight to make a tempo move, and force Black's blockading King away. Unfortunately, White's pawn is an h-pawn. Because of the possibility of stalemate, marching the pawn up the board doesn't provide the answer. It becomes clear that White has difficulty winning. White can't rush his King to the Queenside and win the a3-pawn because it would cost him his own h6-pawn. White's only winning chance lies in using the Knight to create checkmate.

1.Na2!

The winning plan is to have White's King on the g6-square when Black's King is on the g8-square and the Knight is on the b4-square. In this way, the move h6-h7+ will force Black's King into the corner, and the Knight will deliver checkmate. Now that you know the plan, you just have to be precise. Remember, the Knight won't be able to make a pass.

1...Kf8

Black tries to make White's life difficult and opts not to go after 1...Kg8 2.Kg6 Kh8 3.Nb4, which would allow White to achieve the position he wants.

2.Kf6!

This is a better choice than 2. Kg6? Kg8 3.Nb4 Kh8, after which Black gets to where he wants to go. By choosing 2.Kf6!, White wins the opposition and the game.

2...Kg8   3.Kg6 Kh8   4.Nb4 Kg8

Now White is able to execute his win.

5.h7+ Kh8   6.Nc6 a2   7.Ne5 a1=Q   8.Nf7 Checkmate

The Knight had to cover a lot of territory, but in the end he was able to pack a wallop.

From this study, you should realize that when the Knight has to handle a passer on its own, it can still offer assistance across the board. Diagram 171 showed one of the most difficult endings of this type for the superior side to win.

Another ending—and an extremely tricky one—is when the Knight has to play nursemaid to its own pawn. In Diagram 172, White, a Knight to the good, can't win if it's his move. The problem is that his Knight must protect the g3-pawn and stop Black from playing ...h5-h4, trading the Kingside pawns. White's King is forced to lend the Knight protection:

1.Ke6 Kg6!   2.Ne3 Kg5

Black threatens to draw with the ...h5-h4 trade.

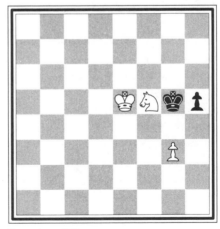

DIAGRAM 172.

159

3.Nf5 Kg6   4.Ke5 Kg5   5.Ke4 Kg4

White's progress is thwarted.

In Diagram 172, if it were Black to move, White would win easily:

1...Kg6   2.Kf4 Kf6   3.Nh4

After this, Kf4-g5 would follow, winning the h5-pawn. Another option also wins: 1…Kg4 2.Kf6 h4 (2…Kf3 3.Kg5) 3.gxh4 Kh5 4.Kg7 Kg4 5.Kg6

How easy to win in one situation, and how difficult in the other! This brings to mind how important tempi and the opposition tactic are to Knight endings. (This is the parallel that is often drawn between King and pawn endings and Knight endings.) Let's look at two more examples of these awkward cases.

The position in Diagram 173 is taken from a game between Joseph Henry Blackburne and Johannes Zukertort, two nineteenth-century chess giants. The active Black King manages to save the day. White can't move his Knight or advance his pawn. His hope is either to drive Black's King backward or to attack Black's g6-pawn with his King.

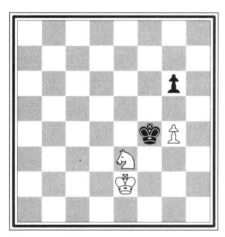

1...Kg3!

It's the only move. If White is allowed Ke2-f2, Black's King would be driven back. This is also seen after 1…Ke4? 2.Ng2! g5 3.Kf2, when Black is forced to retreat. Advancing the g-pawn has a different reason for failure: 1…g5? 2.Kd3 Kf3 3.Kd4 Kf4 4.Kd5! Kxe3 5.Ke5 leads to a winning King and pawn ending.

DIAGRAM 173.
Blackburne–Zukertort, 1881

2.Kd1 Kf3!

Black carefully keeps the diagonal opposition. Both 2…Kf2? and 2…Kf4? lose for the same reason, when 3.Kd2 Kf3 4.Kd3 Kf4 5.Kd4 Kf3 6.Ke5! Kxe3 7.Kf6 Kf4 8.g5! gives White a win.

3.Kd2 Kf2

An unnecessary extravagance. A simpler choice would be to keep the diagonal opposition by 3…Kf4 4.Ke2 Kg3, arriving right back where you started.

4.Kd3

Black is fortunate that White's other option, 4.Nf5 Kf3 5.Nh6 Kf4 6.Kd3 Kg5, draws.

4...Kf3   5.Kd4 Kf4

With this, White is unable to make progress. The ability of the defender to threaten both Knight and pawn and to draw the most hopeless-looking game can be quite frustrating for the superior side. However, using the device of this threat doesn't always guarantee a forced draw.

Diagram 174 seems like a defender's dream. Even though Black is a Knight behind, his active King appears to be able to rescue the game. What can White try?

1.Kd3

White is eschewing the win of a pawn. He doesn't choose 1.Kb4 Ka1! 2.Kxa3, which would leave Black stalemated.

1...Ka1

This is a much better play than 1...Kc1? 2.Nd5 Kb2 3.Nb4, after which White's King is ready to march to the b3-square and munch the a3-pawn. Now it appears that White cannot improve his position.

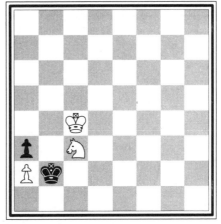

DIAGRAM 174.
J. Berger

2.Na4!

A calculated sacrifice, jettisoning the pawn but weaving a mating net.

2...Kb1   3.Kd2 Ka1   4.Kc1

White forces Black to make the capture.

4...Kxa2   5.Kc2 Ka1   6.Nc5! Ka2

Naturally, 6...a2 7.Nb3 Checkmate would follow.

7.Nd3 Ka1   8.Nc1!

Black is forced to advance his pawn.

8...a2   9.Nb3 Checkmate

A fine ending, and a fine study indeed.

Knight and Pawn vs. Knight

Knight and one pawn against Knight endings are usually drawn because the defending Knight is generally able to blockade the pawn or sacrifice itself to make a draw. Therefore, the superior side needs a further advantage. The pawn needs to be well advanced with good support from its own King.

DIAGRAM 175.
J. Kling, 1867

The position in Diagram 175 has been instructive for generations of chess fans. It is White's move. His only chance of promoting his b-pawn is to dislodge the Black Knight. He will have to do that by using his own Knight.

1.Ng6!

This dual threat, with 2.Ne5+ or 2.Nf8, pushes Black's Knight away.

1...Kd5!

Weaker was 1...Kc5 2.Nf8 Ne5 3.Ka8 Nc6 4.Ne6+ Kd6 5.Nd8, which wins.

2.Nf8 Ne5   3.Kb6

White had his choice of wins. He could also have played 3.Ka8 Nc6 4.Nd7 Kd6 (4...Ke6 5.Nb6 Kd6 6.Nc8+ Kc7 7.Na7! Nb8 8.Nb5+ wins.) 5.Nb6 Kc7 6.Nd5+ Kd6 7.Nb4, which also does the trick.

3...Nc6   4.Kc7

White keeps Black's King at bay and wants to bring his Knight back into the action to interfere with the defending c6-Knight.

4...Nb4!   5.Nd7 Nc6

Black has no choice but this because 5...Na6+? 6.Kb6 (5...Ke6 6.Nc5+) Kd5 7.b8=Q and 5...Kc4 6.Kb6 Nd5+ 7.Ka7 Ne7 8.Ne5+ Kc5 9.b8=Q win for White.

6.Ne5!

A clever way to break up Black's defenses.

6...Nb4   7.Kb6

White wins as the pawn finally promotes.

As this study shows, White needed several positional trumps in addition to the extra pawn. The defender's King wasn't in front of the pawn, and the defending Knight could be dislodged. Advantages such as these don't always come with the extra pawn.

Knight and Passer vs. Knight

The position in Diagram 176 displays a pattern that should soon be permanently impressed on your mind. In a material sense, the game should be an easy draw because of the balance of forces, but the following combination changes the outcome of the game:

1.Nxb7!

A stunning shot. The b7-pawn, which seemed to be so nicely guarded, has been suddenly removed.

1...Nb5

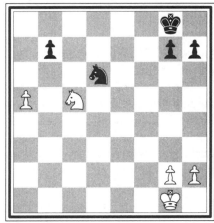

With much sorrow, Black is forced to accept the loss of the pawn. After 1...Nxb7 2.a6, Black is helpless to prevent the promotion of the a-pawn. This pattern is worth memorizing.

2.a6

The position now gives White an extra pawn and the meanest pawn passer of all, the outside a-pawn (the h-pawn passer shares this distinction). Black's Knight

DIAGRAM 176.

must now remain out of the action of the center and the Kingside. Black's only way of rescuing his Knight from its guard duty is to rush his King to the Queenside. Otherwise he will be playing a piece down. However, when Black's King moves to the Queenside, White will start to raid the Kingside.

2...Kf8

This is a better choice because the more active 2...Kf7 is immediately refuted by 3.Nd6+!, which wins.

3.Nd6 Na7   4.Kf2 Ke7   5.Nf5+

White wants the new theater of battle to be the Kingside, so White's pieces converge there.

5...Kf6   6.Ng3!

White had the option of 6.g4 h5 7.h3 hxg4 8.hxg4 g6 9.Nh4, which would also win. However—and this is an important point—White shouldn't be so agreeable about trading pawns. Rather, he should try to keep as many Kingside pawns on the board as he possibly can. In this way, the raid on the Kingside will win two pawns. With 6.Ng3!, he can play Ng3-h5, menacing the g7-pawn.

6...Ke5

Black prepares for his sprint to the Queenside.

7.Kf3

White, too, steps up the board, aiming to raid the Kingside. It would be a mistake to play 7.Ke3 with the aim of going to the Queenside. Instead, White should use the passed a-pawn as a decoy and concentrate his forces on winning on the Kingside.

7...g6

After 7...Kd5 8.Nh5 g6 9.Nf6+ Kc6 10.Nxh7 Kb6 11.Nf8 Kxa6 12.Nxg6, White is left with two connected passed pawns and a winning position.

Now is a good time to discuss advancing pawns. In endings, the tactic of advancing a passed pawn should be held close to our hearts. (Grandmaster Aaron Nimzovitch described this as the passer's "lust to expand.") On the other hand, when you are obliged to push pawns that are not advanced, they often become weaknesses. While the move 7...g6 was necessary, Black's pawns are being lured closer to White's King.

8.Ne4!

White tries to inflict further damage on Black's Kingside structure. The new menace is Ne4-g5, attacking the h7-pawn.

8...h6

Again, Black wants to go to the Queenside, but 8...Kd4 9.Nf6 h6 10.Ng8 h5 11.Kf4 Kc5 12.Kg5 Kb6 13.h4 will cost Black both of his pawns.

9.Nf2!

White continues to lure the pawns forward into the welcoming embrace of White's King. The new threat is Nf2-g4+, forking King and pawn.

9...h5   10.Nd3+ Kf5

As you can see in Diagram 177, Black is doing his best to be as annoying as possible. His last move is intended to block White's King from penetrating the Kingside. Had Black allowed White's King access to the f4-square, his pawns would have quickly fallen. Now White has to combine threats of supporting his a-pawn with his King and his true intention of raiding the Kingside.

11.Ke3

This introduces the threat of Ke3-d4-c5-b6, which Black has to take seriously.

11...Nc6

Black is covering the d4-square. Black could also choose 11...Nb5 12.Nb4 (playing for Nb4-c6 and to advance the a-pawn) 12...Ke5 (12...Na7 13.Kd4) 13.Nc6+ Kd6 14.a7 Nc7 15.Nd8 Na8 16.Kf4, with a winning Kingside invasion.

12.Nf4

With this, he temporarily keeps Black's King tied to the Kingside pawns.

12...h4   13.Ne2 Na7

Black gets out of the way of 14.Nd4+, trading Knights. After 13...Ke5 14.Nd4 Nxd4 (14...Na7 15.Nf3+ picks off the h4-pawn) 15.a7, the pawn promotes.

14.Nd4+ Kf6   15.Nf3 g5   16.Ke4

White continues to make progress. His King has advanced up the center, and he is able to go to either flank. This state of affairs is all because Black's Knight has been forced to play guard duty and is unavailable, being tied to the blockade of the passed a-pawn.

DIAGRAM 177.

16...Nc6   17.Nd4

Vigilance is an endgame requirement. The hasty 17.Kd5?? Nb4+ would have been a cruel loss of the a6-pawn.

17...Na7   18.h3

This pawn step puts Black in zugzwang. His Knight cannot move, as 18...Nc8 19.Nb5 will see the advance of the a-pawn. Because 18...g4 19.hxg4 Kg5 20.Kf3 costs a pawn, Black must move his King. White could also play 19.Kd5 Nc8 20.Nb5 Ke7 (20...Kf5 21.Nd6+ trades Knights.) 21.Ke5, going after the Kingside pawns.

18...Kg6

At last Black has really committed his King to the defense of his Kingside pawns. Now White can go to the Queenside and force a win—not by trading his passer for the Knight as you might expect, but by promoting his pawn and winning with:

19.Kd5! g4   20.Kc5 Kg5   21.Nb5 Nc8   22.Nd6! Na7   23.Kb6

Knight and Pawn Majority vs. Knight

With all the pawns on one side of the board, a defender has an easier time than if his forces were split. The superior side still has winning chances, which shouldn't be underestimated. As usual, the presence of an extra pawn isn't by itself decisive. The superior side needs additional advantages. These advantages are the result of either superior activity of pieces, or weakness in the defender's structure.

DIAGRAM 178.
Y. Averbach, 1955

Domination by activity is exemplified by the position in Diagram 178. In this diagram, White has tremendous advantages that make the position an easy win. The protected passed f6-pawn cramps Black's pieces and, along with White's active King, helps him wrap up the game.

1.Ke6 Kf8

Black is trying to limit White's advance. After 1...Nd8+ 2.Kd7 Nf7 (because with 2...Nb7 3.Ke7, the f-pawn trots home) 3.Ke7, it's a win.

2.Kd7! Kg8   3.Ke7 Nh8

4.Ne5 Kh7   5.Kf8 Nf7   6.Kxf7

This rapid-fire win was probably quite overwhelming for the defender, so we will give him a sporting chance. The position in Diagram 179 is fairly typical of these endings, in which White has a few advantages beyond his extra pawn. As we can see, White has two solid advantages: an extra f4-pawn and more active pieces. Black's structure is very solid. Especially useful is the g6-pawn. White's only plan is to engineer a passed f-pawn using g3-g4 and f4-f5, hoping that he might force his f-pawn up the board. This plan will allow Black to trade a pair of pawns, making the win problematic. With this situation in mind, Black makes an understandable error.

1...h5?

In anticipation of g3-g4, Black optimistically looks forward to White's playing h2-h3 and g3-g4 so that he might play ...h5xg4 and trade off the h-pawns. The text, however, has an immediate drawback: the g6-pawn is weakened. White must try to push away Black's King in hopes of cozying up to the g6-pawn.

2.Nf3

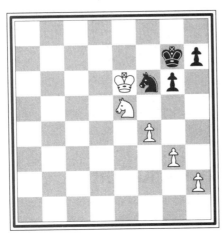

DIAGRAM 179.

White is seeking to bring his Knight to the e6-square with check.

2...Ng4 3.Ke7 Nh6!

Black is covering as many squares on the Kingside as he can.

4.Nd4 Ng8+!

Forced and good. White shouldn't be allowed Nd4-e6+, or else real progress with his King could be achieved.

5.Ke6 Nf6

White hasn't been able to put his initial plan into effect, so he tries something else.

6.Nf3 Ng4 7.h3

As we are about to see, the position in Diagram 180 is an easy one for Black to misplay. He has many ways to go wrong, and we will explore several dead ends: **7...Nf2? 8.Ng5 h4? 9.g4 Nd3 10.Ke7 Nxf4 11.Ne6+ Nxe6 12.Kxe6 Kh6 13.Kf6 Kh7 14.g5** is a winning King

ending for White. Or this: **7...Nf2? 8.Ng5 Nd3** (not: 8...Nh1? 9.Ne4, trapping his own Knight!) **9.Ke7 Nf2 10.h4! Ng4 11.Ne6+ Kg8 12.Nc7**, a line of play that allows White's pieces to put on a squeeze. It is dangerously easy for Black to lose this line. Continuing the play shows us why: 12...Ne3 13.Kf6 Nf5 14.Kxg6 Nxg3 15.Ne6 leads to the h5-pawn's impending fall. Also, 12...Kg7 13.Ne8+ Kg8 14.Nf6+ is a winning King and pawn ending. As these variations show, from Diagram 180, Black must avoid **7...Nf2?**.

DIAGRAM 180.

Another false trail is **7...Ne3? 8.Nh4 Nf1** (And 8...Nc2 9.f5 is similar.) **9.f5 gxf5** (9...Nxg3? 10.f6+! wins.) **10.Nxf5+ Kg6 11.h4 Nd2 12.Ne7+ Kh6 13.Kf7 Ne4 14.Ng8+ Kh7 15.Nf6+ Nxf6 16.Kxf6**, with a winning King and pawn ending.

Black must also avoid getting squeezed by playing the following: **7..Nf6? 8.Ng5 Ng8** (8...Ne8? 9.Ke7 Nc7 10.Ne6+ wins.) **9.Ne4 Nh6 10.Nd6** (Note how White's Knight keeps controlling the squares of Black's Knight.) **10...Ng8 11.Ne8+! Kf8 12.Nf6 Nh6 13.g4 hxg4 14.hxg4** (14.Nxg4 Ng8!) **Nf7 15.Nh7+ Kg7**, after which Black is getting squeezed for space.

DIAGRAM 181.

This analysis now brings us to Diagram 181. White continues to dominate play by **16.Ke7! Nh6 17.Nf6 Nf7 18.g5! Nh8 19.Ne8+ Kg8** (19...Kh7 20.Kf8) **20.Nd6 Kg7 21.Ke6 Kg8 22.Kf6 Kf8 23.Nc4**, with **Nc4-e5** to follow, and White wins.

Studying Diagram 180 carefully, you can fully appreciate Black's difficulties. You can deduce that most of these difficulties stem from the initial mistake 1...h5, which severely weakened Black's Kingside. From the position in Diagram 180, Black should try **7...Nh6! 8.Nd4 Ng8** (8...Nf7 9.Ke7 planning Nd4-e6+) **9.Nb5! Nf6 10.Nc3** (Again, White aims to out-maneuver the Black Knight with his own.) **10...Ng8** (10...Ne8? 11. Nd5) **11.Ne4! Nh6 12.Nd6!**, and the position has transposed to the analysis accompanying Diagram 181.

These examples give you insight into this ending that features a King and pawn majority on one side of the board. The superior side has to press his advantage by activating his pieces and by trying to control his colleague's activity.

DIAGRAM 182.
Seirawan–Utut, 1994

You're *The* Indonesian Grandmaster

This section features an ending from my tournament practice, taken from the final game in a four-game match against Indonesia's best, Grandmaster Adianto Utut. Set up the position in Diagram 182 on your chessboard and play the White side. Your task will be to answer a series of quiz questions. Please cover all moves but the current one with a sheet of paper, and work your way through.

The position appears quite even. The force count is equal, and the only difference in pawn structure is that the d5-pawn is isolated. This slight structural difference—Black with three pawn islands, White with two—gives White an advantage. White has an additional plus in that his King is one step closer to the center. However, if Black can bring his King to the center unhindered, he will be able to equalize the position. Tackle the quiz before making your first move as White.

QUIZ 1: What is the ideal setup for White's King and Knight?

After you answer this question, check it against the solution I've provided at the end of the chapter, and then make your move.

1.Ne2!!

White correctly moves off the d4-square and prepares to attack the d5-pawn. Give yourself credit if you realized that the natural 1.Ke2 Kf8 2.Kd3 Ke7 3.Ne2 Kd6 4.Kd4(?) Ne7 leads nowhere, as Black soon plays ...Ne7-c6, achieving immediate equality. In this variation, both Black pieces transit through the e7-square. Therefore, White has to force Black to occupy this square at once.

1...Kg7

After the game, Adianto was critical of this move, believing that it cost him the game. He was mistaken. His preferred defense, 1...Kf8 2.Nc3 Nb6 3.a4! a5 4.Ke2 Ke7 5.Kd3 Kd6 6.Kd4, leads to an ideal position for White: Black is tied to the defense of the d5-pawn, and White is prepared to play e3-e4, which will win on the spot. The play chosen, 1...Kg7, seeks to bring the King into the center without having to tread on the e7-square. Now that I've revealed a few secrets, what do you decide to play?

2.Nc3

Attacking the d5-pawn in this way is the right choice. If you wanted to play 2.Nf4 Ne7 3.Ke2 Kf6 4.Kd3 Ke5, how did you intend to further use your Knight?

2...Ne7

QUIZ 2: If Black had moved with 2...Nb6, how would you have responded?

Black, with the move he chose, intends to make a flexible defense and wants to keep ...Ne7-c6 as an option when necessary. Your turn. Be careful! This moment is critical, and there is only one way of improving the position.

3.Na4!

If you realized that 3.Ke2 Kf6 4.Kd3 Ke5 achieves nothing and lets Black achieve his ideal defensive setup with ...Ke5-d6 and ...Ne7-c6, give yourself credit. And stay on your toes; the choice you made carries the threat of Na4-c5 winning a pawn.

3...b5

This forcing move makes your decision an easy one. Your turn.

4.Nc5

Such an attack on the a6-pawn forces Black to advance his pawns. Of course, Black would love to activate his King, but not at the cost of a pawn.

4...a5

Black is keeping his material. What will you play now? Just bringing the Kings to the center of the board doesn't achieve an advantage.

5.Nb7!

To continue harassing the Queenside is a good decision.

5...Nc6

Your last move also keeps Black busy defending his a5-pawn.

QUIZ 3: After 5...a4, how could you have won a pawn?

Now that the a-pawn is protected, what's next?

6.Nd6!

Attacking the b5-pawn keeps White's initiative alive. Other moves fail.

6...b4

Now he's protecting the b-pawn.

QUIZ 4: If faced with the counterattack, 6...Nb4, how would you handle it?

QUIZ 5: After 6...Na7, what would you play?

Your turn—think carefully.

7.Ne8+!!

This is a surprising blow to Black, and one that keeps White's advantage alive. Once more, if you realized that 7.Ke2 Kf6 8.Kd3 Ke6 limits White's advantage, you're doing very well indeed.

7...Kf8

Black had a tricky alternative with 7...Kh6, in which the winning plan isn't easy, despite the awkward position of Black's King. Stop for a moment and work out the best line for White.

QUIZ 6: What would you play after 7...Kh6?

Your turn. Take a deep breath and think.

8.Nf6

Forking Black's pawns is a terrific answer! The current position is shown in Diagram 183. Who would have thought that from the starting position of Diagram 182, the h7-pawn would be a target? Now Black has to decide how to create problems for White.

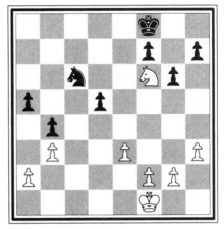

DIAGRAM 183.
Seirawan–Utut, 1994

8...d4!

Adianto makes the best of a difficult choice. He could have jettisoned the d5-pawn by 8...Ke7 9.Nxd5+ Kd6 10.Nb6, which activates his King. He made the better choice, however, because it inflicts long-term damage on White's position. Black's active King would have been only temporary. See what you can do with your turn.

9.Nxh7+

Taking while the taking is good. If you wanted to play 9.Ke2 dxe3 10.Kxe3 h5, you make points for your positional prowess, but why not grab a pawn?

9...Ke7

Your turn.

10.Ng5!

This completes the remarkable journey of the Knight. Did you realize that Black has the potential threat of playing 10...f6, trapping the Knight?

10...dxe3   11.fxe3 Ne5

Black is centralizing the Knight.

QUIZ 7: How would you have handled 11...Na7, which seeks to play ...Na7-b5-c3, harassing the a2-pawn?

Once you've answered, choose your next play.

12.Ke2

Black's last move was designed to keep White's King under guard, but you should be seeking to centralize the King!

12...Kd6

Likewise, Black to tries to keep his King as active as possible. Your turn.

13.Nf3

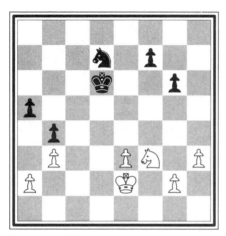

DIAGRAM 184.
Seirawan–Utut, 1994

White correctly seeks to dislodge the e5-Knight to activate his King.

13...Nd7

In Diagram 184. White has won a pawn, but he still has to win the game. How should he do that?

14.Kd3!

Clearly, the powerful role of the King in Knight endings is crucial, and King activity is a defining element in whether an ending wins or draws. With the text, White sets his sites on a Queenside raid.

14...Nb6

Black effectively stops the aforementioned threat. Now what will you play?

15.e4!

As important as King activation is, the real key to strategic play is to limit the activity of the opponent. White's choice to move his pawn to the e4-square takes away the d5-square for the Knight, limiting its hops. If you wanted to play 15.Ke4, give yourself a pat on the back; it is also an excellent move.

15...f6

Black is in deep trouble. He is trying to resist by taking away several squares from the f3-Knight. Your turn.

16.Kd4

There are several good choices here.

QUIZ 8: Which of the candidate moves 16.Kd4, 16.Nh4, 16.Nd2, and 16.h4 are the best? Rank them from 1 to 4.

Check your answer against the solution in the back of the chapter and then move on.

16...a4

Black sees the threat of 17.e5+ fxe5 18.Nxe5 coming, with the potential to endanger the g6-pawn. He also sees White's plan of Ne5-c4 attacking the a5-pawn. Black decides to try to trade pawns. What to do?

17.Ne1

This is a pretty good choice, playing to dominate Black's Knight and to attack the b4-pawn. If you wanted to play 17.e5+ Ke6 18.exf6 Kxf6 19.Kc5, here's a high five. That would have been better than my choice!

17...axb3   18.axb3 Nd7

With victory in sight, precision is called for.

19.Nd3

This is what my last few moves were all about. I had been anticipating that I'd be able to control Black's Knight with the text. Shame on you if you wanted to play 19.Kc4?? Ke5, which gives Black a chance for counterplay.

19...Nf8

Black is aiming to activate his Knight. How to stop him? Your turn.

20.h4!

Well played. After 20.Nxb4 Ne6+ 21.Ke3 (21.Kc4 Nf4) Nc5, Black would be able to regain one of his lost pawns. White's h-pawn simply stops Black in his tracks. After 20...Ne6+ 21.Kc4, Black is facing the inevitable loss of his b4-pawn and a two-pawn deficit. Seeing this, Adianto reluctantly called the game.

While this book was being written, a game that featured an interesting Knight ending was played in Spain. Grandmaster Peter Svidler of Russia, ranked among the world's top ten players, had been trying hard to win against India's Grandmaster Viswanathand Anand, the world's second-highest-ranked player. In Diagram 185, White, on move, abandoned the game and agreed that it was drawn.

QUIZ 9: Do you agree with this decision?

Solutions

QUIZ 1 (DIAGRAM 182): White's ideal is to have his King on the d4-square and his Knight on either the c3-square or the f4-square, when both pieces are attacking the d5-pawn.

QUIZ 2 (DIAGRAM 182): After **2...Nb6**, White should play **3.a4!**, forcing Black to weaken his Queenside. A likely line to follow would be **3...a5 4.Ke2 Kf6 5.Kd3 Ke5 6.f4+ Kd6 7.Kd4**, with play similar to the game.

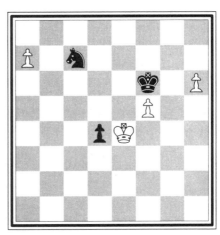

DIAGRAM 185.
Svidler–Anand
Dos Hermanas, Spain, 1999

173

QUIZ 3 (DIAGRAM 182): The play **5...a4 6.bxa4 bxa4 7.a3! Nc6 8.Nc5 Na5 9.Nxa4 Nc4 10.Nc3 Nxa3 11.Nxd5** achieves a Knight and four vs. Knight and three ending, which is a winning material advantage. In hindsight, the latter was Black's best chance.

QUIZ 4 (DIAGRAM 182): The counter-attack, **6...Nb4? 7.a3! Nc2 8.Nxb5**, wins a pawn.

QUIZ 5 (DIAGRAM 182): The defensive **6...Na7? 7.Ne8+!** is a superior version of the game. After **7...Kf8 8.Nf6**, White will fork and win a pawn, with Black's Knight further removed from the action.

QUIZ 6 (DIAGRAM 182): Indeed, the move 7...Kh6 was suggested by most commentators as best. But **8.Ke2 Kg5 9.Nc7! d4 10.Nb5 dxe3 11.Kxe3** highlights the difference between the two Kings. After the subsequent moves in **11...Kf6 12.Ke4**, White should win.

QUIZ 7 (DIAGRAM 183): In **11...Na7**, the simplest solution is to centralize the King by playing **12.Ke2! Nb5 13.Kd3 Nc3 14.a4!**, with **Ng5-e4** to follow. In this case, Black's Queenside is more vulnerable than White's Queenside structure.

QUIZ 8 (DIAGRAM 184): Ranking the moves 16.Kd4, 16.Nh4, 16.Nd2, and 16.h4 is not an easy undertaking. In fact, I'm not sure myself! I liked 16.Kd4 best as it activates the King. My second choice was for 16.h4, planning for g2-g4 and h4-h5 to establish a passed h-pawn, which is a dream passer. My third choice was for 16.Nh4 g5 17.Nf3, with the intention of e4-e5 trying to isolate the g5-pawn. Thus, my arguable answer is for (1) 16.Kd4, (2) 16.h4, (3) 16.Nh4, and (4) 16.Nd2 as ranking in importance.

QUIZ 9 (DIAGRAM 185): It was certainly a mistake for White to offer a draw. After all, he could hardly lose! White has the study-like win: **1.Kxd4 Nb5+ 2.Kc5 Nxa7 3.Kb6 Nc8+ 4.Kc7 Na7** (4...Ne7 5.h7! Kg7 6.f6+ wins.) **5.Kd7 Nb5 6.h7! Kg7 7.f6+ Kxh7 8.f7 Kg7 9.Ke7**. Reliable observers have reported that, upon being shown this line, Peter's cries of anguish sailed over several counties.

Bishop vs. Knight

Of all the opposing pieces, the relationship between Bishop and Knight remains the most difficult to understand. When I was first starting to play chess, my Knights were forever getting pinned by Bishops and eventually captured. When I resolved to keep my Bishops and not trade them for my opponent's Knights, I was constantly victimized by forks. I flip-flopped between a preference for Knights and a preference for Bishops.

Today, with the benefit of a few decades of experience behind me, I have chosen my loyalties. I prefer a Bishop to a Knight. Usually. This was not an easy conclusion to come to, for there are literally thousands of positions where a Knight will be at least equal, if not superior, to a Bishop. That truth notwithstanding, and for reasons that are beyond the scope of this paragraph, the majority of the time I will favor—however slightly—the Bishop. Having said that, in practice, everything depends on the position at hand.

In this chapter, we will aspire to understand the difficult relationship between these two minor pieces, looking at examples of the positions that benefit each piece. To understand the circumstances that favor one piece over the other, let's examine some guiding principles:

- *In the opening and middlegame, the Bishop and the Knight have roughly the same value.*
- *As more and more pawns are traded off the board and the position becomes open, the Bishop starts to emerge as the superior piece.*
- *To be effective, Knights need to be centralized and protected.*
- *Bishops can be effective from the flanks as well as the center, and do not need to be protected.*
- *Knights are more effective in those endings in which pawns exist only on one flank.*
- *Knights are more effective in closed or blocked positions.*

■ *Bishops are more effective in positions where the pawn structure is dynamic (fluid) or where imbalances exist.*

■ *A Bishop is less effective when its pawns are on the same-colored squares as the Bishop.*

■ *In the ending, the combination of two Bishops vs. two Knights strongly favors the two Bishops.*

These general principles will be our guide as we set out to fathom the complexity illustrated in the following examples.

Blocked Positions

As we can see from the guiding principles, blocked positions favor the Knight. The following examples illustrate these principles. Naturally, not all blocked positions will win for the Knight.

In Diagram 186, White is doing very well indeed. The position favors him for several reasons. The position is blocked by the d5-, e4-, d6-, and e5-pawns, a circumstance favorable for the Knight. Black's *blocked* d6- and e5-pawns are on the same color as his Bishop. This means that the Bishop is ineffective, because it is unable to attack White's pawn structure and instead must play a defensive role only. (This structure commonly appears from a King's Indian Defense, a defense I recommend in my book *Winning Chess Openings*.) White's King is more active than its counterpart. White puts these advantages to quick use and wins the game handily.

1.Kb5

White is introducing the threat of 2.Nxe5, clipping a pawn.

1...f6

Black feels compelled to put another of his pawns on the dark squares. After 1...Bg1 2.Kc6 Bxh2 (2...Bc5 3.Kc7!, intending Nc4-b6-c8+, wins the d6-pawn and the game.) 3.Nxd6 Bg1 4.Nb7, White escorts the d5-pawn to promotion.

2.Kc6!

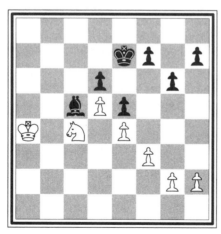

DIAGRAM 186.

176

This prevents Black's King from playing …Ke7-d7, which would elbow White's King out of the game. White bears down on the targeted d6-pawn.

2…Bb4

Black "passes" with his Bishop, as he is unable to make a constructive move.

3.h3

This is arguably an unnecessary finesse but an instructive move. White places all of his pawns on light-colored squares to rob Black of the type of counterplay just mentioned.

3…Bc5   4.g4

White gains space and continues trying to keep his pawns on light squares.

4…Bc5   5.Kc7!

White wants to keep Black's King bottled up. This is the final preparation for the winning maneuver.

5…Bb4   6.Nb6!

This satisfying move shows the advantage of a Knight over a Bishop. The Knight, being able to hop to all 64 squares on the board, will uproot Black's King. The threat is Nb6-c8+, winning the d6-pawn.

6…Ba5   7.Kc6

Here's the same threat again: Nb6-c8+, which wins the d6-pawn.

7…Bxb6

This is a required capture, because 7…Kd8 8.Nc5 forks the d6-pawn and Bishop.

8.Kxb6 Kd7   9.Kb7

The King and pawn ending is an easy win. Black will soon be exhausted of pawn moves, and the d6-pawn will fall.

This theme of bad Bishop vs. good Knight in a blocked position is repeated in Diagram 187. White has at least two distinct advantages: better minor pieces and, most important, a very active King. Black's pawns are all *on the same color as his Bishop, which renders it ineffective.* White wins rather quickly.

1.Kg8! Bg4

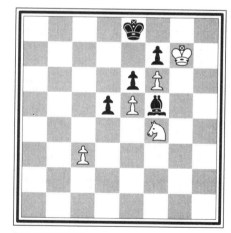

DIAGRAM 187.
Szily–Balogh
Hungary, 1947

Black must keep his e6-pawn protected because 1...Be4 2.Nxe6 fxe6 3.f7+ wins at once.

2.Ng6!

White offers up a similar sacrifice as before. The point of the move is that White is targeting the f7-pawn.

2...Bd1   3.Nh8 Bh5   4.Kg7!

Black is placed in zugzwang and must lose the f7-pawn and the game.

Open Positions

Let's take a look at two diagrams that will illustrate the Bishop's ability to excel in open positions. Just as not all blocked positions will win for the Knight, not all open positions will win for the Bishop! A position that beautifully illustrates the strengths of a Bishop over a Knight is shown in Diagram 188, a study by Grandmaster Yuri Averbach.

Despite having extremely reduced material, White is winning. This is because Black's Knight, in order to prevent White's a-pawn from promoting, needs to be protected, but is not. White has no such problems with his Bishop.

1.a7! Kg4   2.Kf2 Kf4   3.Ke2

White's King treks toward the b6-Knight and is not worried that Black might trade his h-pawn for the Bishop. Black is forced to come back to defend his Knight.

3...Kf5

After 3...Kg3 4.Ke3 Kh2 5.Bb7 Kg1 6.Kd4 h2 7.Kc5 Na4+ 8.Kb4 Nb6 9.Kb5, White wins.

4.Ke3 Ke5   5.Kd3 Ke6

6.Kc3 Kd6   7.Kb4 Kd7

8.Kb5 Kc7   9.Ka6

DIAGRAM 188.
Y. Averbach, 1958

178

White wins anyway. This example also illustrates the dangers for Knights of passed pawns on opposite sides of the board. The Bishop is often able to influence the play across the board while blocking a passed pawn, whereas a Knight, when forced to blockade a pawn, can influence only its immediate vicinity.

Perhaps you were thinking that the position in Diagram 188 was a bit of a fluke? That if only Black's h-pawn had been protecting his Knight, the position would be drawn? In Diagram 189, we have a study by Alexey Selezniev that drives home the similar point that a Knight can be dominated in an open position even when protected.

In Diagram 189, Black appears to have a comfortable draw because his Knight is well protected. The problem is that his King is bottled up, and through a series of zugzwangs, Black will forcibly lose his c7-pawn and the game.

1.Bc6! Kd8   2.Kf5

This position would hardly qualify as a study if White were able to play 2.Kf7 Kc8 3.Ke8 and win on the spot. That was why the composer had 2.Kf7?? Nc8! 3.a8=Q stalemate in mind!

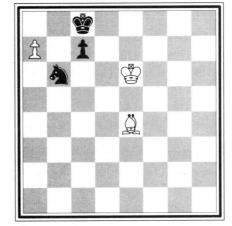

2...Ke7   3.Ke5 Kf7   4.Kd4 Ke6

5.Kc5 Ke5   6.Kb4! Ke6

7.Ka5! Kd6   8.Kb5 Ke6

9.Ka6 Ke7   10.Kb7 Kd6

11.Bg2 Kd7   12.Bf3

Here we see the Bishop's ability to lose a tempo.

12...Kd6   13.Bc6!

DIAGRAM 189.
A. Selezniev, 1915

Zugzwang. Black must forfeit his c7-pawn.

13...Kc5   14.Kxc7

Zugzwang again. This time the b6-Knight is lost.

A final look at Diagram 189 yields an interesting revelation. If Black is on move, he has a fine way to draw: 1...c6! 2.Bxc6 Kc7 3.Be4 Na8! 4.Bxa8 Kb6, and Black is in time to capture the a-pawn.

Pawns on One Flank

When a position like that in Diagram 190 is reached with all the pawns on the same flank, it generally favors the side with the Knight. This position must be assessed as a draw or as "equal" because White would need some advantages—such as an active King, a bad Bishop, or better structure—to win such a position.

The position in Diagram 191, analyzed by International Master Nikolay Minev, is an instructive one. White has a number of advantages: an extra pawn, better pieces, and the prospect of winning the f6-pawn. White was shocked, after playing 1.Ne8+? Kh6 2.Nxf6 Bxf6 3.Kxf6, to discover that his dominance had turned to stalemate, which led to a draw. Nikolay Minev shows what White should have played:

1.Ne4! Bb2

Black wants to stop White's intended g4-g5 and makes this choice over two other possibilities that both lead to failure:

- 1…h6 2.Ke7! (2.Nd6 Kf8) Bb2 3.Nd6 Ba3 4.Ke6 Kf8 (4…Bxd6 5.Kxd6 is a losing King and Pawn ending.) 5.Ne4, winning the f6-pawn.

- 1…Kh6 2.Kf7! Bb2 3.Kg8! (White is going after the h7-pawn.) 3…Be5 (3…Bd4 4.Nd6 Kg5 [to escape the threat of Nd6-f7 Checkmate] 5.Kxh7 Kxg4 6.Kg6, winning.) 4.Nc5 Bb2 5.Nd7 Bc3 (5…Ba3 6.Nxf6 Kg5 7.Kf7 Bb2 8.Nxh7+ Kxg4 9.Kg6 wins.) 6.Nf8 Bb4 7.Nxh7 Be7 8.Kf7!, which wins all of Black's pawns.

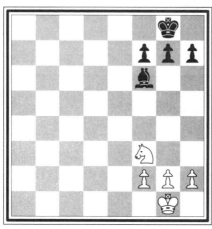

DIAGRAM 190.

DIAGRAM 191.
Georgiev–Kyriakides
Novi Sad Olympiad, 1990

2.g5 fxg5   3.f6+ Kh6

Again the best defense, because after 3...Kg8 4.f7+ Kg7 5.h6+ Kf8 6.Nxg5, there will be checkmate on next move. And after 3...Kf8 4.Nxg5 h6 5.Nh7+ Kg8 6.f7+, White's pawn is allowed to queen. Finally, 3...Bxf6 4.Nxf6 Kh6 5.Kf5 g4 6.Kxg4 Kg7 7.Kg5 Kh8 8.Ne8 Kg8 9.Kh6 Kh8 10.Nd6 Kg8 11.Ne4 Kh8 12.Ng5 means White wins the h7-pawn and the game.

4.Ng3! Ba3

Black is trying to cover the f8-promotion square. Black's Bishop would have been blocked after 4...g4 5.Nf5+ Kxh5 6.f7 Ba3 7.Ne7, with White winning.

5.Kf5!

A crafty retreat, the point of which is soon revealed.

5...Bd6

The point being that Black is forced to play this because White's retreat would pay off with 5...Bb2 6.Kg4! Bxf6 7.Nf5 Checkmate!

6.Kg4!

Here again is the same threat of Ng3-f5 Checkmate.

6...Bxg3   7.Kxg3 g4   8.Kh4! g3   9.Kxg3 Kxh5   10.f7

The way is opened, and White's pawn promotes.

After seeing an example in which a Knight and an extra pawn on the same flank make a win, you probably wonder how easy is it for the Bishop to produce the same result. The position in Diagram 192 gives you a clue. White has a healthy extra pawn and a more active King. However, the defense is very easy for Black. All he has to do is keep his f6-pawn well protected, look forward to a pawn trade, and sacrifice his Knight for the remaining pawn. In the ensuing play, Larsen is unable to make an impression in Black's fortress.

1.Bf5 Nc6   2.Kg4 Ne5+

3.Kf4 Nc4   4.Bc2 Nd6!

Black's Knight takes up residence on a fine square. White's King is not afforded an easy entrance into Black's camp.

5.Ke3 Ke6

DIAGRAM 192.
Larsen–Miles
Reykjavik, 1978

It would have been foolhardy to play 5...f5??, which puts the pawn in obvious jeopardy. White would then win after 6.Kf4 Kf6 7.Bb1 Ke6 (7...Kg6? 8.g4) 8.Kg5 Nf7+ (8...Ke5 9.f4+ Ke6 10.Kg6 Ne4 11.g4) 9.Kg6 Ne5+ 10.Kg7 Ng4 11.f4 Ne3 12.Kg6, placing Black in zugzwang.

6.Kd4 Nb5+   7.Kc5 Nd6!

The Knight should remain close to its King for protection. After 7...Nc3? 8.Bd3 Nd1 9.f3, the Knight could easily find itself trapped.

8.Bb3+ Ke7   9.Kd5 Ne8   10.Bc2 Nd6   11.Bg6 Kd7

Now the players agreed on a draw. If White tries to advance his g-pawn by 12.f4 Ke7 13.g4 Nb5 14.g5 fxg5 15.fxg5 Nc7+ 16.Ke5 Ne6, the Knight will sacrifice itself for the remaining pawn.

From the previous examples, we are able to deduce that it is easier to force through a victory by using a Knight with a material advantage of an extra pawn—all pawns on one side of the board—than using a Bishop.

Pawns on Both Flanks

The most common minor piece ending is one in which there are pawns on the flanks for both sides. In such a case, Bishops usually provide an advantage because they can exertt pressure on both sides of the board. More than any other player, chess' twelfth World Champion, Robert James (Bobby) Fischer, loved his Bishops. One of my favorite chess stories involves the position shown in Diagram 193.

DIAGRAM 193.
Fischer–Petrosian
FIDE Candidate Finals
Buenos Aires, 1971

The scene is the press center of the FIDE Candidate Finals in Buenos Aires, Argentina, in 1971. Bobby has just taken the lead with a difficult win in game six, and now, in the seventh game, has a big advantage. (The advantageous position is shown in Diagram 193.) White's pieces are obviously superior to their counterparts, and the Soviet grandmasters and Soviet journalists are gloomily watching the monitors. Could Tigran "The Iron Tiger" Petrosian save the game and get back in the match?

Suddenly, Argentine Grandmaster Miguel Najdorf explodes out of his chair. "My God!! Idiot!! What has he done?? He's crazy!! How can he give up Knight for Bishop??" The Soviets are suddenly jumping around, embracing each other.

The cause for all the commotion was Bobby's astonishing twenty-second move: 22.Nxd7+, trading the beautiful c5-Knight for what was perceived as Black's "bad" d7-Bishop (the d5- and a6-pawns being on the same color as the Bishop). Grandmaster Robert Byrne, of the *New York Times*, filled in the rest of the story for me.

> I had kept quiet during all the celebration because I really didn't know what to think. For years the Soviets had been underestimating Bobby, and they all thought that he had blundered. Had Bobby really misjudged the position so badly? After about ten more moves and as it became clear that Petrosian's position was hopeless, the Soviet players began to sit down. Grandmaster Alexey Suetin stared in open-mouthed horror and said, "He plays so simply." Then I knew Bobby had 'em. You see, to Bobby's way of thinking, capturing that Bishop was like driving the final nail into the coffin. The position was already open and Bobby loved his Bishop.

This story provides a nice segue to Diagram 194. The position is from the fourth match game of the FIDE Candidate Quarterfinals. Bobby had a crushing lead over Grandmaster Mark Taimanov, having won the first three games. Here, in the fourth, he had the advantage of his beloved Bishop. There are several reasons why the position favors White. Taken individually, they are subtle, but when added together they are overwhelming. With pawns on both sides of the board, the Bishop is superior to Black's Knight. Black's Kingside structure—all of his pawns are positioned on light squares—is susceptible to attack from White's Bishop. Black has no counterplay. White's King has a potential march to the b5-square, which is likely to be a decisive penetration. Now let's see how Bobby puts together a convincing win.

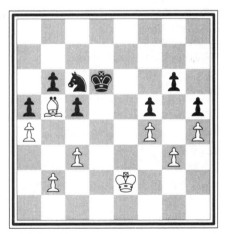

DIAGRAM 194.
Fischer–Taimanov
FIDE Candidate Quarterfinals
Vancouver, 1971

1.Kd3

He introduces the first decisive threat.

White is ready to play 2.Bxc6 Kxc6 3.Kc4 Kd6 4.Kb5 Kc7 5.Ka6 Kc6 6.c4 Kc7 7.Ka7 Kc6 8.Kb8, with a winning King and pawn ending. Black's Knight must give way.

1...Ne7 2.Be8!

White grabs the opportunity to menace the g6-pawn, and in the process also vacates the b5-square for his King.

2...Kd5 3.Bf7+ Kd6 4.Kc4 Kc6 5.Be8+ Kb7 6.Kb5

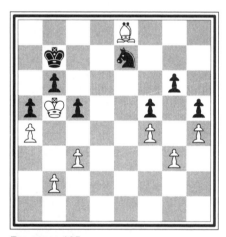

DIAGRAM 195.
Fischer–Taimanov
FIDE Candidate Quarterfinals
Vancouver, 1971

As we can see from Diagram 195, White has accomplished his first goal. Now his King is quite active, and Black's choices will become more limited.

6...Nc8!

This was the best defense, as we shall soon see. Black sets up the transparent trap 7.Bxg6?? Nd6 Checkmate, which White avoids with his next move:

7.Bc6+ Kc7 8.Bd5!

White centralizes his Bishop again and prepares to make further advances by Kb5-a6, in conjunction with Bd5-f7, which attacks the g6-base.

8...Ne7

Black makes the better choice because an attempt at active play using 8...Nd6+ 9.Ka6 Ne4 10.Bf7 Nxg3 11.Bxg6 Kc6 12.Be8+ Kc7 13.Ka7 Ne2 14.Bxh5 Nxf4 15.Bf7 with h4-h5 to follow wins for White. Grandmaster Mark Taimanov knows full well that allowing White a passed h-pawn would be fatal. Thus, the text:

9.Bf7

White is reestablishing the threat to the g6-pawn and freezing Black's Knight. Black's King must keep guard for the b6-pawn.

9...Kb7

This keeps White's King out of the a6-square. Despite the aggressiveness of White's pieces, Black appears to have a fortress. How can White make further progress? He has maximized his pieces, having tied Black's King and Knight to the base-pawn of their pawn chain, but further inroads seem to be ruled out. Bobby now comes up with a brilliant series of moves to create a zugzwang.

10.Bb3! Ka7

Black is not conceding White's King an entry. Choosing 10...Kc7 11.Ka6 Kc6 12.Bf7 would transpose to the game.

11.Bd1! Kb7   12.Bf3+ Kc7

Black is forced to concede the a6-square because after 12...Ka7? 13.c4!, Black's Knight is compelled to give way and allow White's King to decisively penetrate with 13...Ng8 14.Kc6 Nf6 15.Kd6 Ne4+ 16.Ke5 Nxg3 17.Kf6, winning. All of Black's Kingside pawns, at this point, are doomed to fall.

13.Ka6!

This further limits the ability of Black's King to move.

13...Ng8

Again, Black's Knight must give way. Weaker was 13...Nc6? 14.Bxc6 Kxc6 15.c4 Kc7 16.Ka7 Kc6 17.Kb8, with a winning King and pawn ending, a circumstance we've seen before.

14.Bd5 Ne7

Taimanov is avoiding 14...Nf6? 15.Bf7 Ne4 16.Bxg6 Nxg3 17.c4! Kc6 18.Ka7 Kc7 19.Bf7 Ne2 20.Bxh5 Nxf4 21.Bf7, in which White's h-pawn is decisive.

15.Bc4 Nc6

Alternatively, 15...Kc6 16.Bb5+ Kc7 17.Be8 transposes into the game.

16.Bf7 Ne7   17.Be8!

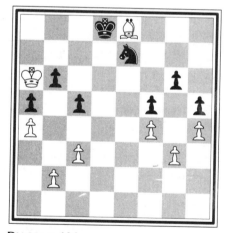

The position in Diagram 196 is what Bobby has been aiming for. Black is forced to abandon the defense of his b6-pawn to attack White's Bishop.

17...Kd8

Weaker is 17...c4? 18.Bf7, which would cost Black his c4-pawn.

18.Bxg6!

This winning sacrifice has been beautifully set up. The sacrifice works well because Black's Knight is placed on an unfortunate square where it is a long way from causing any damage.

18...Nxg6   19.Kxb6 Kd7

DIAGRAM 196.
Fischer–Taimanov
FIDE Candidate Quarterfinals
Vancouver, 1971

In his adjournment analysis, Bobby worked out the following winning line: 19...c4 20.Kxa5 Nh8 21.Kb5 Nf7 22.Kxc4 Nd6+ 23.Kd5 Ne4 24.Ke5 Nxg3 25.c4.

20.Kxc5 Ne7   21.b4 axb4   22.cxb4 Nc8   23.a5 Nd6

Black wouldn't have been able to hold on after 23...Kc7 24.b5 Kb7 25.b6 Ka6 26.Kd5 because Black's Kingside pawns would also fall.

24.b5 Ne4+   25.Kb6 Kc8   26.Kc6 Kb8   27.b6

A flawless endgame by Bobby, and one that forcibly drives home the strengths of a Bishop over a Knight.

Countering that demonstration, and as a proof that not all open positions with pawns on both flanks on the board favor the Bishop, I offer Diagram 197, featuring one of the most stunning moves in the endgame that I've ever seen.

According to our principles, the position in Diagram 197 should favor the Bishop over the Knight, but it does not. It is easy to spot the culprit, or rather culprits, behind the Bishop's failure to be the better piece. Black's pawns, the a6-, b5-, d5-, and h5-pawns, are all on light squares, making Black's Bishop a "bad" one. Kasparov's last move, ...g5xh4, was an unfortunate choice. Anxious to solve the Kingside tension, he falls victim to an absolutely brilliant counter.

DIAGRAM 197.
Karpov–Kasparov
FIDE Championship
Moscow, 1984–85

1.Ng2!!

A superb move, which requires some explanation. To win, White must open the Kingside so that his King will have a way to penetrate the position. Kasparov had been expecting 1.gxh4 Ke6 2.Kg3 Bd3 3.Kf4 Bb1 4.Nf1 Bd3 5.Ng3 Bg6, after which White is unable to improve his position because his King is effectively blocked. By choosing to go with 1.Ng2!!, White temporarily sacrifices a pawn to open a route for his King.

1...hxg3+

A bad choice would be 1...h3? 2.Nf4 Bf5 3.Nxh5, when White will round up the h3-passer by g3-g4 and Kf2-g3, winning.

2.Kxg3 Ke6

Kasparov decides to return the pawn at once. After 2...Bg6 3.Nf4 Bf7 4.Kh4, White would similarly regain the sacrificed pawn.

3.Nf4+ Kf5   4.Nxh5!

White takes the more dangerous Black pawn. The d5-pawn isn't running away. With this choice, White threatens 5.Ng7+ Kg6 6.Ne8 with the plan of Ne8-c7, winning the a6-pawn. Because of this threat, Black's King is forced to make a fast retreat.

4...Ke6

Black's King lets go of its active position because 4...Kg5? 5.Nf4 Ba2 6.Ne6+ Kf5 7.Nc5 would have won the a6-pawn.

5.Nf4+ Kd6   6.Kg4

White has successfully traded off the Kingside pawns, and this operation gives his King opportunity to advance, as we can see in Diagram 198.

6...Bc2   7.Kh5! Bd1   8.Kg6 Ke7!

The best chance is to jettison the d5-pawn straight away. After 8...Bxf3 9.Kxf6, White would easily win by forcing zugzwang with 9...Bg4 10.Nd3 Bh3 11.Nc5 Bc8 12.Kf7 Kc6 13.Ke7 Kc7 14.Ke8 Kb8 15.Kd8, when Black loses material and the game.

This note shows how dominant a Knight vs. "bad Bishop" ending can be, and how easy it is for the side with the Knight to make decisive inroads into a position.

9.Nxd5+ Ke6?

This unfortunate error costs Black the a6-pawn. White would have had a considerably more difficult time winning after 9...Kd6! 10.Nc3 Bxf3 11.Kxf6 Bg4, although it would be possible. White's winning plan would consist of playing his King back to the e3-square and continuing Nc3-e4-c5, anchoring Black's Bishop to the c8-square. White would then use his King to push his d-pawn forward.

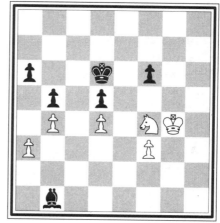

DIAGRAM 198.
Karpov–Kasparov
FIDE Championship
Moscow, 1984–85

10.Nc7+!

Karpov is quick to realize his good fortune and immediately goes for the a6-pawn.

10...Kd7

It is necessary for Black to attack the Knight. After 10...Ke7? 11.f4!, White has time to save his f-pawn.

11.Nxa6 Bxf3   12.Kxf6 Kd6

As shown in Diagram 199, White has made considerable progress since Diagram 197. But there is a strange irony. Black, by losing two of his bad pawns—the a6, and especially his d5-pawn—improves his defensive chances of holding the game. He threatens to play 13...Kd5, win the d4-pawn, and rush to try to capture White's remaining Queenside pawns. This is possible because, although White has won two pawns(!), his pieces are scattered. Karpov masterfully rebuilds his position into a cohesive unit.

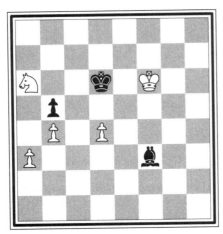

DIAGRAM 199.
Karpov–Kasparov
FIDE Championship
Moscow, 1984–85

13.Kf5! Kd5   14.Kf4!

White gains a tempo by attacking the Bishop and thereby saves his d4-pawn. Herein lies an important lesson: *While vigilance is always important in the game of chess, it is especially important that a player remain vigilant in the endgame.* Although you might be able to recover from a mistake in the opening or the middlegame, you will enjoy no such luxury in the ending. In the ending you must be especially precise because victory or defeat is only a tempo away.

On with the game. White could have erred by 14.Nc7+? Kxd4 15.Nxb5+ Kc4 16.Nd6+ Kb3, allowing Black to save his bacon.

14...Bh1   15.Ke3 Kc4!

Black's exceptionally active King gives him good chances to save the game. From this perch, Black is ready to play ...Kc4-b3 and pounce on the Queenside pawns. Karpov must show great accuracy to win.

16.Nc5 Bc6

Black marks time with his Bishop on the long diagonal. Had he tried 16...Bg2 17.Nd3! Kb3 18.Nf4 Bb7 19.Kd3! Kxa3 20.Kc3!, his King would be trapped, and the advance of the d-pawn would cost him his Bishop and the game. This point is reinforced in the upcoming play. White is willing to sacrifice his a3-pawn and try to meet its capture with the move Kd3-c3, thereby boxing in Black's King.

17.Nd3 Bg2

Black continues to mark time. He avoids 17...Kb3 18.Ne5 Bd5 19.Kd3 Kxa3? 20.Kc3, which sets up the ideal position for White.

18.Ne5+

Delighted, White disturbs Black's King from its lofty perch.

18...Kc3!

Kasparov puts up heroic resistance. Once more, 18...Kb3 19.Kd3 Kxa3? 20.Kc3 is the position that Black must avoid. Also worth avoiding is 18...Kd5? 19.Kd3 Bf1+ 20.Kc3, which would neutralize the active possibilities of Black's King.

19.Ng6!

White is presenting a new threat: 20.Nf4 Bb7 21.d5, bringing a winning advance of the passed pawn.

19...Kc4! 20.Ne7!

Both players are navigating well through this enormously complex ending. Here, Karpov avoids 20.Nf4 Bb7 21.d5? Bxd5 22.Nxd5 Kxd5 23.Kd3 Ke5!, which leaves Black a pawn down, but allows him to secure a draw in a King and pawn ending.

20...Bb7

Black throws in his best chance, curtailing his desire to grab the Queenside pawn. The grab, 20...Kb3? 21.d5! Kxa3 22.d6 Bh3 23.Nd5 Kb3 24.Kd4 Be6 25.Kc5 Bd7 26.Nf6, gives the win to White by advancing his d-pawn.

It has taken a lot of effort to make it to the position in Diagram 200, but White is now able to cash in on his advantages.

21.Nf5!

Here it is, the winning move, as the invasion of the d6-square proves to be decisive.

21...Bg2

Let's analyze why Black makes this choice. The retreat 21...Kd5 22.Kd3 Ba8 23.Ne3+ Ke6 24.Nd1! Bc6 25.Nc3 Kd6 26.d5! Bd7 (26...Bxd5 27.Nxb5+) 27.Kd4 wins for White. So would 21...Bc6 22.Nd6+ Kc3 23.Nc8 Kb3 (23...Kb3 24.Kd2 Kb2 25.Nf5 Kb3 26.Ne3 wins. Or 23...Kd5 24.Nf7! Be8 25.Ne5, which freezes Black's King out of the c4-square.

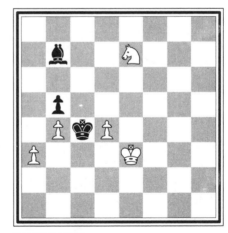

DIAGRAM 200.
Karpov–Kasparov
FIDE Championship
Moscow, 1984–85

White would then play Ke3-d3-c3 before repositioning his Knight.) 24.Kd2 Kxa3 25.Kc3, leaving Black in a hopeless position.

22.Nd6+ Kb3   23.Nxb5 Ka4   24.Nd6

Kasparov finally hangs up his spurs. After 24…Kxa3 25.b5, this time it will be the b-pawn that will cost Black his Bishop. Then the d-pawn will make a triumphant march.

Two Final Lessons

This brings us to the last combination before we test what you've learned. In general, a minor piece and two protected passed pawns vs. a minor piece must win, but there are some guiding principles regarding this combination.

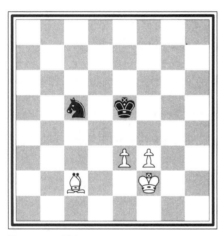

The position in Diagram 201 is a winning position for White, but it can easily go wrong. As a general rule, *the pawns should advance only when the Bishop covers the squares in front of them.* Furthermore, *the pawns should be advanced to the squares opposite the color of the Bishop.* White should proceed with:

1.f4+!

From the above principles, a horrendous error would be 1.e4??, a move that puts White's pawns on the same color as the Bishop. Black would play 1…Ne6! 2.Ke3 Nf4, with an immediate draw because he has an impregnable fortress.

DIAGRAM 201.

1…Kd5   2.Kf3 Ke6

Black must avoid 2…Ne6? 3.Bb3+, which would allow White to trade pieces, leading immediately to a winning King and pawn endgame.

3.e4! Kf6   4.Ke3 Nd7   5.Kd4

White controls more and more squares and seeks to *control the squares in front of the pawns.*

5…Nf8   6.e5+!

A dreadful move would be 6.f5?? Ne7, allowing another drawing fortress.

6...Ke7   7.f5 Nd7   8.Bb3!

White is correctly trying to *control the squares in front of the pawns*. Their progress is inexorable.

8...Nf8   9.f6+! Kd7   10.Kd5 Ke8

Not 10...Ne6 11.Ba4+, which wins the Knight.

11.e6 Nh7   12.Ba4+! Kd8   13.Ke5

Voilà! The e-pawn safely promotes.

This technical winning ending becomes far more awkward when the passers are moved a few files over. Diagram 202 shows the type of position that can lead to problems. The crucial point that the White player must be constantly aware of is that he has the "wrong Bishop." Take off the g3-pawn and the f5-Knight, and the game is drawn. This knowledge immediately places us on high alert! With our "Spidey senses" tingling, the winning plan for White will be to gradually push Black's pieces back.

1.Bf3!

White correctly recognizes the state of affairs. Black's pieces are ideally placed but, after this quiet move, one of them has to move! Of course, there are a number of ways for White to go wrong: 1.h3?? Nxg3 and 1.h4+?? Nxh4 are

DIAGRAM 202.

egregious examples. Far subtler is 1.g4? (violating our principle of advancing pawns to the same color as the Bishop) 1...Kf4! (offering the Knight for capture!) 2.h3 Nh4 3.Be2 Nf5!, which makes it difficult for White to progress.

1...Nh6

With Black's King ideally placed, this choice seems to be the most stubborn. An alternative, 1...Kf6 2.Be4! Nh6 3.Kf3 Kg5 (3...Ke5 4.Bc2 Nf7 5.Kg4 Kf6 6.Kf4 Ng5 7.Bf5 prepares the advance of the pawns.) is similar to our main line.

2.Be4 Ng4+   3.Kg2 Nh6!

Black is avoiding 3...Ne3+? 4.Kf3 Ng4? 5.h4+ Kh5 6.Bg6+, which wins on the spot. To have any chance, Black must try to provoke a premature advance of the h-pawn.

4.Bd5 Nf5

White's progress is easier after 4...Kf6? 5.Kf3 Kg5 6.Be6 Kf6 7.Bd7, when Black has voluntarily moved his King.

5.Be6 Nh6

Black must not misplace his Knight with 5...Ne3+? 6.Kf2 Nd1+? 7.Kf3, when White's pawns will start to march.

6.Kf3 Kf6   7.Bd7 Kg5   8.Ke4

White sets up the threat of 9.Be6 Kf6 10.Kd5, in which the Bishop dominates the Knight.

8...Kf6

Black is forced to retreat becasue 8...Nf7 9.Be6 Nd8? (9...Nd6+ 10.Ke5) 10.Bd5 again dominates the Knight.

9.Kf4 Nf7   10.g4!

At last the pawn can move forward. Had it done so earlier, ...Nh6xg4 would have been the painful response.

10...Nd6

Not all "wrong Bishop" positions are drawn. After 10...Ne5? 11.g5+ Kg6 12.Bf5+ Kh5 13.Kxe5 Kxg6 14.h3 Kh6 15.Kf6 Kh5 16.Kg7, Black's King wouldn't make it back to the corner. Also, 10...Nh6!? 11.g5+ Kg6 12.Be6! Kh5 13.h4! Kg6 14.Ke5 Kg7 15.h5 Kh8 16.Kf6 Kh7 17.Bf5+ Kh8 18.Bh3 Ng8+ (18...Kh7 19.Be6 Kh8 20.Kg6) 19.Kf7 Nh6+ 20.Kf8 wins.

11.h4 Nf7   12.g5+ Kg7!

Black's best chance is to go with the defense of *keeping his King in front of the pawns* and to hope for a "wrong Bishop" position. Black had to avoid 12...Kg6? 13.Be8, which wins.

13.Bf5 Nd6

This makes sense because we know that 13...Nh6? 14.Be6 dominates the Knight. In the ensuing play, White will try to keep the Knight "away" from the Kingside.

14.Bg4 Nf7

Black's best move is with his Knight; if he moves his King with 14...Kg6? 15.h5+ Kg7 16.Be6, he allows the pawns to advance. As we can see from Diagram 203, White has made steady progress since Diagram 202. The key to winning is to boot the Knight firmly away from the Kingside.

15.Be6! Nd6

The Knight has a shortage of squares; if Black tries either 15...Nh8? 16.h5 or 15...Nd8? 16.Bd5 Kg6 17.Kg4, he loses.

16.Ke5! Ne8   17.Bd7!

White is relentless in his hounding of the Knight.

17...Nc7   18.Kd6

An arguable decision, but White is on a roll and wants to send Black's Knight into oblivion. Black's King will be unable to handle the combination of connected passed pawns and Bishop.

18...Na6   19.h5! Nb4

20.h6+ Kg6   21.Bf5+!

A fine move, which has the added bonus of covering the b4-Knight.

21...Kf7   22.g6+ Kf6   23.g7

There's the win. Interestingly enough, when the roles are reversed and the

DIAGRAM 203.

player with the connected passed pawns has a Knight, the win is more straight-forward. The reason for this is that the Bishop must be able to sacrifice itself for both pawns, because a King, Knight, and any pawn (provided that the pawn hasn't advanced too far) is a win.

In Diagram 204, I've chosen an analysis by Grandmaster Yuri Averbach that is difficult to win. In general, the winning procedure is to *advance the pawns with the escort of the King and Knight while trying to avoid a potential blockade.* This presents a challenge because the a3-pawn must be protected at the same time that White is trying to enforce the b3-b4 advance. The winning procedure is instructive:

1.Nd5!

White begins with the winning threat of 2.b4+ Kb5 3.Kb3 so that he can advance his pawns—a plan Black will do his best to foil.

1...Bg7+!

Black finds the best way to annoy his opponent. The other try, 1...Kb5 2.b4 Kc4 3.Ne3+ Kd3 (3...Kb5 4.Kb3 is just what White wants.) 4.Ng4! Kc4 5.Ne5+! Kd5

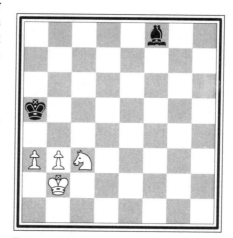

DIAGRAM 204.
Y. Averbach, 1958

6.Ng6, gains a crucial tempo on the Bishop. After the Bishop moves, White plays Kb2-b3 and then races forward with his a-pawn.

2.Ka2 Kb5!

Black isn't able to prevent b2-b4, and so anticipates playing ...Kb5-c4 as a response. Weaker choices include 2...Be5? 3.b4+ Ka4 4.Nb6+ Kb5 5.Nd7, with a tempo against the Bishop. Once more, White would be ready to play Ka2-b3, winning with the advance of the a-pawn. Another failure is 2...Bd4? 3.b4+ Ka4 4.Nf4! Bc3 5.Nd3!, in which White is just in time to protect the b4-pawn and drive away Black's King. White's next move would then be Nd3-b2+, followed by Ka2-b3, winning.

3.Nf4!

White draws the Knight back to a better square from where it can support the advance of the pawns. Black would have excellent drawing chances after 3.b4? Kc4! 4.Ne3+ Kd3 5.Nd1 Kc2, when Black's active King is more than a nuisance.

3...Bf6

He's doing his best to restrict White's King. After 3...Bf8 4.Nd3 Bd6 5.Kb2! Be7 6.b4! Kc4 7.Kc2!, White is poised to drive Black's King into retreat with Nd3-b2+ and Kc2-b3, a winning line.

4.Nd3

As we see in Diagram 205, White introduces a different plan of expansion. This time he aims for 5.a4+ Ka5 6.Ka3 Be7+ 7.b4+, winning. This is the key difference between the minor pieces in such endings: Although the Bishop can be wrong-footed, the Knight is able to win with any pawn. After 7...Bxb4+ 8.Nxb4 is played, White's Knight and passed a-pawn will win the game.

DIAGRAM 205.
Y. Averbach, 1958

4...Be7 5.b4!

At last, White is sufficiently prepared to support this advance. A poor move would be 5.a4+?? Ka5, which would give Black an ideal Queenside blockade.

5...Kc4

This is the only way to stop Ka2-b3 because 5...Ka4 6.Nb2+ Kb5 7.Kb3 is ineffective.

6.Nb2+ Kc3

Other moves allow Ka2-b3, which wins.

7.Na4+ Kc4

Black has to maintain contact with the b4-pawn. The advance 7...Kc2? 8.b5! Bd6
9.b6 Kd3 10.b7 Kc4 11.Nb6+ Kb5 12.Nd7 Kc6 13.b8=Q Bxb8 14.Nxb8+ shows that
Black's King has strayed too far forward.

8.Nb6+ Kb5   9.Nd5

White gains the tempo against the Bishop so that he has time to activate his King.

9...Bd8   10.Kb3 Kc6   11.Kc4

Now that White has solved the issue of advancing his pawns, the next step is to
keep his pieces as active as possible and to further escort them up the board.
Ideally, White would like to drive Black's King away from the Queenside. As we
have learned, the defender *must keep his King in front of the pawns.*

11...Bg5   12.a4 Bd8   13.a5 Kb7

This is more of a fighting chance than the winning analysis, 13...Kd6 14.a6 Kc6
15.b5+, provided by Grandmaster Yuri Averbach. Black tries to hold up the advance
of the a-pawn.

14.Kb5

White temporarily steps in front of his pawns. He wants to dominate Black's King
and prevent ...Kb7-a6, in which case the threat of ...Bd8xa5 would lead to a draw.

14...Bh4   15.Nc3 Be1   16.Na4 Bd2   17.Nc5+ Ka7

Black is doing his utmost to make White's progress as difficult as possible by
staying in front of White's pawns.

18.Ka4

White prepares for the march of the
b-pawn, as we can see in Diagram 206.
Black tries to spoil this plan.

18...Be3   19.Nb3 Bf2   20.b5

In general, the superior side should try
to *advance its pawns abreast of one another* if possible, keeping them from getting too far apart.

20...Kb7

Black can't give up the g1-a7 diagonal,
which he would do with 20...Be1? 21.Nc5
Bf2 22.b6+ Kb8 23.Kb5—it's too easy
for White.

DIAGRAM 206.
Y. Averbach, 1958

21.Kb4 Kc7   22.Kc4 Be3

Black hangs on to that diagonal by avoiding 22...Be1 23.b6+ Kc6 24.Nd4+ Kb7 25.Kb5, which wins.

23.Kd5 Bf2   24.Nc5

At last, White has completed his preparations, and now the pawns glide home.

24...Be3   25.b6+ Kb8   26.Kc6 Bf4   27.Na6+ Ka8   28.Nc7+ Kb8

Black holds out a little bit longer, not wanting to give White—with 28...Bxc7 29.bxc7 Ka7 30.c8=R! Kxa6 31.Ra8 Checkmate—such an elegant finish.

29.a6

It's an elegant finish anyway. While this operation took White a lot of time, we must admire its methodical execution. Slowly, slowly, White nursed his pawns up the board, taking the time to properly position his pieces so that the pawns might be escorted. This is the heart and soul of chess endgames: a careful exploitation of the advantages inherent in a position. Chess is a game that requires both the subtle and the brutal.

A full understanding of these opposing minor piece endgames takes work. In time, you'll notice the characteristics of the positions that benefit Bishops and Knights, and you'll learn to discern which is the better piece for a given situation.

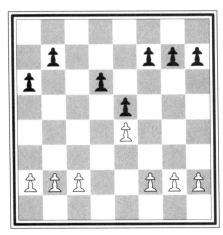

DIAGRAM 207.

Test Your Skills

In the following quizzes, your task is to decide which minor piece is preferred for the pawn position at hand. Be prepared to articulate the reasons for your answers. Good luck!

QUIZ 1: Look at Diagram 207. As White, which minor piece would you prefer and why? Where would you place it? Now, as Black, answer the same questions.

QUIZ 2: In Diagram 208, we have an extremely common balanced pawn position that can come from nearly any opening. Which minor piece would you prefer and why? On which square would you place it? (Because the pawn positions mirror one another, your answers to which piece and why would apply to both sides.)

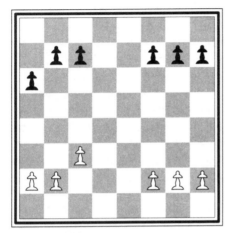

DIAGRAM 208.

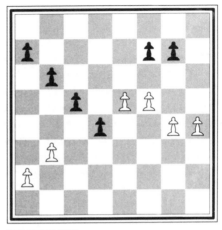

DIAGRAM 209.

QUIZ 3: Diagram 209 illustrates a rich pawn structure that allows for a wealth of creative ideas. Is this a position for Knights or Bishops?

QUIZ 4: In the position in Diagram 209, what are White's best pieces, and where should they go? Answer the same question from Black's point of view.

QUIZ 5: Look at Diagram 210. Assuming that both players have Knights, where are they best placed? Also, suppose that Black has a dark-squared Bishop; would you place it on the c3-square or on the d6-square?

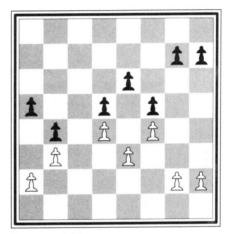

DIAGRAM 210.

Solutions

QUIZ 1 (DIAGRAM 207): This structure commonly occurs in games featuring the Sicilian Defense. To White, this is a trick question—all of White's choices are bound to be good. A dark-squared Bishop is nice because of Black's central pawn structure. A Bishop on the b6-square would be brilliant. A light-squared Bishop on the d5-square would be very powerful in its ability to restrain the backward d6-pawn and attack Black's Queenside structure. Finally, a Knight would find gainful employment on the d5- and f5-squares, where the *Knight would be protected*. (Study those principles!)

Black's choices are also rather clear. The one piece *he does not want* would be a *dark-squared Bishop*, which would have a rather sad existence defending the center. A Knight on the f6-square, protecting the d5-square and attacking the e4-pawn, would be well placed. A Knight on the d4- or f4-outpost wouldn't be that great, as these squares aren't stable. Black's best choice would be for a light-squared Bishop on the e6- or c6-square, protecting the d5-square and playing for ...d6-d5, to get rid of the backward d6-pawn.

QUIZ 2 (DIAGRAM 208): This is a clear example of a position that favors Bishops. It favors a Bishop of either color, as the pawns are fluid. If Black's c-pawn is on the c4-square, the possibility of a Knight on the d3-square would be attractive.

QUIZ 3 (DIAGRAM 209): Another trick question, as this is a situation for either Knights *or* Bishops. Arguments can be made for either piece, so your solution was definitely right!

QUIZ 4 (DIAGRAM 209): The offsetting pawn majorities will require that both players remain vigilant in watching the passers. Even with five pawns on the light squares, a light-squared Bishop on the d3- or c4-square would be quite useful. It would hold up Black's pawns while supporting White's Kingside passers. A White Knight on the d3-, d6-, or c4-square would be brilliant. A dark-squared Bishop might not be as useful in such a position, although I might feel better about it if it were posted on the d6-square.

Because Black has to be concerned about a potential passed h-pawn, owning a Knight might be seriously disadvantageous. Then again, if it were on the e3- or c3-square, it would definitely be useful. Overall, my preference would be for a Bishop. A light-squared Bishop supporting the advance of the central majority would work well.

QUIZ 5 (DIAGRAM 210): This is a position for Knights if there ever was one. The position is well blocked, with only a pair of pawns traded. White's natural outposts are the c5- and e5-squares; for Black it's the c3- and e4-squares.

If Black had a dark-squared Bishop, it wouldn't be particularly effective on the c3-square because it wouldn't control either of White's natural outposts. However, on the d6-square it would cover both outposts.

Rook vs. Minor Pieces

As a chess beginner, I struggled to understand why a Rook was stronger than a Knight or a Bishop. I was told that a Rook was worth 5 points in the force count and that minor pieces were worth 3, and that seemed to be that! My understanding of why the Rook was so much more highly valued didn't come easily, but it did come, eventually, in my study of the endgame. In the opening and middlegame, the strength of the Rook can be camouflaged by the presence of pawns and other pieces. When the camouflage is stripped away, the situation is obvious. In this chapter, we will come to realize exactly how a Rook is superior to a minor piece, and we'll get to know the conditions under which a Rook can win.

Rook vs. Bishop

In a straight-up fight between a Rook and a Bishop, the Bishop has no chance. But this doesn't mean that the Rook will win. In fact, although a defender's Bishop and King will be pushed around by the Rook, the defender can hold on for a draw—if he knows what to do!

The two principles that the defender should be aware of are:

DIAGRAM 211.

■ *Avoid King opposition.*

■ *Avoid the corner squares that are the same color as your Bishop.*

In Diagram 211, we have a typical situation that should be a draw. As we will see, it is, in fact, very easy for Black to lose. Let's follow a sample of poor play by Black, which at first glance appears rather reasonable.

1.Ra5 Kd6? 2.Kd4 Bc6

3.Ra6 Kc7? 4.Kc5 Bb7

5.Ra7 Kb8??   6.Kb6 Bf3   7.Rf7 Bg4   8.Rf8+ Bc8   9.Rd8

Black is checkmated in the next move.

Well, that was certainly a poor excuse for chess! But how bad was it? Wasn't Black being forced backward? Indeed he was, but he didn't have to be so cooperative. In the first place, Black should have *avoided King opposition,* for it is only by allowing opposing Kings that Black has to backpedal. The next point—and this is a crucial one—is that *the King should go to the corner opposite the color of his Bishop.* In our example of bad play, Black headed to the a8-corner, a white square, when his Bishop was also on a white square. The result, as we saw, was a quick loss.

Let's go back to Diagram 211 and improve Black's play:

1.Ra5 Ke6!   2.Kd4 Bf3

Black avoids 2...Bc6 3.Ra6, which would force him backward.

3.Re5+ Kf6!

Black is avoiding 3...Kd6, which would create a King opposition. White could then play 4.Rf5 Bg4 5.Rf6+ Be6 6.Rh6, pushing Black backward. After the text, White has to try another approach to force back Black's King.

4.Re1 Bc6   5.Rc1 Bg2   6.Ke3 Bb7   7.Kf4

With the Kings in opposition, White readies a Rook check.

7...Ke6!

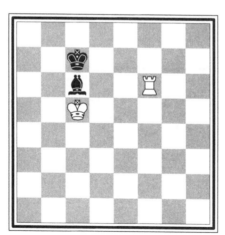

DIAGRAM 212.

Black quickly steps out of the opposition. White isn't able to force Black's King to the side of the board.

In Diagram 212, I've given White a greater starting advantage. As we can see, with the Kings in opposition, White will be able to force Black's King to the side of the board.

1...Bg2   2.Rf7+ Kd8!

Black backs away from the a8-square.

3.Kd6 Ke8   4.Re7+ Kf8

Black avoids the trap 4...Kd8?? 5.Rg7 with the duel threat of Rg7-g8 Checkmate and the capture of the Bishop.

5.Ke6 Kg8   6.Kf6 Bf1   7.Rg7+

In Diagram 213, White has been able to achieve his maximum, creating a bit of a crisis by forcing Black's King to the side of the board.

7...Kh8!

Despite its appearance, Black's King is actually quite safe in this corner. What Black wants to avoid is 7...Kf8, when the Kings are in opposition. With the Kings in opposition, White would create a mating net with 8.Rg1 Bd3? (This accelerates defeat, but 8...Be2 9.Re1 Bf3 10.Re3 Bg2 11.Re2 Bf3 12.Rf2 Bc6 13.Rc2 Bd7 14.Rb2! Kg8 15.Rb8+ Kh7 16.Rb7 wins.) 9.Rd1 Bb5 10.Rd8+ Be8 11.Rc8, winning the Bishop.

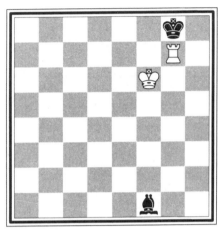

DIAGRAM 213.

8.Kg6 Bd3+ 9.Kh6

It now appears that White can win, because he has been able to set up opposing Kings by force. Because of the threat of stalemate, Black can still hang on to a draw.

9...Bc4 10.Rc7 Bd5 11.Rc8+ Bg8

White's dominant pieces are a bit too dominant. He must release the stalemate.

12.Rc3 Ba2 13.Rc2 Bb3 14.Rc7 Bg8

White can't improve his position, and the game is drawn.

Rook vs. Knight

Driving the inferior King to the side of the board is even more difficult with a Rook against the Knight. It is harder for the superior side to create King oppositions, and therein lies the difficulty, as we're about to discover in Diagram 214.

1. Rb5 Ke6 2.Ke4 Nc4

Black holds back White's Rook by covering the b6-square.

3.Rc5 Nd6+

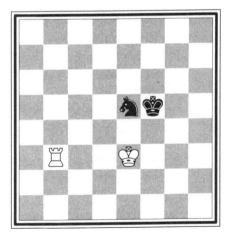

DIAGRAM 214.

This simple move shows the strength of the Knight in breaking up the opposition with check.

4.Kf4 Nf7   5.Ra5 Nd6   6.Re5+ Kf6   7.Rh5 Ke6   8.Rc5 Nf7

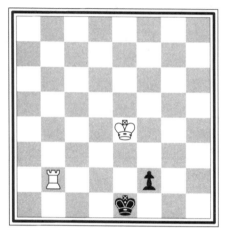

DIAGRAM 215.

White isn't able to make progress. As before, we have to give White a little assistance, shown in Diagram 215.

1.Ke3

This will force Black into an under-promotion, a common occurrence in Rook and pawn endgames. This position is from Chapter Four, Diagram 105.

1...f1=N+   2.Kd3

After the underpromotion, Black has a moment or two of discomfort. His King is trapped on the back rank, where it is vulnerable to potential checkmating nets. The key to saving the game is very simple: The inferior side *must keep the Knight close to the King.* If the Knight is forced far away, the defender loses. In the next phase of play we see White trying to separate Knight and King.

2...Ng3   3.Rg2 Nf1!

A mistake would be 3...Nf5?? 4.Rg4! Nd6 5.Rf4, in which the Knight would find it-self trapped and ensnared. Again, the Knight must stay close to its King.

4.Re2+ Kd1   5.Rf2 Ke1!   6.Rg2 Kd1

Black doesn't fear the opposing King position as long as the Knight is near.

7.Ra2 Ke1   8.Re2+ Kd1   9.Re7 Ng3   10.Rg7 Nf1   11.Rg1 Ke1

12.Rg2 Kd1

White hasn't made any progress. Does this mean this ending is always drawn? Not at all. When you have a Knight vs. a Rook, you have to avoid the corners at all costs, for it is there that defeat lurks.

Diagram 216 is similar to Diagram 215; I've just scooted the passer over a few files, which makes a big difference because it instantly puts Black's King in a mate.

1...h1=N+   2.Kf3

Immediately Black is lost. Undoubtedly, we feel Black has been cheated. His Knight hardly had a chance! Let's try a few other starting positions in which Black's chances look pretty good.

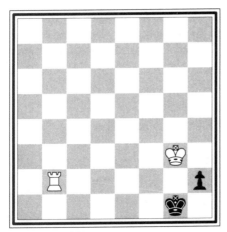

DIAGRAM 216.

DIAGRAM 217.
J. Kling and B. Horowitz, 1851

The study in Diagram 217 looks rather reasonable, doesn't it? But White has two ways of instantly winning! Here's the first:

1.Ke6 Ke8   2.Rg8+ Nf8+   3.Kf6

White wins Black's Knight and—the point that the authors of this study intended— lures Black's King into the corner.

Here's the second way to win:

1.Kg6 Kg8   2.Rg3! Nf8+

A better choice than 2…Kh8 3.Rh3, which wins the Knight.

3.Kf6+ Kh8   4.Kf7 Nh7

5.Rg8 Checkmate

It seems cruel to have to put Black's Knight on a bad square. Well, let's be more sporting. In Diagram 218, we see the danger of separating the King and Knight, and we know how to take advantage of this circumstance. While admiring the following play from the position in Diagram 218, let yourself be astonished by its publication—1257! The analysis is as valid today as it was then.

1.Kd6!

DIAGRAM 218.
Arabic Manuscript, 1257

This is a bit of a surprising move, but right on the mark for the plan that's unfolding. White's King covers the e7- and e5-squares, which are key to containing the Knight. In this study, Black's King isn't the target; rather, White discovers that it is much easier to trap the Knight.

1...Nf4

Black has a few other tries at escaping:

- **1...Nf8 2.Rg5! Kb6** (2...Kc8 3.Rg8 pins and wins.) **3.Ke7 Nh7 4.Rh5,** traps the Knight.

- **1...Nh8 2.Ke6 Ng6 3.Rd4! Kc6** (3...Kc7 4.Rg4 Nf8+ 5.Ke7 Nd7 6.Rc4+ wins the Knight.) **4.Rc4+ Kb5 5.Rg4 Nf8+ 6.Ke7** wins.

- **1...Nh4 2.Rh5! Ng2** (2...Nf3 3.Kd5 Kc7 4.Rh3 Ng5 5.Rg3 Nf7 6.Rg7 wins.) **3.Ke5** (threatening Ke5-e4 and ensnaring the Knight at once) **3...Ne3 4.Kd4 Nc2+** (4...Ng4 5.Rf5 Kc7 6.Rf4 Nh6 7.Ke5 Kd7 8.Kf6 Ke8 9.Kg7 wins the Knight.) **5.Kc5!** (A beautiful and surprising move. Instead of going directly after the Knight, White simply controls its future possibilities. The threat is Rh5-e5-e2, winning the Knight.) **5...Ne1 6.Rf5!** (A similar controlling move. White is weaving another trap. The intent is for Kc5-c4 and Rf5-f2 to ensnare the Knight.) **6...Ng2** (The other try, 6...Nd3+ 7.Kc4 Nb2+ 8.Kb3 Nd3 9.Kc3 Ne1 10.Rf2, is a winner.) **7.Kd4! Nh4 8.Rf6!** (White continues to control the Knight while bringing his King closer.) **8...Kc7 9.Ke4 Kd7 10.Rh6 Ng2 11.Rh2 Ne1 12.Re2,** and the Knight is lost.

After this lengthy pause we now return to the author's solution.

2.Rd2!

This pattern of controlling the Knight is worth memorizing. Note how White's two pieces control the Knight by being two *diagonal* squares away from the Knight. With this in mind, replay the above variations and look for this characteristic. By using this pattern against the Knight, you make it peculiarly vulnerable.

2...Kb6

If Black's Knight tries to scamper away with 2...Ng6 3.Rf2! Kb6 4.Rf6! Nh4 5.Ke5+ Kc5 6.Ke4 Kc4 7.Rc6+ Kb5 8.Rh6 Ng2 9.Rh2 Ne1 10.Re2, the Knight, as we've seen before, ends up trapped.

3.Ke5 Ng6+ 4.Kf6 Nf4 5.Kf5 Nh5 6.Rg2!

White wins the Knight after 7.Rg5, while Black looks on helplessly.

QUIZ 1: If you have a minor piece and your King is stuck on the a1-square, which minor piece would you want?

Knight Hunting

When I was a young man, one of my favorite sports was Knight hunting. Alright, it's an exercise, not a sport, but it's a good one! To try your hand at it, look at Diagram 219. The idea is for White to hunt down the Knight by coordinating his King and his Rook. Whenever he likes, Black can make a "pass move" as if he has a King. This "sport" will help you recognize the unique patterns of this ending.

Even after this brief discussion, we can sum up some of the principles that govern the Rook:

DIAGRAM 219.

- *Like Bishops, Rooks do not need protection. On the contrary, they go eagerly into pursuit, even in enemy territory.*

- *The Rooks can be effective from a long range, not needing to be "close" to the action.*

- *Although Rooks can be bullies and push the minor pieces around the board, they are able to coordinate well with the King and all piece combinations.*

- *Like Bishops, Rooks are long-range pieces that prefer open positions.*

Rook and Pawn vs. Knight and Pawn

In the following section, we cannot extensively explore all of the Rook and pawn vs. minor piece and pawn combinations. Instead, I will simply point out the winning methods that the side with the Rook is able to employ.

The position in Diagram 220 on the following page is fairly typical of this type of ending. If White is able to drive back the defender and win the d6-pawn, the win is a snap. But in this case, Black is burrowed in pretty well, and it is impossible to coordinate the King and Rook in such a way that the d5-pawn is not jeopardized. For instance, if White sends his King to the b7-square, Black waits by moving his King back and forth on the d7- and d8-squares. If White sends his King to the h5-square with the intent of running to the f7-square, Black's King squeezes out and plays ...Kc7-b6-c5, and wins the d5-pawn. How is White to win?

DIAGRAM 220.

Simple: Whenever White can create the conditions for a winning King and pawn endgame, he can sacrifice his Rook! White has two winning procedures.

    1.Kf4 Kd8   2.Rh8+ Kd7

    3.Rh7 Kd8   4.Rxe7 Kxe7

    5.Kg5! Kf7   6.Kf5 Ke7

    7.Kg6 Kd7   8.Kf7

White can also win on the other side by:

    1.Kd4 Kd8   2.Kc4 Kd7

    3.Rh7 Kd8   4.Rxe7 Kxe7

    5.Kb5 Kf6   6.Kb6! Kf5

    7.Kc7! Ke5   8.Kc6

Rook and Pawn vs. Bishop and Pawn

It is even more discouraging for the minor piece to have to defend the same ending with a Bishop. This is especially true when the pawn is on the same color as the

DIAGRAM 221.

Bishop. The defender has virtually no chance of creating a blockade. Using a similar position to the one in Diagram 220, in Diagram 221 we see the Bishop getting clobbered. In this case, White smartly forces Black's King aside and wins the d6-pawn.

    1.Rh7+ Kd8   2.Kf5 Bc5

    3.Ke6 Bb4   4.Rd7+ Kc8

    5.Rxd6 Bxd6   6.Kxd6

A winning King and pawn ending. Nothing changes, even if we allow Black to move first so that he avoids having his King being pushed to the back rank. If he tries 1...Kc7 2.Rh7+ Kb6 3.Kf5 Kc5 4.Ke6 Kc4 5.Rd7, the d6-pawn falls.

Sometimes the superior side has difficulty winning these endings because he has advanced his pawn too far, and so his Bishop isn't tied to the defense of its own pawn. Diagram 222 is representative of such cases.

The position in Diagram 222 is an ideal one for the defender. His f7-pawn covers the e6- and g6-entry squares, and the Bishop covers the f6- and d6-squares. The position is actually quite sharp, with the outcome determined by which side is on move. If it's White's move, Grandmaster Yuri Averbach shows us how White wins:

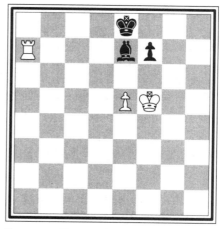

DIAGRAM 222.
Y. Averbach, 1981

1.Ra8+!

If he played 1.e6? Kf8!, White would blow the win completely.

1...Kd7

Blocking the check with the Bishop would bring a quick response: 1...Bd8 2.e6! Ke7 3.exf7, and the Bishop would be lost.

2.Rh8 Bd8

Black is stuck for a move. His King can't move, because Rh1-h7 will then win the f7-pawn. Likewise, a Bishop move that gives up control of the f6-square, such as 2...Bc5 3.Kf6 Bc3 4.Rh7, will cost the f7-pawn.

3.Rh7 Ke8   4.e6! f6

The loss is now inevitable, but 4...fxe6+ 5.Kxe6 Kf8 6.Rh8+ wins the Bishop. Black is now helpless in a King and pawn ending.

5.Rh8+ Ke7   6.Rxd8 Kxd8   7.Kxf6 Ke8   8.e7

Clearly, Black lost the position because his King was separated from the f7-pawn.

Let's go back to Diagram 222. If it is Black's move, he can draw the game.

1...Kf8!

This guards against a back rank check, because Black's King will be perfectly comfortable on the g7-square. Black has to avoid 1...Bd8?? 2.e6, which loses on the spot.

2.Ra8+ Kg7   3.Rb8

This sets up an important test for Black. Where will he move?

3...Bh4!

This is the only move to save the game. It is vital for Black to control the f6-entry square. After 3...Bc5?? 4.Rb7 Kg8 5.Kf6, Black would lose the f6-pawn. The retreat, 3...Bf8?, loses for a different reason: 4.Rb7 Kg8 5.e6 fxe6+ 6.Kg6!! traps Black's King in the wrong corner. The win, then, would be the straightforward 6...e5 7.Rb8 e4 8.Re8 e3 9.Rxe3 Kh8 10.Re8 Kg8 11.Ra8, with checkmate next move. Now, despite Black's precarious position, the Bishop's d8-h4 diagonal is just long enough to draw the game.

Create Your Own Endgames

We now come to one of the most important tips in this whole book. Every chess teacher will advise his or her student, "Think for yourself," and "Make your own move." However, these well-meant phrases don't always hit the mark. How can students think for themselves? I know this question on the face of it seems absurd. But is there a way of *training* oneself to do one's own thinking? Yes, there is. My friend International Master Nikolay Minev has advised me well over the years, and I pass this favorite lesson on to you: *Don't just study the positions in the book. Change them yourself!* At the end of the last game, I gave you an important clue about the position in Diagram 222. The clue is in this concept: "...despite Black's precarious position, the Bishop's d8-h4 diagonal is just long enough to draw..." This might cause you to muse, "If we were to shorten Black's diagonal by moving the position a file to the right, would the position then be lost?" Let's try it.

As we can see in Diagram 223, in this new position it seems that White does indeed win, because Black must give up control of the g6-square. However, this time Black's King is in the right corner and he can draw with a stalemate:

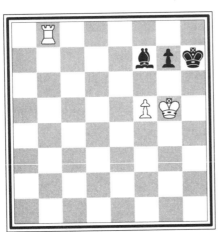

DIAGRAM 223.
Reader's Inspiration, 1999

   1...Bg8   2.Rb7 Kh8

   3.Kg6 Bh7+   4.Kg5

Otherwise, 4.Kf7 Bxf5 costs the f5-pawn.

   4...Bg8   5.f6 gxf6+   6.Kh6 f5

   7.Rb8 f4   8.Rf8 f3

   9.Rxf3 Bd5   10.Rf8+ Bg8

And there's the draw.

Thus, we have an excellent method to help us understand chess endings. When an author gives a position and indicates who is on play and what the outcome will be, take the time to understand the solution, but then *change* the position slightly. Try to understand how a subtle change would affect the outcome. Sometimes you might want to add a pawn or more. This exercise will help your understanding *and* prevent you from becoming a studying robot!

Let us now return to Diagram 222 and where we left off. Black is on play.

1...Kf8 2.Ra8+ Kg7 3.Rb8 Bh4! 4.Re8

White attempts to shorten the Bishop's diagonal. If White tries either 4.Rb7 Kf8 or 4.Ra8 Be7!, he makes it too comfortable for Black. After the text, Black is forced to give up control of the f6-square. Fortunately for him, this isn't fatal.

4...Be1 5.Re7 Bh4 6.Rd7 Kf8

White isn't able to make progress, because Black will spend his tempo to retreat with his Bishop to the e7-square.

What went wrong for White in Diagram 222? What was the culprit? The problem for White was that his e5-pawn was too far advanced. He could penetrate the position with his King through the f6-square only. Had White's King been posted on the e5-square and his e-pawn on, for example, the e4-square, White's King could have simultaneously threatened to enter through the d6- or f6-square, and this penetration could not have been prevented.

Rook and Pawn vs. Bishop: An Exception

I certainly didn't appreciate the significance of Diagram 224 (shown on the next page) when I started to play chess, but after my play had "matured" and I had become a registered tournament player, I found the position to be quite vexing. "My goodness," I realized, "White has a major piece worth 5 points against a minor piece worth 3 points and an extra pawn. A plus-3 lead in the force count, yet the position is drawn!" (This bit of news coincided with the stunner that a wrong Bishop and h-pawn or a-pawn are drawn too.) The culprit—again—is that White's pawn is too far advanced. White's King has to step on a light square to advance, and the Bishop can shoo it away. If the pawn were on the f5-square, the move Kg5-f6 would, of course, win at once. Let us see how Black is able to save his skin.

1.Rc7

The first test. White would like to play 1.Kg6, but 1...Bd3+ would displace the King. The text intends to push the Bishop to a losing square.

1...Ba2

DIAGRAM 224.
E. Del Rio, 1750

It is vital that 2.Kg6 be prevented, so Black's Bishop moves to a square that will allow him to check on the b1-h7 diagonal. That's why both 1...Bb3? 2.Kg6 and 1...Be6? 2.Kg6 would lose. Another good alternative to the text is 1...Bd5, when 2.Kg6 is met by 2...Be4+, chasing away White's King.

Another big but instructive mistake would be 1...Bb5? 2.f7! Kg7 (stopping Kg5-f6, which is a winning threat) 3.Kf5 (with the threat of Kf5-e6-e7, which Black's Bishop has to prevent) 3...Ba4 4.Rb7! (guarding the b3-square and also making Kf5-e6 possible) 4...Bd1 (to attack the f7-pawn from a different diagonal. Weaker is 4...Bc6 5.Ke6 Bxb7 6.Ke7, winning.) 5.Ke6 Bh5 6.Rc7! (a subtle pause in the action as Black's Bishop is lured to a vulnerable square) 6...Bg6 7.f8=Q++! Kxf8 8.Kf6, resulting in the dual threats of Kf6xg6 and Rc7-c8+, which gives White the game.

2.Rc1

Again, White sets up the threat of advancing with his King. White could have played 2.f7, which he will look at later. For now, White is testing his opponent, hoping for a mistake.

2...Bd5

Black also avoids 2...Bf7? 3.Rc8+ Be8 4.Kf5 Kf7 5.Rc7+ Kf8 6.Ke6, which wins.

3.Kf5 Kf7!   4.Ke5 Bb3

The Bishop's diagonal is just long enough to be able to cope with the position. With his next few moves, White continues to create problems that have only one solution.

5.Rc7+ Kf8   6.Rb7 Bc4   7.Rb4 Ba2!

The only move. We've seen that 7...Bf7? 8.Rb8+ is a winner. Also out of the question is 7...Bg8? 8.Rb8+ Kf7 9.Rc8 Bh7 10.Rc7+ Kf8 11.Ke6 Bg8+ 12.f7, winning for White.

8.Kf5 Bd5!

Again, the only move, because 8...Kf7? 9.Rb7+ Kf8 10.Kg6 wins.

9.Kg6 Bf7+!

With the e4-square covered, this is Black's only check.

10.Kg5 Bd5! 11.Rh4

White takes another approach, hoping to disrupt Black's defenses.

11...Bb3 12.Rh8+ Kf7

13.Rh7+ Kf8 14.f7

The game has now reached the position shown in Diagram 225. Black faces a new test. What would you do?

14...Ke7!!

A brilliant move that sidesteps the loss awaiting this alternative: 14...Bxf7? 15.Kf6 Ba2 16.Rh8+ Bg8 17.Kg6, which wins the Bishop. The text prevents Kg5-f6 and prepares to capture the f7-pawn.

DIAGRAM 225.
E. Del Rio, 1750

15.Kg6 Bc4

Black must not be tempted by 15...Bc2+?? 16.Kg7, which wins for White.

16.Rg7 Bb3 17.f8=Q++

White cannot improve his position further and so jettisons his remaining pawn.

17...Kxf8 18.Kf6 Ke8

Black safely draws.

This main line brings us right back to Diagram 224. Consider what would happen if White had tried the most straightforward approach:

1.f7

White pulls out this threat, planning Kg5-f6 to win. Can you guess Black's only move?

1...Kg7!!

A mirror reflection of the earlier line. The pawn is poison: 1...Bxf7? 2.Kf6 Bh5 3.Ra8+ Be8 4.Rb8 Kg8 5.Rxe8+ wins the Bishop and the game.

2.Kf5 Bxf7 3.Kg5 Kg8!

This move is the key to the draw. We've seen that 3...Kf8? 4.Kf6 is a loser.

4.Kf6 Bd5

We've seen it before: a draw.

This brings an end to this section on the Rook vs. minor pieces. Clearly, this overview was deliberately biased in favor of the Rook. It was my intention to show how a Rook is superior to, and can overcome, a minor piece in the majority of endings. One of the Rook's greatest strengths is its ability to trade itself to allow a winning King and pawn endgame. I'll leave you with a suggestion: when you play through grandmaster games, pay particular attention to those endings that feature a player an exchange ahead. Observe how the grandmaster puts his Rook to work to outplay the minor piece.

QUIZ 2: (Do not set this position up on a chessboard.) Imagine that you are White in the following position: Kg5, Rc7, and a pawn on h6. Black has Kh8 and Bb1. Can you win?

Studies to Enjoy

As you've undoubtedly realized, I particularly enjoy studies that are practical to the game, so instead of completing this chapter with a series of tests, I'd rather share with you some of my favorite studies featuring the pieces topical to this discussion.

DIAGRAM 226.
Vancura, 1916

As I've mentioned, in January 1999 I played a ten-game match against Grandmaster Michael Adams in Bermuda. In the first game I had played one of the best games of my career and had achieved a winning position, only to badly blunder the exchange and lose the game in just a few moves. My friend Grandmaster Lubosh Kavalek wrote me an e-mail message to tell me not to worry, that I had played well and would get the point back. To cheer me up, he sent me the Vancura study you see in Diagram 226, and soon the loss was all but forgotten.

The Bishop—a long-ranging piece—has on average better chances than a Knight when dueling against a Rook. Of course, the truth of this generalization depends on the specific position. The charm of this study is the intriguing twist in the way the Bishop dominates the Rook. White seems to have two strategies for a win. The first, moving his King, fails:

1.Kh3 Kc7　2.Kh4 Kd7　3.Kh5 Ke6　4.Kh6 Kf7　5.Kxh7 Rg8

Black draws. Perhaps a different move by the King would work:

1.Kg3 Kc7　2.Kf4 Kd7　3.Kf5 Re8　4.Kf6 h5　5.Kf7 h4

6.g8=Q Rxg8　7.Kxg8 Ke8　8.Kg7 h3　9.Bd6 h2　10.Bxh2 Kxe7

This also draws. So White can't win by advancing his King. Thus, he tries the second strategy:

1.e8=Q! Rxe8   2.Bf8

Suddenly Black appears lost because the g-pawn is ready to promote. Simple, right? So what about the "spike" checks that Black now tries?

2...Re2+   3.Kh3

White can't step on the g-file, because 3.Kg3 Re6 4.Bd6+ Kb7, followed by ...Re6-g6+, saves the game for Black.

3...Re3+   4.Kh4 Re4+

Black is obliged to keep checking because 4...Re1 5.Bd6+ Kb7 6.g8=Q Rh1+ 7.Kg4 Rg1+ 8.Bg3 blocks the check and saves the Queen. White's Bishop seems to be everywhere!

5.Kh5 Re5+   6.Kh6 Re1

Now Black is prepared to check from behind and skewer the newly created Queen. Both 6...Re3 and 6...Re2 7.Bd6+ cover the h2- and g3-squares and lead to a win. Now it looks like a draw because the checks seem too strong.

7.Bc5!

White covers the g1-square and threatens to Queen with check. Black has to retreat.

7...Re8   8.Kxh7

White is now ready for Bc5-f8, and the g7-pawn promotes.

8...Rd8

Black takes another defensive stance. Now the intent is ...Rd8-d7, pinning the g-pawn. Weaker was 8...Kc7? 9.Bf8 Re1 10.g8=Q Rh1+ 11.Bh6!, blocking the check and saving the Queen yet again.

9.Be7!

Blocking Black's threat with tempo.

9...Rc8

There is no other choice, because 9...Re8 10.Bf8 transposes into the weak line mentioned after the eighth move.

10.Bf8 Rc7   11.Bd6

Pinning the Rook—an amazing example of the Bishop's ability to be seemingly everywhere! Note how many critical squares the Bishop needed to cover: f8, e7, d7, c7, h6, g1, g3, and h2. The Bishop blocked the Rook on the seventh and eighth ranks as well as the h- and g-files, all while starting from the a3-square.

Neither was Vancura satisfied with this line of play, which allows a Bishop to embarrass the Rook! He found a beautiful way to show how a Knight could upstage its more powerful adversary as well, as we'll now see.

DIAGRAM 227.
Vancura, 1925

In Diagram 227, White's Knight appears to be so badly placed, it is hard to imagine that Black would be unable to sacrifice his Rook for the g7-pawn and make a draw. How on earth can White win this position? White's first move is nothing short of amazing:

1.Kh5!!

Contrary to the natural idea of supporting the passer, White's King steps backward to allow the Knight the g6-square. The obvious fails: 1.Kf7? Rf3+ 2.Ke7 Rg3 is a draw, and 1.Kf5? Re8 2.Ng6 Kd6 3.Nf8 Ke7 4.g8=Q Rxf8+ draws as well.

1...Re8

This is Black's best chance, because 1...Re5+ 2.Kh6 Re8 3.Ng6, intending Ng6-f8 (3...Rg8? 4.Ne7+ forks.), wins for White. Also, 1...Rh3+ 2.Kg4 Rh1 3.Ng6 Rg1+ 4.Kf5 Rf1+ 5.Ke6 Re1+ 6.Ne5+!, interposing with check, wins for White as well.

2.Ng6 Kd6

Black chooses this, knowing that he has an extremely tricky defense in 2...Ra8, when White must play precisely to win: 3.Kh6! (The immediate 3.Nf8? Ra1 4.Ne6 Ra8! is equal.) Now the threat is 4.Nf8 Ra1 5.g8=Q Rh1+ 6.Kg7 Rg1+ 7.Ng6, saving the Queen.) 3...Kb5 (Trying to escape the Knight forks and making ...Ra8-g8 a threat. Although it seems that Black's King has a host of squares to move to, in fact he has none. He can't step on the seventh rank, 3...Kb7 or 3...Kc7 4.Nf8 Ra6+ 5.Kh7, because Black can't pin the g-pawn on the seventh rank. If Black tries 3...Kd5? 4.Nf8, the g-pawn will promote with check. Finally, 3...Kc5 4.Nf8 Ra6+ 5.Kh5 Ra1 6.Ne6+ Kd6 7.g8=Q Rh1+ 8.Kg6 Rg1+ 9.Ng5 wins.) 4.Nf8 Ra6+ 5.Kh5 Ra1 6.Ne6! Ra8 (If 6...Rh1+ 7.Kg6 Rg1+ 8.Ng5, the g-pawn promotes.) 7.Nc7+ Kc6 8.Nxa8—completing a remarkable journey as the Knight hops from one corner to the other.

3.Nf8 Re1

214

The position, shown in Diagram 228, has shifted. It seems that Black is ready to give checks from behind and make a draw. White now makes a magical move.

4.Ne6!!

Beautiful play. Black's Rook is prevented from returning to the e8-square and must try to stop the pawn from behind.

4...Re5+

Once more, 4...Rh1+ 5.Kg6 Rg1+ 6.Ng5, and the pawn promotes.

5.Kg4! Re1   6.Kf5! Rf1+

After 6...Re5+ 7.Kf4, Black has run out of useful checks. White wins in the next two moves:

7.Kg6! Rg1+   8.Ng5

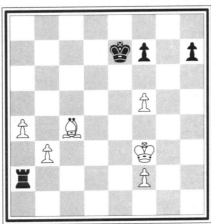

DIAGRAM 228.
J. Vancura, 1925

A charming example of the Knight's ability to interfere and support a passed pawn.

Well, those were certainly two enjoyable studies, but let's recall the main story: The Rook is the better piece, and history has proven it over and over again. Diagram 229 features the final position of the most celebrated match in chess history. The position shown is from the twenty-first game of the 1972 Spassky–Fischer match in Reykjavik, Iceland.

After 31 moves, the players have reached the position shown in Diagram 229. The position hardly seems lost, does it? Two connected passed pawns on the Queenside and an equal force count is all that White can console himself with, because Black's Rook is just too powerful. The three keys to the position are that the Rook, which is behind White's connected passed pawns, keeps them frozen; the doubled f-pawns have limited value; and Black's passed h-pawn is the best one on the board. This combination of "better piece and best pawn" is a lethal mix.

31...f6

DIAGRAM 229.
Spassky–Fischer, 1972

Black is taking the pawn off a light square where it is vulnerable to attack, and fixing White's f5-pawn on a light square where it is a defensive liability.

32.Bg8

White is unable to spend the time to bring his King to the Queenside, because the h-pawn is too strong. Also, 32.Bb5 Kd6 33.b4 Rb2 will cost White his b-pawn. By going with the text, White temporizes by moving back and forth, hoping he can create a fortress to hold the position.

32...h6   33.Kg3 Kd6

Black's King is headed to the central e5-square to harass the f5-pawn and White's King.

34.Kf3 Ra1!

Black is preparing for ...Ra1-g1, cutting off White's King so that the h-pawn can advance. Black also avoids 34...Kc5?? 35.b4+ Kxb4 36.Bxa2, which would be an abysmal failure.

35.Kg2 Ke5   36.Be6 Kf4!

Black further limits White's choices, and White is quickly running out of moves.

37.Bd7 Rb1   38.Be6 Rb2!

White is in virtual zugzwang, and something must give.

39.Bc4

Offering up the f5-pawn.

39...Ra2!

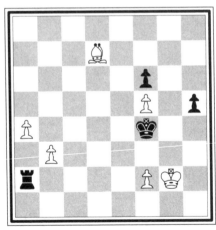

DIAGRAM 230.
Spassky–Fischer, 1972

Declined! After 39...Kxf5 40.a5 Ra2 41.a6, White has been allowed to activate his passers.

40.Be6 h5   41.Bd7

The position, shown in Diagram 230, was adjourned. After a night of study, Spassky decided to throw in the towel and resigned the game. Bobby became the new World Champion and didn't play a public game of chess for the next 20 years—a shame. As for the game, Bobby would have won by escorting his h-pawn up the board: **41...Kg4 42.b4 h4 43.a5 h3+ 44.Kg1 Ra1+ 45.Kh2 Rf1 46.a6 Rxf2+ 47.Kg1 Ra2 48.b5 h2+ 49.Kh1 Kg3,** with checkmate on the next move.

Solutions

QUIZ 1: You would want a light-squared Bishop. The a1-corner is a dark square and a light-squared Bishop is needed to draw. A Knight would likely lose.

QUIZ 2: The position is drawn. Black's King is in the right corner. After **1.h7 Bxh7 2.Kh6 Bg8**, the game will likely end in a stalemate.

The Rare and the "Perfect"

Queen vs. Rook

A Queen vs. Rook ending is a rather rare ending. In my tournament career of nearly three decades, I can recall having played this particular endgame only once! I had the Rook and lost. So why devote a whole chapter to an esoteric ending that hardly appears in practice? That is a good question, and one I pondered as I was planning this book, until I realized how vital an understanding of this particular ending is in grasping the powers of the Queen. Understanding the Queen, in turn, leads to a better understanding of the Rook's limitations. Now that we have extolled the powers of the Rook against a minor piece, this chapter will show us which piece really is the boss on the chessboard. It's the Queen!

Despite the rarity of this ending, it has the *potential* for appearing often, and

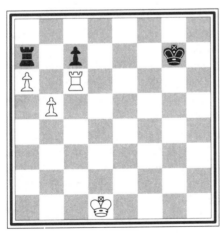

DIAGRAM 231.

it can appear out of nowhere. Diagram 227 in Chapter 8 featured the line 1.Kh5 Re8 2.Ng6 Ra8 3.Kh6, when Black could have tried 3…Kd6 4.Nf8 Ke7 5.g8=Q Rxf8, creating a Queen vs. Rook position. Often when players with the Rook realize that they will have to face the Queen, they resign rather than play on!

In Diagram 231, White might have other ways of winning the position, but most grandmasters would play 1.Rxc7 Rxc7 2.b6, when one pawn will queen. A likely continuation is 2…Rd7+ 3.Kc2 Rd6 4.b7 Rxa6 5.b8=Q, which puts us in our topical ending.

In this manner, Queen vs. Rook endings can easily appear from that most common endgame of all, Rook vs. Rook. How difficult or easy is this ending? When Queen vs. Rook was first taught to me, the ending was viewed as being pretty straightforward. The superior side would march his King toward its adversary. Combined with the powers of the Queen, the defending King would be forced to the side of the board, eventually getting crammed into a corner, and then would be forcibly separated from the Rook it was trying to protect. The Queen would then give a series of checks, effectively skewering the King and Rook, and win the game. This prevailing view of an easy win was held for many centuries. However, a certain programming friend of mine, Ken Thompson, of Bell and UNIX fame, upset this cozy understanding.

A Bit of Mischief

Ken's computer program revealed that the Queen vs. Rook ending is much more difficult than anyone realized. With mischief in mind, Ken began looking for a grandmaster victim to champion the superior side.

When considering whom to challenge, Ken didn't have to look further than his own backyard. America's illustrious Grandmaster Walter S. Browne, a six-time U.S. champion, has an established reputation for accepting daring challenges. He was Ken's immediate choice. Ken's challenge was that Walter would either win the Rook, or checkmate the computer using the Queen and 50 moves. Unsuspicious of the problems, Walter was unable to win in the allotted number of moves. Miffed, Walter demanded a rematch, and after a few days of careful study, managed to win. Both puzzled and annoyed by his earlier failure, Walter expressed new appreciation for this ending that had brought him to some new insights. The computer had made one of its first marks on the chess world.

What had the computer revealed that no one had previously been able to see? In the past, a defender would do his utmost to keep his Rook under protective cover of his King, allowing their separation only when forced. The Queen would then pounce, checking the King to skewer the Rook by a series of checks, and the game was over. What the computer showed was that the defender should, in certain positions, *voluntarily move his Rook away before being forced to do so*. In such cases, the Queen is unable to create a skewer, and only a quiet move does the trick of forcing a win. In this way, the eventual loss can be postponed but not avoided. I must confess that all the nuances of this ending still escape me, but the principles behind this winning procedure have worked for hundreds of years and are easy to learn.

In a nutshell, the superior side has to bully the defender as if the Rook didn't exist at all! The following principles lead to a skewering of the Rook and a win:

- *The defending King must be driven out of the center to the sides of the board.*

- *Once the defender's King is decentralized, the superior side should crowd the defender into the corner.*

- *After the King has been cornered, the Rook is forced away from the protection of the King.*

Let's see how this endgame was taught by the old masters. Diagram 232 is a starting position given by Grandmaster Paul Keres, and we follow his analysis.

1.Qf3+ Ke5 2.Qe4+ Kd6 3.Kd4 Rc6

Keres readily admits that this move is by no means forced. It's not even the best move, pointing out that 3...Ra5 would likely hold out longer. For now, we are just interested in the method employed by White.

4.Qe5+ Kd7 5.Kd5 Rc7 6.Qe6+ Kd8

As shown in Diagram 233, White has made considerable progress, having forced Black's King to the board's edge. Now White has to make an adjustment of his pieces.

7.Qg8+

White is not falling for the devilish 7.Kd6?? Rc6+ 8.Kxc6, which brings a stalemate.

7...Ke7 8.Qg7+ Kd8 9.Qf8+ Kd7

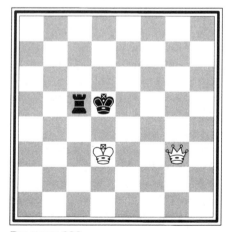

DIAGRAM 232.
P. Keres, 1973

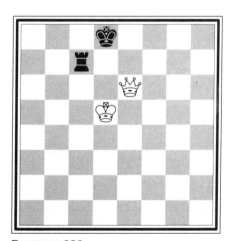

DIAGRAM 233.
P. Keres, 1973

DIAGRAM 234.
P. Keres, 1973

In Diagram 234, White would now like Black to have the move, so he aims to repeat the position, with Black to play. White has to find a way to lose the move.

10.Qf4

Although there are other ways to lose the move, this seems straightforward, because Black's Rook is dominated.

10...Kc8

Black's King steps back. If the Rook had moved instead, 10...Rc2? 11.Qf5+ and Qf5xc2, 10...Ra7? 11.Qf7+ and Qf7xa7, 10...Rb7 11.Qf7+ Kc8 12.Qe8+ Kc7 13.Kc5! Ra7 14.Qe7+ Kb8 15.Qd8+ Kb7 16.Kb5! Ra8 17.Qd7+ Kb8 18.Kb6 wins.

11.Kd6!

White presses forward with his King, controlling more and more squares.

11...Kb8

Quicker losses await 11...Rd7+? 12.Kc6, which wins for White, or 11...Ra7? 12.Qf8+ Kb7 13.Qf7+! Kb8 (13...Kb6 14.Qb3+ Ka5 15.Kc6 Ra6+ 16.Kc5 wins.) 14.Qe8+ Kb7 15.Qd7+ Kb8 16.Qd8+ Kb7 17.Qc7+ Ka6 18.Qc6+ Ka5 19.Kc5, which also wins.

As so often happens in this ending, White doesn't get anywhere by forcing checks. From the position in Diagram 235, as in Diagram 234, White must make a quiet move, which strengthens his position while giving the move to his opponent.

12.Qe5! Rb7

Black is being squeezed into the corner because the text was unavoidable: 12...Kb7 13.Qb5+ Kc8 14.Qa6+ Kb8 15.Qb6+ Rb7 16.Qd8+ Ka7 17.Kc6, and White's King conquers the c6-square as in our main line.

13.Kc6+! Ka8

DIAGRAM 235.
P. Keres, 1973

The first two principles of play are now complete. The final step is to force the Rook to move away.

14.Qa1+ Kb8 15.Qa5

Diagram 236, showing a position that was analyzed by Philidor in 1777, indicates that Black has no choice but to move his Rook away.

15...Rb1

Black's Rook can run, but it can't hide. Three equally undesirable options exist:

- 15...Rh7 16.Qe5+ Ka8 17.Qa1+ Kb8 18.Qb1+

- 15...Rf7 16.Qe5+ Ka7 17.Qe3+ Kb8 18.Qe8+

- 15...Rb3 16.Qd8+ Ka7 17.Qd4+ Kb8 18.Qf4+ Ka7 19.Qa4+

DIAGRAM 236.
F.A.D. Philidor, 1777

All lead to the capture of the Black Rook. After the text, as we expect, a forced series of checks picks up the Rook.

16.Qd8+ Ka7 17.Qd4+ Kb8 18.Qh8+ Ka7 19.Qh7+

Because the King and Rook are skewered, White wins.

This example shows how White has to be careful not to permit a stalemate. An exception to this win occurs if White's King starts in a bad position, as shown in Diagram 237. This analysis by Domenico Lorenzo Ponziani (1719–96), an Italian priest, shows that White's Queen is too powerful, and Black is able to keep up a perpetual check:

1...Rh7+ 2.Kg5 Rg7+

3.Kf5 Rf7+ 4.Kg6

White returns to the Kingside, because 4.Ke5 Re7 draws.

4...Rg7+ 5.Kh6 Rh7+!

Black gets his point. He is allowed his perpetual, or 6.Kxh7, stalemate.

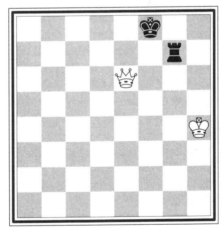

DIAGRAM 237.
D.L. Ponziani, 1782

Computer Analysis

Ever since the highest-rated chess player, Garry Kasparov, lost a celebrated match in 1997 to IBM's computer chess program, Deep Blue, a disturbing trend in chess has developed. This new trend considers technology to be a "higher authority" than the human. I don't want to go too deeply into the details about the 1997 Kasparov–Deep Blue match, but I will say that Kasparov's loss was grossly premature. Kasparov made two blunders. In game 2 of the six-game match, he resigned a drawn position. In game 6, he made an all-too-common human mistake, something chess players describe as a *finger failure*: He moved the wrong piece in the opening. With this mix-up, he fell into a standard opening trap and lost the game before it was even begun. Deep Blue merely followed its preprogrammed library of opening moves, and by the time Deep Blue had to make an original move, the position was already won. Kasparov lost game 6 in the first hour of play after a mere 19 moves, the quickest loss of his career. Two gross failings in a short six-game match were too much to overcome.

The match's final score of 3½–2½ was in no way reflective of the computer's "strength," even though Kasparov badly blundered away games 2 and 6. (He also failed to win positions that were clearly to his advantage in games 3, 4, and 5.) The public saw the final score, and that was all that mattered. The computer had won, and now the public thought both Deep Blue and computers in general were better than any human chess player. This simply is not true. It is doubtful that IBM's Deep Blue program is even the best in the world. I have played some of the best computer chess programs in tournament conditions and have scored 16½ points from 18 games. One of these programs, Fritz, defeated Deep Blue in the Computer Chess World Championships. I have no doubt that I, as well as a few dozen of my colleagues, could defeat Deep Blue in match play.

Having said that, there are many areas of chess where computers *are* far stronger than the best players in the world. Two key strengths are that a computer's memory of openings is perfect, and that a computer has the ability to follow the main line of even the most harrowing of openings with absolute precision. Then there are chess endgame databases composed of five or fewer pieces and pawns. For these endings, the Kings count as two pieces. For instance, the King and Queen vs. King and Rook ending is a four-piece ending. In these endings in which the material is greatly reduced, every conceivable move, right down to checkmate, can be analyzed with absolute precision. The same cannot be done with positions that have many pieces and pawns on the board.

The Ken Thompson program mentioned earlier worked out every conceivable position that might occur between the four-piece ending, King and Queen vs. King and Rook. Regardless of where or how the pieces are placed, in a nanosecond the computer will state precisely how many moves there are until checkmate. No chess player has such an ability. I can only match that level of accuracy in stating that the side with the Queen should win!

Therefore, in such special cases, players do indeed have to bow before the "higher authority." Since Deep Blue's victory in 1997, computer hardware and software have improved substantially, making chess programs ever stronger. Still, I believe that it will be another decade or more before computers will, with certainty, defeat the very best human players.

In the following section, let's look at some computer variations for the Queen vs. Rook ending. I set up some tests using Ken Thompson's endgame databases, put out by Tasc ChessSystem©. I ran two random positions through the computer, comparing the methods of the computer with the methods of the old masters. The play, as you'll see, was quite similar, with one major detectable difference: The computer's Rook moved away from the protection of its King earlier than is considered—in the world of humans—good form. There were, as you'll also see, a greater number of optimal moves for both sides than I had realized.

For my first test I chose the position in Diagram 238 for its similarity to the position presented by Keres. The computer soon revealed that with optimal play by both sides, White gives checkmate in 27 moves. (The numbers in brackets after each move indicate in how many moves checkmate will be reached. I've also shown the alternative "optimal" moves for both sides.)

1.Kd3 [27] Rc6 [26]

2.Qg5+ [26]

Clearly a "human move." Surprisingly, **2.Qd4+**, **2.Qf3+**, and **2.Qe4+** are all as good.

2...Kd6 [25]

Also, **2...Ke6 [25]** lasts just as long as the text.

3.Kd4 [25]

An obvious and strong choice. I was surprised that **3.Qb5** was just as good.

DIAGRAM 238.
Computer Database, 1997

3...Kd7 [24]   4.Qb5 [24]

The computer likes this move and so do I. Also, **4.Qg7+** was optimal.

4...Kc7 [23]

The best resistance. Most players would have chosen 4...Kd6, which would lose faster.

5.Ke5 [23]

This one is not such an obvious choice. I'd have chosen 5.Kd5, which is weaker, while **5.Qb4!?** is as good as the text.

5...Rg6 [22]

This is a definite computer move, as *the Rook moves away of its own volition*. The human move, 5...Rb6, would have accelerated the defeat.

6.Qc4+ [22] Rc6 [21]   7.Qb4 [21] Rh6 [20]

Once more, the computer is able to see that the Rook is not to be skewered. Happily, the more human moves, **7...Rb6** and **7...Kd7**, were also optimal.

8.Qe7+ [20] Kc6 [19]   9.Qe8+ [19] Kc7 [18]   10.Kd5 [18]

This was the move I wanted on move 5.

10...Rd6+ [17]

Also, **10...Ra6** would last as long.

11.Kc5 [17] Rd7 [16]   12.Qe5+ [16] Kb7 [15]

DIAGRAM 239.
Computer Database, 1997

I choose to defend away from the center, because **12...Kd8 13.Kc6** looks dangerous, although both moves will lose in 15 moves.

13.Kb5 [15] Rc7 [14]

14.Qe8 [14]

White doesn't go with the expected 14.Qe6 or 14.Qd6, which both cut off Black's King and claim the sixth rank. Those moves just delay the victory.

14...Rc1 [13]

As you might guess from Diagram 239, such a move provokes a growl. If a human opponent played this against me, I'd spend the following few minutes trying to calculate a series of checks to grab the Rook. I realize I'd be wasting my time against a computer! The trick is not to spend tempi on fruitless checks, but to strengthen White's grip by controlling more squares. The first thing to do is to cover the b1-square to prevent checks.

15.Qe4+ [13] Kc8 [12] 16.Kb6 [12] Kd7 [11]

Also, **16...Kd8** holds out for 11 moves. But both moves cost the Rook.

17.Qd3+ [11]

With **17.Qd4+**, White also wins the Rook.

17...Ke6 [10] 18.Qe3+ [10]

With **19.Qxc1** next, mate will be forced in the predicted number of moves.

To make the challenge as difficult as possible, I set up Diagram 240 for one more test. Let's see how the computer wins:

1...Rc4 [34] 2.Ka2 [34]

I select the human move of trying to activate the King. Also, **2.Qf5, 2.Qd1+, 2.Qg6,** and **2.Qf1** are all optimal. These latter two moves mystify me.

2...Rc3 [33] 3.Kb2 [33]

The most difficult moves to grasp, **3.Qg6** and **3.Qf1**, are also optimal.

3...Rf3 [32]

Black could also choose from **3...Re3, 3...Rc4,** and **3...Rc6**, all of which in some way cut White's King and resist for 32 moves.

4.Qg1+ [32]

White had three choices here: 4...Qg6 [32], 4.Qc1 [32], and 4.Qe1, in addition

DIAGRAM 240.
Computer Database, 1997

to the text. I chose the last option because I liked the idea of controlling the f2-square with check.

4...Ke4 [31]

As reasonable is **4...Re3**, hanging around in the center.

5.Qg4+ [31]

The choices **5.Kc2** and the surprising **5.Qh1!?** are as good.

5...Rf4 [30] 6.Qe6+ [30]

I like this move because White tries to pull Black's King down to the first rank, where it is closer to White's King. It is also the best move.

6...Kd4 [29]

Black is trying to cling to the sweet center, although **6...Kd3** is rated as good.

7.Qd6+ [29] Ke4 [28]   8.Kc3 [28] Kf5 [27]

Surprisingly, **8...Rf3+** is as good. So much for the expression, "Patzer sees a check, patzer plays a check." (A *patzer* is an inept chess player.)

9.Kd3 [27] Rf3+ [26]   10.Kd4 [26] Rf4+ [25]   11.Kd5 [25] Rf3 [24]

I enjoyed that series of moves because I felt I really understood what was going on. Now, *with the King centralized*, it is time to *push Black's King to the side*.

12.Qe5+ [24]

With **12.Qf8+**, White would accomplish the same goal.

12...Kg4 [23]

Although **12...Kg6 13.Qe4+ Rf5+ 14.Ke6** picks up the Rook, would you have guessed that after **12...Kg6 [7]**, Black is mated in seven moves?

13.Ke4 [23] Rf1 [22]

It seems more secure to play **13...Rf2**, which is also optimal. I deliberately chose the text, which seems more like a computer move. As we see in Diagram 241, White

has made marvelous progress, and Black is to be driven to the side of the board. What should White play next?

14.Qg7+ [22]

If you had played **14.Qe6+**, you would have chosen another optimal move. The text just seems more "reasonable."

14...Kh5 [21]

15.Qg3 [21] Rf8 [20]

As strong was **15...Rf6 [20]**; however, the text, which goes "as far away as possible," seemed best.

16.Ke5 [20] Rf7 [19]

17.Qd3 [19]

DIAGRAM 241.
Computer Database, 1997

An astonishing move. Unexpectedly, White must force the King and Rook back together again. Once they have to rely on one another for mutual protection, it is easier to force the defender back, which allows White's King to get closer. The text prevents Black's Rook from going to a large number of squares.

17...Kg5 [18]   18.Qd8+ [18] Kg6 [17]   19.Qg8+ [17] Rg7 [16]

Now that Black's pieces are huddled together, White can make gains.

20.Qe6+ [16] Kh7 [15]   21.Kf5 [15] Rg2 [14]   22.Qf7+ [14]

Here there were five other perfect moves: **22.Qd5, 22.Qd7+, 22.Qe5, 22.Qe4,** and **22.Qe3**; all force mate in 14 moves.

22...Kh6 [13]   23.Qf6+ [13] Kh7 [12]   24.Qd4 [12]

In this familiar retreat, White covers the f2-square and threatens to advance with his King. Also, **24.Qh4+** mates in a dozen moves.

24...Rg6 [11]   25.Qe4 [11]

Bravo to Paul Keres! The old masters sure knew what they were doing!

25...Rg7 [10]   26.Kf6+ [10] Kg8 [9]

Black is hiding with 26...Kh8, which also lasts for nine moves. How far we've come since Diagram 240! Corner to corner.

27.Qa8+ [9] Kh7 [8]   28.Qe8 [8] Ra7 [7]

This time the Rook's departure is forced.

29.Qg6+ [7]

This move is the most forcing, even though **29.Qh5+** and **29.Qe4+** are also optimal.

29...Kh8 [6]

In looking at Diagram 242, it's hard to believe that White will mate in just six moves. Can you spot the first move?

30.Qg1 [6] Rh7 [5]

Also, **30...Rd7** is good for five more moves, but **30...Ra6+ 31.Kf7** accelerates Black's defeat.

31.Qg3 [5]

Another nice choice is **31.Qe3**, covering the h6-square.

31...Rb7 [4]

Here Black prevents Qg3-b8 mate. By choosing **31...Ra7** or **31...Rh6+**, Black still gets to lose in four moves.

32.Qh3+ [4]

The check **32.Qh2+** wins in four moves as well.

DIAGRAM 242.
Computer Database, 1997

32...Kg8 [3]   33.Qg2+ [3]

It's the same deal, with 33.Qc8+ scooping up the Rook.

33... Kh7 [2]   34.Qxb7+ [2] Kh6 [1]   35.Qh1 Checkmate

So ends this most interesting peek at the future of chess. I hope this section on computer analysis hasn't given you the impression that I dislike computers. Nothing could be further from the truth. In fact, I'm in awe of them and all the wonders that accompany them: their perfect recall, the database engines that analyze tirelessly and without complaint, and their "willingness" to play day or night. These qualities all make computers a modern chess player's indispensable tool. My annoyance is directed at the trend that considers them to be a "higher authority" for all positions. I enjoyed the TV series *Star Trek*, in which Dr. Spock (Leonard Nimoy) plays three-dimensional chess against the spaceship's computer, which plays "perfectly." In one episode Spock wins, thereby proving that someone has fiddled with the computer's program. In fact, no such level of perfection yet exists, and for many positions, the computers have a long way to go. It will be intriguing to see, undoubtedly within my lifetime, a game with "perfect play" by both sides.

I recall an amusing story from the 1997 AEGON tournament, the human vs. computer competition. International Master Roberto Cifuentes had slipped and was in a Rook ending, a pawn behind. With a loss looming, Roberto began to dig down and wrack his brain, trying to find a way to save the game. Suddenly, the computer operator calmly informed Roberto that it would be "mate in 47 moves." Talk about intimidation! Later, I roared with laughter—at Roberto's expense of course—happily explaining that I would have resigned on the spot because I was sure that I would not be able to find the "optimal" move to last all 47 moves. Like a nightmare, the programmer would inform me after each of my moves that I had accelerated my own defeat!

In closing, a hearty thanks for reading this book on the endgame from cover to cover. If I've inspired you toward a greater appreciation of chess, I am pleased. It has been a great pleasure to introduce you to the intricacies of endings.

Resources

The author would like to express his appreciation and respect for the following books, periodicals, and software, which have made this work so much richer:

Akiba Rubinstein: The Later Years, IM John Donaldson, IM Nikolay Minev
Akiba Rubinstein: Uncrowned King, IM John Donaldson, IM Nikolay Minev
Basic Chess Endings, GM Ruben Fine
Comprehensive Chess Endings: All Volumes, GM Yuri Averbach
Chess Endgame Lessons, GM Pal Benko
Chess in a Nutshell, Fred Reinfeld
Chess Informants, Volumes 1–76, Chess Informant
Chess Personalia: A Bibliography, Jeremy Gaige
Domination in 2,545 Endgame Studies, Ghenrikh M. Kasparyan
Encyclopedia of Chess Endings, All Volumes, Chess Informant
Endgame Play, GM Chris Ward
Endgame Strategy, Mikhail Shereshevsky
Grandmaster Preparation, GM Lev Polugaevsky
How to Play Chess Endings, Eugene Znosko-Borovsky
Impact of Genius, Richard Fauber
Kings, Commoners and Knaves, Edward Winter
The Oxford Companion to Chess, David Hooper and Ken Whyld
Practical Chess Endings, GM Paul Keres
Practical Chess Endings: A Basic Guide to Endgame Strategy for the Beginner and the More Advanced Chess Player, Irving Chernev
Reinfeld on the End-game in Chess, Fred Reinfeld
Skola Saha: Zavrsnice, GM Borislav Ivkov

British Chess Magazine (BCM)
Chess Life Magazine, United States Chess Federation (USCF)
Chess Monthly, London Chess Center
Inside Chess Magazine, International Chess Enterprises, Inc. (ICE)
New In Chess Magazine, Interchess BV

Chessica, Tasc ChessSystem©
Ken Thompson's Endgame Databases, Tasc ChessSystem©
M-Chess Program, Marty Hirsch

Index

About the Author

International Chess Grandmaster Yasser Seirawan is one of the top U.S. contenders for the World Championship title. The first American contender for the world title after Bobby Fischer retired in 1975, Seirawan qualified for the World Championship in 1985, 1987, and 1997, and has earned numerous other titles including 1979 World Junior Champion, U.S. Champion (three times), and 1989 Western Hemisphere Champion. He is an eight-time member of the U.S. Olympic chess team and earned a gold medal for best individual score in the 1994 Chess Olympics. He has defeated the two top-ranking players in the world, Garry Kasparov and Anatoly Karpov, in tournament play, and he is the only American to have played in the World Cup cycle. Seirawan has been the highest-rated American player by the FIDE (Fédération Internationale des Échecs) and WCC (World Chess Council), and is currently the highest-rated American according to both associations on their January and July 1999 rating lists.

Born in Damascus, Syria, in 1960, Seirawan moved with his family to Seattle at the age of 7. His chess career was launched at the age of 12, when he began to play in local and regional tournaments. Seirawan is married and lives in Seattle, Washington. He has authored 13 books on chess, including a five-book award-winning series published by Microsoft Press. Readers are invited to write him at yasser@insidechess.com and to follow his tournament career via his Web site at *www.insidechess.com.*